# NATURAL VALUE

# NATURAL VALUE

BY

FRIEDRICH VON WIESER

EDITED WITH A PREFACE AND ANALYSIS

BY

WILLIAM SMART

[ 1893 ]

REPRINTS OF ECONOMIC CLASSICS

Augustus M. Kelley · Publishers

NEW YORK 1971

First Edition 1893
( London: Macmillan & Company, 1893 )


Reprinted 1956 & 1971 by
AUGUSTUS M. KELLEY · PUBLISHERS
REPRINTS OF ECONOMIC CLASSICS
New York  New York  10001


· · · · · · · · · · ·


I S B N  0 678 00821 3
L C N  56 4895

· · · · · · · · · · ·


PRINTED IN THE UNITED STATES OF AMERICA
by SENTRY PRESS, NEW YORK, N. Y. 10019

# EDITOR'S PREFACE

In the preface to my *Introduction to the Theory of Value*, in which I attempted to make clear to English readers the main lines of that theory as expounded by the Austrian School, I said that, in justice to Professor Wieser, I stopped short of his application of the value theory to distribution, preferring to put the translation of his brilliant and suggestive work into the hands of one of my former students. The rendering of *Natural Value* which follows will, I think, justify at once my reserve and my selection of a translator.

The theory of value, of which the Austrian economists are now the chief exponents, is the Final or Marginal Utility theory, best known to English economists through Jevons's great work published in 1871. In the same year, and quite independently, appeared Menger's *Grundsätze*—a work typical of Teutonic thoroughness and strength. This was followed, in 1884, by Wieser's *Ursprung und Hauptgesetze des wirthschaftlichen Werthes*. The *Positive Theory of Capital* of Böhm-Bawerk (1889) contains a masterly exposition of value, price, and costs, on which the author bases his well-known theory of interest. Previous to that, in 1887, Sax published his *Grundlegung*, in which he applied the value theory to the economic functions of the state. Finally came the present work, which at once catches up many loose ends in previous expositions, and carries the whole theory, with its applications, to a higher level of completeness.

The main purpose of *Natural Value* may be read in chap. vi. of Book II. (p. 60). The general reader, however, will possibly find the most suggestive matter in chapters incidental to this main development, particularly in the attacks on Socialist theory. To English economists, again, I venture to think that there are three points which will specially commend themselves as original contributions to our science. These are, the re-setting of the elementary conception of value in Book I., the application to distribution in Books III. and IV., and the bringing of the law of cost of production within the compass of the general Marginal Law in Book V. If an editor's preface has any function it is, I imagine, to elucidate points which his, presumably, close study of the book have shown to be difficult, and my connection with the Austrian School may, perhaps, justify me in putting these points in my own way.

The first book contains the general statement of the theory of value according to the Austrian School. Its main lines are as follows.

The man in the street, asked the simplest questions about value, betrays the popular belief that value originates in Utility, while he is, at the same time, aware of many phenomena which seem to contradict this faith. For instance, free gifts of nature have no value : some confessedly very useful things have little value : scarcity, as well as use, confers value : cost seems the very antithesis of value. It is a fundamental principle of the school that the investigation of value is the investigation of human acts of valuations, and, accordingly, no theory of value can be satisfactory which does not bring these contradictions under its law.

A slight analysis shows that, in the last resort, the " use " of goods—or the use we get from them—is nothing but the satisfaction of want, or rather of desire. Goods which do not satisfy some desire are of no use to anybody : if we could satisfy desire without goods we should have no desire for goods :—these two considerations point to the conclusion that it is not goods in themselves that are either desirable or desired, but satisfactions. We must, first, then, look deeper into the nature of wants and satisfactions.

Gossen's law gives us a correct analysis. According to it, want or desire diminishes with every successive draught of satisfaction till the point of satiation is reached. This is true of all desires, higher and lower, if we are careful to consider the same desires and not other varieties of them, and if the desires in question are full grown, and not merely awakening or in course of development. Thus the satisfaction of every want describes a falling scale, and, at each degree on the scale, the sensations of want are of different intensity.

But here are two things which may be spoken of as " want " : the want as a whole, or kind, or class, and the individual sensation of want. However we classify the kinds of want—according as we look at them from a moral, or hedonistic, or intellectual standpoint —the more important kinds of want remain the more important. But, in these kinds, the *sensation* of want varies from an indefinite higher point down to zero, according to the circumstances of provision for it. Taken day by day, the appetite for food is constant and important : at any point of the day, its importance depends on the satisfaction afforded by the last meal.

Thus, however we arrange the wants as classes, we constantly find that a want, belonging to what we would recognise as an important class, has no great importance for us in the circumstances. Of two wants the one, of its class, important, the other unimportant, the latter will be felt by us as important if unsatisfied, in comparison with the former if satisfied. In measuring satisfactions of want, then, we have to take both of these into account. The possibilities of want are according to the class; the actualities, according to the satisfaction already reached. It is only in exceptional circumstances that we know much about the possibilities of want within us, just as hunger to most is merely a pleasurable anticipation.

Utility being the general capability of satisfying human want, or, as Jevons defined it, "a circumstance of things arising out of their relation to man's requirements"; if the "use" of goods amounts to satisfaction of want, and if satisfaction depends, partly, on the importance of the class to which the want belongs, and, partly, on previous satisfaction attained, we have already come in sight of that influence of quantity or Supply on the estimate of utility and of use which becomes so prominent in the estimate of value. It is a commonplace that value is not inherent in things : it is not so well recognised that neither is utility. There is nothing "useful" except in relation to a being who finds it so, but even the useful is not "of use" if that being has already enough or too much of it.

Here we reach the point of view from which the utility of goods is defined and measured. It is only as we find that satisfaction depends on having, and non-satisfaction follows on not having or losing goods, that we transfer our interest in satisfactions to the material conditions on which these satisfactions are dependent. We attach no importance to goods when they are to be had in superfluity—not even to that portion of them which we use, because satisfaction is not *dependent* on those we use. If our wants were few we should perhaps attain something like superfluity of goods as regards many of them, but the fact that our wants are many and varied makes us desire many goods, and distribute our effort at acquisition over a wide field. Thus we find that, as a rule, the supply of commodities in the control of any person is not sufficient for all the possible and even actual sensations of want for these commodities. There must, then, be a point, short of complete satiation, at which satisfaction is broken off. This is the marginal satisfaction : the least utility economically obtainable in the circumstances. It is this Marginal Satisfaction that determines the value of goods to us.

It will be noted that this marginal satisfaction is not the general capacity of use, nor even the actual use made of goods, but the last or least use in the circumstances of the individual demand and the individual supply. Suppose that commodities were represented and ranked in importance according to the letters of the alphabet. A being the most important, we should strive to obtain it first, but only till such time as some supply of B became more desirable than a further supply of A. In the same way we should leave off accumulating B whenever the decreasing satisfaction from it made it more desirable to obtain some supply of C. In A and B, then, there emerges a marginal satisfaction—the least permissible in the concrete circumstances. We say that this is the economic margin, inasmuch as persistence in accumulating A or B would result in the total sum of satisfaction attainable being less than by drawing the marginal line at a point short of further satisfaction, and proceeding to the satisfaction of C.

When goods are valued by themselves there is no comparison of utilities, and, therefore, no marginal utility; in this case goods do get their value from the actual use made of them; and, of competing uses for the good, it is, of course, the highest which decides the value. But few goods are valued in this way : they are generally valued as items in a stock or supply of similar items. Suppose that a person gradually acquire several of these items, he will successively put them to less and less important uses. But however many or few goods he has, there will always be a least use—unless the good is a " free gift "—to which he puts the goods. The larger the stock the less will be this marginal use. But if the goods are similar, any one of them may be the last used. The value of each item, then, cannot be more than the least : and the value of the whole stock must be a multiple of that least. In a stock of ten goods—assuming unchanged demand—the value of each good cannot be more than the tenth use to which the goods are put ; and the value of the whole is ten times the tenth use. Of a stock of a million items, the total value is a multiple of the millionth use. Thus, then, all these uses above the marginal ones are unrepresented in value, and it is on the same principle that the uses actually obtained from free goods are not represented in value at all. Here in the main is the solution of the contradictions with which we started. If iron is little valued, it is not because its usefulness is little, but because the supply is so great that the marginal use of iron is quite insignificant, and the total value of iron is a multiple of this insignificant use. If air is not held of any value, it is because the supply is so abundant that the marginal use is never reached, and its total is multiplied, if we may say so, by zero.

But this determination of value by marginal utility brings with it a paradox of its own. If increase of supply has lowered marginal utility till value disappears with superfluity, it is evident that somewhere there has come a point at which further increments of supply not only did not increase the total value, but actually diminished it. Suppose that one item yields ten units of satisfaction, and two items eight units each—corresponding with the diminution in desire with successive satisfaction—and three items six units each, and four items four units each. The total value is the same when I have two items as when I have four, viz. sixteen ($8 \times 2$ and $4 \times 4$), and is less when I have four than when I have three ($4 \times 4$ and $3 \times 6$).

This, however, is paradoxical only so long as we think of value as simple and positive. It comes from confusing usefulness or use with value. True, the usefulness of goods to man cannot decrease with the supply of them. True, also, that the total use of the four goods to me is $10 + 8 + 6 + 4 = 28$, because the use I actually obtain from the goods is no less although the actual use of each is less than that of those preceding it. But if we remember that value disappears with superfluity, although with superfluity use is assured in the highest degree, we shall remember that value involves not only use but dependence. The interest we have in a satisfaction we transfer to a good, but we cannot do so unless we find the satisfaction dependent on that good. With a given want craving satisfaction, my dependence is less when I have four goods with which to satisfy it, than when I have three. At every fresh increment of goods the stock of useful things increases, but the dependence decreases, and the amount which represents the dependence is cumulative : it comes not only off the last good, but off all the goods. If I have one good the dependence of satisfaction on the good is perfect : value reflects the whole of the use (10). If I have two goods the dependence is less, *ex hypothesi*, by 2, but, as equal goods must have equal values, the 2 comes off each of the goods, so that, instead of 18 ($10 + 8$) the value is 16 ($8 \times 2$). If I have three goods, two more comes off each good, representing the further failure of dependence, and so on.

Thus value is a combination of positive and negative—of satisfaction gained and of dependence lost. It is a residual amount. Up to a certain point value accompanies the addition of goods, although in slower progression,—because the gain of utility is greater than the loss of dependence. But when the supply reaches a certain point the loss of dependence is greater than the gain of use, and the total value diminishes. So it comes that, in certain cases, the negative element may overpower the positive, and a greater number of similar items have a less total value than a smaller. We should not, however, be surprised at this, if we did not think of value as synonymous with usefulness or with use.

If, then, value were the highest principle in economic life, that is, if economic action were mainly guided by the pursuit of the highest value, we should have a constant antinomy such as Proudhon asserted. But, first, no antinomy emerges till the " down grade " of value has been reached, and this is seldom the case as regards any commodity. With most goods, increase of quantity brings increase of total value, although, of course, the value of the item falls. And, second, it is not true that value is the end of economic action. The highest principle is Utility. When the two conflict, value has to take the second place. As things are, however, utility and value generally go the same way—in the "up grade,"— and no harm is done in economic effort following the lead of value. The true service of value consists in being the calculation form of utility. In economic life everything stands every moment in need of measurement. Thus value is always with us, while the utility which is obtained, but does not come under its measure, is forgotten, and we get the impression that value is the chief end. All the same, the continual effort of the economic world to make things " cheap," might remind us that, in the last resort, we are trying to bring things as near as possible to those " free gifts " which have boundless usefulness but no value.

In the second book Wieser briefly, and for the sake of comparison, shows the connection of value as thus conceived—thereafter called Use Value or Natural Value—with exchange value or the value of ordinary business life. Far from being something with which political economy has little to do, the former is no less than the foundation of the latter. Take the normal case of sellers competing to sell goods made for sale, and buyers competing to buy them. Each buyer, if he knows his business, comes to the market with a maximum offer in his mind. This maximum will be determined by two valuations ; first, by the value in use of the goods to him, and, second, by the exchange value of the purchase money to him—which latter will vary indefinitely with wealth and income. It is that sum of money whose exchange value is equal to the anticipated use value. Considering the individual differences in wants and in wealth, it is evident that this maximum will vary quite indefinitely. Nor is the maximum a mere possibility—a subjective limit which has little relation to actual price. In the degree that competition is perfect, the competition of buyers to secure purchases, and of sellers to sell at the best price they can get, will force the buyers to their maximum. In these circumstances, if one good is put on the market, price will settle between the maximum of the most capable buyer and that of the next capable (but excluded) buyer. If fifty goods are put on the market, the price—under the same assumption—will settle between the maximum of the fiftieth and the fifty-first (the excluded) buyer, and so on. The price is a marginal one, determined just as we have seen value generally determined. No one, whatever his wants or means, pays more than the weakest buyer who succeeds in buying, and the price of the whole supply is a multiple of the units by this marginal price ; in other words, it is determined by the subjective maximum of the marginal buyer.

It scarcely requires demonstration that the same principle obtains where several items are offered and bought. In this case the buyer has a different maximum per item, falling with the quantity of items he will take, but it is always a subjective maximum determined in the same way, by anticipated use value calculated in terms of exchange value of the purchase money—and it is always a marginal price. In all this there is obviously a close relation between the law of price and the law of value. But there is one important difference; that here demand does not represent simply degree of want, but degree of want as expressed in purchasing power. The most serious effect of this is that, in the present bad distribution of wealth, the direction of production is given, not only by the wants and necessities of the community, but by the desires of rich men expressed in large figures.

In the modern economy, where the life of most men is occupied in making some one thing not to use but to sell, a new and powerful impulse is given to the formations of exchange value. While within each individual economy use value retains its place, the form of value which obtains between the exchanging commodities comes into new prominence, inasmuch as it is carried on by means of a medium which has, practically, no use value. Buying and selling—the whole mechanism of exchange—is carried on by money, and money itself is always estimated according to its exchange value. But what is this exchange value of money but the anticipated use value of the things which can be obtained for it?—money being merely the commodity we reserve for this particular use. The law of the one, then, is the law of the other. It is the same with goods made to sell; that is, to exchange: their ultimate basis is always use value—the use value of the things for which they exchange. It is the same, again, with goods that are replaceable at a cost less than their utility. In short, exchange is another form of use: one of the uses of goods in general, but the sole use of money. " Exchange value in this sense and use value are of the same nature: the former is derived from the latter, and is one of its forms of development. Both are subjective, and the amount of both varies according to personal circumstances."

Thus Wieser, in the manner of his school, while confessing that the two values cannot be subsumed under one definition, vindicates the neglected Use Value, showing that exchange value is founded on it, and cannot be understood without it. To exchange equal values is meaningless unless equal (objective) values purchase unequal (subjective) values.

Thus far the value of consumption goods alone has been considered, and the estimate of value has been analysed as if goods, like bankrupt stocks, were thrown on a market to sell without consideration of the circumstances of their production. If the theory went no further than this, Wieser might deserve the reproach sometimes levelled at the Austrian School, that they look at value too exclusively from the side of demand and neglect the "supply schedule." But what we have considered hitherto is only foundation. In the third book we pass to the value of the means of production, in which is implicated the relation of the value theory to distribution of income and wealth generally.

Inasmuch as production goods are, economically, consumption goods in the making, the utility of the one is the utility of the other, and, so far as they are not to be had in superfluity, they also receive value from their utility. We do not, however, in ordinary life connect the value of production goods with the satisfaction of wants from which all value ultimately comes : we do not need to go further than the value of their returns, for the reason that this value is already based on the satisfaction of wants. Thus production value is, practically, *return* value, or, rather, anticipated return value. Just as the value of a stock is determined by its dividends, so do all elements of production get their value from the value they help to produce—an illustration which will be found very helpful generally.

Now no productive element works alone, but always in combination. We evidently need a principle which will separate up the return into quotas attributable to each element. Experience shows that this calculation is actually made every day, and that not only by individuals, but by great masses of people at particular periods. Production, indeed, could not be carried on at all if the leaders of production could not say to which element success or failure was due, *i.e.* if they could not attribute parts of the return to individual factors. Strangely enough, the few writers who have seen that to analyse and explain this common procedure was the first problem, have made solution impossible by stating it as a problem of physical causation. They have tried to discover which share, physically considered, each factor has produced—which is about as reasonable as asking how much of the child is due to the father and how much to the mother.

The neighbouring science of jurisprudence suggests the solution. In deciding on a murder case, the office of a jury is the limited one of finding which, among all the conditions and instruments necessary to the murder, is legally responsible and punishable. So our problem is to find, from among all the co-operating causes, those which are *economically* responsible for the return. In calculating return, the farmer takes no cognisance of the past history of his land ; nor of the use of it to other creatures than man ; nor of the forces of nature working in it which are not as yet under human control ; nor of that part of it belonging to the free gifts of nature.

Although knowing perfectly that all these causes co-operate, he rightly imputes the return of the farm solely to the causes which he, as a farmer, has to consider if he is to attain the particular end which he aims at. And if he goes further, and, having found the crop as a whole attributable to particular economic factors, proceeds to divide it up and impute particular portions to particular factors, it is simply an extension of the same process. If two fields, similar in size and situation, are cultivated with precisely similar capital, labour, and brains, and yet show a different return in harvest, the surplus return will be attributed, probably, to some virtue in the soil, although without the co-operating factors there could have been no surplus at all. So it is in all branches of production. But what the ordinary business man does the economist can surely do. In fact, unless we can theoretically apportion and impute return to separate factors, we must say that the actual methods of attributing quota of return are under grave suspicion, and that, so far as we can see, the present distribution of income and wealth is quite arbitrary.

Before going further one solution must be cleared out of the way. The Socialists claim all return for labour—and have this much of justification that the mere fact of obtaining income is no argument for production of it. It may be a proof even of fraud or force. But one argument seems decisive. Imagine a communistic state distributing the income "jointly produced" equally to its citizens. Would it, all the same, ascribe all the return to the *labour* of its citizens? Would it be any more possible than now to produce equal crops from all soils, or equal returns from labour irrespective of the capital it worked with? Would the communistic state not count rich land and suitable tools as wealth, and attach value to them just because they affected the return to the effort of the whole community? It is evident that the *economic* return to various factors is quite independent of any ordered distribution of income. If rent and interest are no argument for the landowner and the capitalist, wage is no argument for the labourer.

Among previous attempts at solution Menger has just missed the right one. In estimating the value of a supply of similar goods, the clearest way of finding the value of one of them is to assume its loss, as this at once defines the marginal utility dependent on it. Menger applies this to production goods also, thinking thus to find what production loses in losing a factor. But what is true of homogeneous consumption goods may not be true of heterogeneous production ones co-operating towards one result. Menger forgets the common element of the co-operation. In any productive group whatever, if one factor is lost the co-operation is dissolved, and much more is lost than the factor in question. We have to consider what the remaining factors will do in new combinations. In short, the problem must be put positively : it is not what we lose, but what we gain by the co-operation of different factors towards a single end.

Wieser's own solution, then, is the following. Suppose a man's life were to depend on his last shot. The value of rifle and cartridge together is clear enough, but there is no means of ascertaining the value of each. Here are two unknown quantities and but one equalition:— $x + y = 100$. How does this differ from the value turned out by the co-operating factors in any organised production ? In this, that each factor enters into multitudes of different combinations, with returns of different values. There are multitudes of equations between production goods and values of return, and every production good can be traced as it enters into other equations. For instance, if labour works with various materials, and the return in each case has a different value, while, at the same time, each material enters into many labours, and the return in each case has a different value, it is possible, from the number of equations, to come to quite accurate understanding of what is due to each separately. If $x + y = 100$, and $2x + 3z = 290$, and $4y + 5z = 590$, $x = 40$, $y = 60$, and $z = 70$.

If, then, we take a sufficiently large field, we can find, by this comparison of equations, the share in the return which is credited to each individual factor. This evidently is very far from being anything like the physical return, and to distinguish between the total return to the production and the return to each share, Wieser proposes to call this the "productive contribution" (*Beitrag*).

The Productive Contribution of any element of production is that portion of the return in which is contained the contribution of the individual productive element to the total return, and the sum of all the contributions exactly exhausts the value of the total return. But, as the return is an anticipated one, it cannot be every return, nor is it the average return. It is, of course, the marginal return. Of all goods, production goods are most evidently valued not by themselves, but in stocks ; and, as the value of one item must here be the value of all, it can only be the marginal value obtained that determines the value of each item. In other words, what determines the value of the production good is the marginal product, or the share in the marginal product. To find the value of iron I go first to the value of iron products. That value is already a marginal one, and, in taking that as basis for the value of the iron, I at once put that value on a marginal level. But the case is not so simple as it appears, for iron enters into many products and in many different amounts, and, as these products do not obtain, and indeed cannot obtain, the same marginal value, the value of the iron, if thus determined, could not be uniform. Yet, as a matter of experience, the value of iron in stores is uniform for the same quality, and that uniform value corresponds to the value obtained by the marginal one among the many employments. If iron goods, employed in different combinations, yield respectively 8, 9, and 10, the value of the iron will be 8.

It will be obvious, however, that this determination of imputation by equations of return tells us nothing more than that certain shares *are* imputed to certain elements. We have further to ask, What are the factors which determine the amount of these particular shares? To find, for instance, that labour gets one half of the return due to the co-operation of labour, land, and capital, is so far satisfactory; but we are at once driven to ask what it is that determines that labour should get exactly this half, and that land and capital should get the other half. Into this, however, the compass of a preface will not permit me to enter, and I could at any rate add nothing to the lucidity of pp. 100-107, where the determinants of the respective shares are exhaustively discussed. Suffice it to say generally that each factor gets a greater share imputed to it according as its supply is scarce, as demand for it is great, as technique increases, and *vice versâ*, and that there is no absolute amount due to any factor.

Hitherto it has been assumed that production goods are like items in a warehouse, precisely similar in quality. But this is not always the case. Of two goods of the same kind, co-operating with similar amounts of other goods, one will give a return of higher value. The principle of employing such goods presents no difficulty. If we have a number of them we shall first employ those which give the larger return, and only afterwards those which give the lesser. When we do, the returns imputable to the better qualities will be greater by the difference between the returns. If, of these production goods, the lowest quality be present in superfluous amount, we shall impute no return to it, and the better qualities will have imputed to them all the return.

Now, of such differential production goods, the prominent one is land, and on this Ricardo exclusively fixed his attention. But if we look carefully into his theory, and at the same time into its corollaries—notably the possibility of a general rent for land—we shall find that what Ricardo said of land is true of all instruments of differential value : that the better instruments have imputed to them a share in the return greater than the poorer ones in proportion to the difference in their quality. The personal income which some land yields — and which Ricardo thought peculiar to land—is, in the last resort, dependent on the fact that this land, when co-operating with other factors, gives a return such that, when the shares imputable to capital and labour are deducted, there remains a part which must, on natural laws, be imputed to the land and to the land alone. It is not only a problem of the division of income, but of the distribution of the return, and, as such, must emerge and be solved by Socialism as it is now.

When, however, we pass to capital, we have greater difficulties, for here a preliminary question meets us;—no less than the question whether a net return is indeed always imputable to capital.

In the case of land, it was obvious that a part of the return must be attributed to it, as the land yields its crops net: that is to say, after every crop the field remains, practically, unimpaired. So labour also yields an obvious net product, as the labourer, practically, is none the worse for producing. But, in contributing to production, capital disappears, and the problem is how capital should yield a recurring return just as land does. For, if it does so, this productive instrument must do what the others do not: it must yield enough to *replace* itself, and leave besides a net surplus.

The problem is the following. The return to capital is primarily a gross return: the capital disappears in it. If capital is to do as land does, this gross return must be sufficient to replace entirely the capital destroyed, and to leave a surplus. Carefully distinguishing, then, between physical productivity and value productivity, and remembering that it is the former we have now to prove, we find that, over the field of industry, and as a general rule, the total return of the three factors working together *is* large enough to replace the capital consumed and to leave a surplus. This, at any rate, needs no proof. The millions of people maintained, while millions of capital are accumulating, leave no doubt of this. If so, when it is asked whether, of this net return, a share may be imputed to capital, we may rather retort, why should it be denied it? If capital is an economic factor—one which influences the return, as we have shown—why should it alone be denied a share in the net return?

It is enough to point out (*a*) that, where a machine replaces labour, the share formerly accruing to labour — which was a share in the net return—must be imputed to the machine: and (*b*) that, when additional capital increases the productiveness of any industry, the extra product cannot be imputed to anything else than the capital. And we must conclude that, like land, every form of concrete capital of better quality has a higher return imputed to it than the concrete capital of lower quality, and that this return is measured by the amount of increase in productive results which the employment of the better quality brings. "When we compare qualities of capital it is the net return, not the gross, that decides the imputation."

In stating all this, it must be remembered that the physical productivity of capital cannot be proved directly. A machine does not reproduce itself, but something foreign to it. Indirectly we see that the introduction of a machine leaves labour free to employ itself in creating capital, and so leads to a great increase in product. But, in modern economic life, before the net surplus can emerge, the products — the gross returns of all the various industries—must be exchanged against each other. However circuitous the route may be, theoretically it comes to this, that every lb. of coal consumed in production normally produces another similar lb. of coal, and a surplus bit of coal besides.

Having shown now on what principle value is imputed to production goods, and the factors which determine the amount of imputation, and having shown that to capital also must be imputed a share in the net return, we come back, in the fourth book, to the "natural" value of the various productive factors.

The general principle, as we know, is that the value of the productive factors is derived from the value of their returns. When we turn to apply this to the various factors, we meet again with the greatest difficulties as regards Capital. The problems are the following. (*a*) According to the principle laid down, capital gets its value from its fruits. If, then, we wish to know the final return to any production, and so deduct from the value of the fruits the value of the capital consumed, the result is zero, for in production all capital passes into the fruits. The fruits and the capital are the same, and to deduct the one from the other leaves nothing over. If so, how is interest to be explained?—for the lender of capital demands not only a return of his capital but a surplus under the name of interest. (*b*) And suppose we find that interest exists, and that capital lent out reproduces itself year after year with a net return, why does the value of the capital not represent that infinite amount of return?

The solution rests on our previous analysis of the productivity of capital. We have just seen that in production capital transforms itself into a gross return, and that this gross return does contain the reproduction of the capital and a physical surplus. From this we infer, first, that the value of the capital can never be greater than the value of the gross return: it is thus limited and finite. The capital which changes into 105 can never be greater in value than 105. And we infer, second, that, if the gross return always contains a physical surplus, the capital value cannot be credited with the entire gross return. It must be less than 105. Thus given physical gross return and net return, and we have the solution.

In ordinary life this process is known as "discounting." We find the present value of a money claim due at a future date by deducting the usual interest. Similarly with all capital : we find its value by taking the sum of products into which it will be transformed and deducting the surplus net return. In the case of fixed capital the valuation is more complicated. The essential feature here is that the successive returns have all to be discounted, and complications enter from the fact that repairs, reconstructions, etc., must also be anticipated, and their value discounted. In the case of fixed capital of a very permanent character capitalisation takes the place of discounting, for interest, being a definite part of capital value, and capital value a multiple of interest, it is evident that we may get at the value of capital either by discounting the future interests or by multiplying the present one. The result is mathematically the same.

When we come to the natural valuation of the second productive factor, Land, we find the justification of our procedure in taking capital first. For the method of arriving at the value of the production good, land, by considering the value of its products or crops, is simply that employed in calculating the value of a fixed capital of infinite permanence. We capitalise rent as we capitalise net returns—with this difference that the return to land is always net. This, however, tells us why it is that, till capital had attained to some position in industry, there could be no accurate valuation of land. In capital we have parent wealth reproducing itself with a surplus, and, given this gross and net return, we can find the value of the parent capital. In the case of land, we have nothing but net returns, and therefore can have no principle for calculating the value of land but that which would make it an infinite sum — corresponding to its infinite possibility of rent. But when capital comes on the field, when it is employed on land, and when land and capital begin to be compared and exchanged with each other, a standard is found for the capitalisation of rent. Capital and land become commensurable in their products : the same amount may be reaped by sowing more land or by applying more capital. Under a communism there would, indeed, be no exchange of land and capital, but there would still be the equations resulting from their co-operation.

As to the third productive factor, Labour. While the free labourer is no longer an object of valuation, as he was once in the days of slavery, his individual acts are so. The method here is similar to the others. The imputation decides what share of return may be ascribed to each service of labour, and the value of each share thus ascribed determines the value of the service. Thus the value of each service, like the value of all factors, depends on supply and demand, on the support it gets from complementary goods, and on the state of technique ; and this applies to all services, from the highest monopoly services down to the unskilled labour which figures as a mere " cost good."

Socialism would value labour by time of work, taking no further note of difference: an hour of skilled labour should be counted, say, two hours of unskilled. The Socialists here forget the double service of value to the present economy; that it serves not only as a title to income but as the organ of economic control. In the game of income-making, every one receives the value of his stake, and wealth and labour equally figure as stakes: he who puts in much wealth draws out much income. This Socialism might change. But it is this same value that weighs goods and employments against each other, and determines the conduction of production goods to the best possible economic results. Would the change in the distribution of income compensate for the utter disorganisation which would come of neglecting the determinations of value? Is land to have no value because Hodge is to get as much as the squire, or the effect of capital on the total return to industry to be ignored because Jack is as good as his master?

In the fifth book we come to the subject which will probably meet most criticism from English economists. In it Wieser takes the classical theory that value is determined by cost of production, and finds in cost nothing less than the most general form and measure of utility. The argument in brief is the following. The value of production goods is derived from their products. But production goods, which are not subject to monopoly, and which enter into the making of many products, receive their value from the least valuable of these which is still produced: that is to say, from their marginal product, or, more correctly, from their contribution to this marginal product. But once they have got this value, as a rule they retain it in the products into which they pass, and thus the value of these goods—significantly called, in this relation, "Costs"—proximately determines value. But, inasmuch as it is the marginal utility of the marginal product which first determines the value of these costs, the law of cost of production is merely a special case of the general Marginal Law of value.

This is the most difficult and subtle part of the book, and I make no apology for trying to put the main contention in another setting.

There can be no doubt that a mineral spring gets its value from the fact that its water is found adapted to certain wants of humanity. If the chemical constitution of the water should change, the value attached to the spring will entirely disappear. This is, perhaps, as clear a case as could be desired of the value of a production good being determined by the value of its product. How does this differ from the case of production goods in general?

It is in this, that the mineral water is the one and only product of the spring, while such production goods as coal, iron, unskilled labour are, as it were, wells of many waters. Their products are innumerable in extent and variety and value. On the same principle, however, as we determine the value of the mineral spring, we should naturally say that the value of coal, iron, and labour must be determined by the value of the totality of the commodities into which they enter. But this totality is a thing that does not come under empirical observation. No statistics can cover its infinite variety. It is so huge and so heterogeneous that its influence on the productive elements from which it comes must be obscure. In the means of production, on the other hand, we have homogeneous goods existing in great stocks and easily inventoried. In comparison with products they impress us by their very vastness and homogeneity. It is easy enough to see why we think of them as determining and of products as determined.

Turning now to the individual employer, we find that he has a very good reason for this same belief. He does not, as a rule, make any of his means of production from the beginning. He buys them; and the impressive thing to him is that his coal and iron and labour already have a price. This price he must pay, and thus the first step in his production process is an outlay, a sacrifice, what he experiences as a "cost." The commodities he makes are indeed intended to replace the value he destroys, but while the one value is anticipated the other is real. His first principle, then, being that the price he asks must conform to the price he pays, it is obvious enough why he comes to think that the price he asks is determined by the price he has paid.

And certainly if we look at the large undertakings which are now covering so much of the field of industry, it seems absurd to deny that it is cost of production that determines value. In any trade which is compact enough to be studied closely, we find one or two large firms, with large capitals, controlling the prices. If competition is keen we see these firms taking advantage of every reduction of wage, or replacing of labour by machinery, or large buying of material, or improvements in size and arrangement of buildings, to reduce prices. The market is not consulted at all. Prices go down without waiting on demand, on the well-known experience that, as a rule, every decrease in price taps a greater area of consumption. And, in whatever position the other firms are, they have simply to conform their prices to the costs of production of the one or two who are in the best position. Is it not clear that the change in price directly follows the change in cost?

Here the classical theory of Mill leaves the matter. The Austrian theory, however, does not deny all this, but, granting it all in the fullest manner, it asks:—Whence do all these things consumed in the production get the value they admittedly transmit? The product after all is nothing but the product of labour and capital co-operating. Now labour enters into the co-operation at a certain wage, while mills are built, machinery erected, and materials bought at a certain price. What determines that these wages and prices and no others are paid ? Logically, the answer of the classical school must be that the goods get their value from previous costs of production. But this is only putting the question a stage further back, and lands us in a perpetual regress till we turn the vicious circle. Suppose that, in the continual regress to more remote costs of production, capital itself should be reduced, as the Socialists would have it, to its first elements of labour, the question still is : What gives its value to this primary labour ? Unless it also is determined by its cost of production—a "monstrous idea," as Wieser calls it, which is powerfully attacked in Book V. chap. vii.—the answer can only be that labour gets its value from its products. To determine value by cost of production, then, leads us finally round the circle till we find ourselves determining cost of production by value.

Wieser's answer, on the other hand, takes us back to the one and only law of value. Products in the shape of consumption goods get their value from the dependence of human want on the possession of them, and production goods get their value derivatively from that of products. "Costs" are the ordinary and universal production goods, capable of many employments and entering many equations of value. That such costs transmit their value to products is only to say that they fulfil the purpose of their existence ; if they did not reproduce their own value in their products they would not be produced at all. But costs of themselves could give no value unless they first received it. What they receive, however, is not the total value of their products, any more than the value of goods reflects the total utility of the goods ; it is the value of their marginal product. That being so, it is only the marginal value which they, of themselves, can transmit, but this amount they are able to transmit because it is a marginal value. Raw iron of similar quality fetches one price, not because all products of iron fetch this one price, but because, although they fetch all sorts of prices according to the combinations into which they enter, there is always a lowest or marginal price. Therefore the risk of buying iron at that one price, and producing iron products from it, is a minimum ; it is merely the risk of getting the lowest price going, while the slightest increase of demand for the products, or shortening of their supply, will secure a higher price. Producing at cost therefore means destroying value in one form in the expectation that it will be reproduced in another form, and the expectation is justified because the cost represents the marginal value already being realised over the field of industry.

The law which determines value by cost of production, then,

is correct so far as applicable; that is, so far as products are "freely produced," and so far as they are considered in relation to their means of production, and not in isolation. But it is only a law of relative amounts of value. A complete theory requires a law to measure the absolute amounts of value, and this is given in the imputation to costs of the value of the marginal product. The complete law, then, will run thus :—Similar production goods maintain, in the product, similar value, and that value is derived from their marginal productive contribution.

To put it concretely. If iron is 40s. a ton, it is that, in virtue of constant and intimate communication between buyers and sellers, the fact is established that, over the field, a ton of iron, embodied in products, is fetching at least 40s. No producer will give 40s. unless he can get it. It is safe to pay 40s. for the raw iron, because the iron, appearing in the new life of a product, represents at least that value. Or, again, if the unskilled labourer is paid 15s. a week, it is not because it costs the community 15s. to keep him alive and induce him to marry and supply the labour market, but because, over the whole field of employments in which unskilled labour co-operates, 15s. has been imputed to the labourer as his share—his marginal share—in the whole.

The most striking thing in this theory is, perhaps, that it proceeds on an analysis of Cost which regards the word as having a very definite meaning. The English reader will, no doubt, remember Cairnes's attack on Mill, and his vindication of the word "cost" as meaning "sacrifice." It is this sense that Wieser gives to the expression, although his conception of what the sacrifice consists in is very different. But, like Cairnes, Wieser does not identify cost with capitalist's cost. "Cost" with him is what it costs the community. He never loses sight, as so many economists do, of the fact that the wealth of the world is "not a fund but a flow": or, rather, a lake that is always being drawn away from below and replenished from above. To keep value in existence, wealth has to be constantly remade. Every employer knows what he risks in throwing materials and labour into the melting pot of the production process. It is more difficult to see that the rising level of the community's wealth is gained by the continual change of that wealth into new forms, and that it is possible, by putting it into unwise forms, to make the community very much poorer. Production "at cost," with Wieser, indicates the level where production means bare reproduction of value already attained, and where the community would suffer actual loss unless products recovered the value suspended in producing.

Suppose we take labour and materials, pay £100 for them, embody them in a fabric, and that fabric, in course of wear, is consumed and disappears, the community has had, we may assume, £100 worth of use out of it. It has taken that amount of wealth out of the common granary : we do not regret the disappearance, because it has fulfilled its end in giving us its equivalent in satisfaction of want. It has reproduced itself in the sense that material wealth has passed into vital wealth. But if we take labour and materials, pay £100 for them, embody them in a machine, and that machine is worn out afterwards in making something which will not sell for £100, we have committed an economic offence against society. We have taken £100 worth of wealth out of the world's stock, and have neither "got the use" of it, as we say, nor repaid it. Here we have capital and labour put in a dynamic form, with the deliberate purpose of reproducing at least their own consumed value of £100 ; not a product which might or might not have value, but capital and labour which might have been otherwise employed, and in other employments would, we know, have brought £100 worth of value.

In this point of view, then, the ordinary and universal production goods are really Costs, and that both positively and negatively. Positively : because the making of any good from such elements "costs" the consumption of these elements or the suspension of them. Negatively : because, when wealth is bound up in one form of production, the production of other cognate commodities is to that extent limited.

Thus, concludes Wieser, if we ask why products produced at cost have value at all, and why they have a definite value which corresponds with the value destroyed in making them, the answer is that it comes to them from utility—not, of course, the utility realised by themselves, but the marginal utility of the totality of utility realised by products made from similar costs over the whole field of employment. That costs have been expended is only a symptom : it is the marginal utility that sanctions the cost value.

Utility is always the source of value. The distinguishing thing here is that marginal utility is no longer confined to the *class* of which it is the marginal utility : it communicates with all the field of cognate products, and allows all cognate products to be put in a similar ratio of value. Thus products, different to all appearance, come into the same value relations as do different parts of a stock. It would be difficult indeed to compare consumption goods, if, within each class, we had always to find the marginal utility of each. But, in virtue of costs carrying with them a value already determined, and giving it out to products, commodities of the most diverse kind are compared with each other very much as if they were items of the same stock. Thus it comes that the law of costs is by far the most usual form assumed by the general law of value.

The question which will suggest itself here is : Has Wieser, in this matter of costs, remained true to his first principle, that value is what ordinary people recognise as value ? The very logic with which the contention is pressed will make the English economist suspicious. Without committing myself to everything the author has said, perhaps my practical knowledge, as an old *entrepreneur*, will justify me in saying that his analysis of costs is one which will bear criticism from the man in the street. So far as the individual is concerned, the analysis seems to me no less correct than subtle.

The simplest determination of cost is that of the commission merchant. Executing an export order means to him simply the purchase of the commodities required by his client. If he pays cash, the execution of the order costs him an amount of money which, perhaps, he has taken from bearing interest in his own bank. "Cost price" is exactly this outlay. What it costs the foreign indentor, of course, is that price, plus carriage and the merchant's commission, which commission covers office expenses, interest on money, profit, and perhaps risk. The question is more difficult when we pass to the manufacturer. If I know anything about a "costing," it is this. Any large manufacturer who knows his business has a standing list of certain expenses ; this list includes, probably, specific amounts paid for wages, coal and furnishings, and percentages for wear and tear of machinery and buildings, for office expenses, and for interest on money. To these he adds the definite amounts paid for raw material, and this makes up his "cost." Thus a cotton-spinner has a costing of what it takes to manufacture each number of yarn, and, when asked for his prices, he has only to add to it the current delivered price of the cotton, and the result is his "cost." This, however, is not the price he will quote. That price includes a percentage to cover profit and risk. The costing acts, practically, as a minimum. There are many occasions on which a manufacturer is content to quote at cost— principally when it is a question of keeping his wheels going or of letting his organisation be impaired. But below cost he cannot, normally, go.

It may be thought, however, that each man in his costing is a law unto himself. But as a fact it is unusual for manufacturers to make a costing for themselves. It generally comes to them as a tradition of the trade, or an open secret. In this case, what is accepted as *the* cost is not determined by the expenses of this factory or that, but is a calculation at which, on the average, labour can be bought, factories built, and mills run. In other words, it is a marginal calculation. If the individual manufacturer cannot produce at this cost, so much the worse for him : it is the most that competition will allow him, and if he is to keep in the running he will have to be content with a smaller percentage of

" oncost." If the costing were not based on wages for which labour can generally be obtained, and on percentages of manufacturing expenses which can be realised by any one who has the necessary capital to undertake such a business, it would not be a costing for the trade at all.

If, then, we analyse this trade costing, it will be found based on something quite apart from the empirical expenses of this or that producer. The price of labour it assumes will be the wage paid over a wide field to a class of labour of technical ability. The price of factories will be the price over a definite area of erecting stone and lime. The price of machinery will be the cost of metals, capable of innumerable uses, wrought up into definite shapes by mechanics who could turn their hand to almost any kind of manual work. The price of materials will be determined by the price realisable for the many fabrics into which the material enters. In short, all the factors of production, so far as they are not monopolies, are what Wieser conceives of as Cost Goods ; that is, goods of many and various employments, with a value which may be called predetermined, because it is the marginal one of the many values actually being realised by the products into which these costs enter.

It will not have escaped notice that, among costs, Wieser includes unskilled labour, which—as Wieser indeed has explicitly claimed elsewhere—involves that labour power is a form of wealth. It is true that man, as man, is the end of economic activity, but man, as labourer, is a mean as well as an end ; and, economically, the arms that guide the plough are, equally with it, forces expending themselves in producing more wealth. This becomes clear if we consider how really poor a community would be which had dynamic wealth in abundance and had not labour enough to employ it. But however we may differ as to the propriety of including labour power in wealth, we can scarcely deny that, when labour power is employed in one way, an essential factor in the producing of wealth is withdrawn and withheld from any other employment. The particular production certainly " costs " the community this particular labour, just as clearly as the world is the poorer for the death of a good worker.

Further than this I cannot go. The important points which follow are :—the inquiry into the place of rent and interest among costs, the trenchant criticism on that conception of " cost " which identifies it with the pain of labour and the abstinence of capital, and the concise but pregnant treatise which occupies Book VI., on the place of the marginal law in the economy of the state. If I pass over these here, it is not because they are of less value, but because modesty must set some limit to an editor's preface.

I am bound to add that, according to the author's conditions, I have made myself responsible for the economic accuracy of the present rendering, and have revised it word by word. For the translation of the Author's Preface, ·and the drawing up of the Analytical Table of Contents, I alone am to blame. In all other respects the translation is Mrs. Malloch's, and although, as the inspirer of her undertaking, I am debarred from giving my own opinion as to its excellence, it is no more than justice to quote what Professor Wieser says regarding it :—" der Text schien mir in Ihrer Ueber-setzung wieder klareren und tieferen Sinn gewonnen zu haben." To Professor Wieser himself my grateful acknowledgment is due of the singular patience and clearness of explanation with which he has answered my numerous queries, and finally revised the entire proofs.

WILLIAM SMART.

GLASGOW, 1893.

# AUTHOR'S PREFACE

IT has been said that one finds in Adam Smith nearly all the explanations of value which have ever been attempted. What is certain is that, in his explanation, Adam Smith has put together two views that contradict each other. To put it shortly: he gives two theories, one philosophical, the other empirical. In the first he tries to make clear what should be thought of as the characteristic attribute of value; what it is we ascribe to some things and deny to others that, to all appearance, are entirely the same; what it is of which we ascribe a great deal to certain things and very little to other things which, measured by outside standards, seem infinitely superior. In this view value is an attribute *per se*, coinciding with no other that we know, and, least of all, with the usefulness of things. In carrying out this attempt Adam Smith first of all abstracts from the complicated circumstances of ordinary economic life, and confines himself to the simple, primitive, natural state. In this state he finds that it is labour in which value originates. Goods are worth to us what they cost in labour, and what, therefore, their possession saves us in labour. The idea of value thus arrived at Adam Smith goes on to apply to the empirical instances of the phenomenon of value. Thereafter when he comes across value he sees nothing mysterious in it; he has a means of distinguishing it from the other attributes of things; he knows how to get to the heart of it; indeed, through its relation to the labour from which it receives its content, he can even measure it.

But, independently of this, Adam Smith describes—and here

we come to his empirical theory—the causes of value and of the more or less of value, as he finds them in actual life. He sees clearly that labour which he has recognised as, philosophically, the sole cause of value, is not also, practically, its sole cause. As a rule three factors together, he thinks, make up the exchange value of products; besides the labour of production there is also interest on the capital required and rent of the land required. This is not to say that the "value" of observed experience is of another nature from the "value" of philosophy. That value which is created by land and capital is of the same nature as that created by labour. As regards it also, it is labour to which we must refer, if we are to grasp its content and measure it. The only sign of his being aware that there is any contradiction between his philosophical and his empirical explanation is where he passes from describing the primitive natural condition of economic life to describing a society based on private property in land and capital. Here he cannot resist a gibe at those who "love to reap where they never sowed," although, once within the kingdom of reality, he takes interest and rent into his system as self-intelligible facts.

Nearly half a century passed, and then Ricardo tried to clear his master's doctrines of their imperfections. Ricardo deeply felt the contradiction which Adam Smith had scarcely noticed. How did he seek to remove it? In a way that, more than Adam Smith's mistake, betrayed how young a science political economy was. To-day when, in virtue of the labours of these great pioneers of the science, we stand face to face with the problems which are to be solved, it is scarcely possible to put ourselves back into those conceptions in which they first gave shape to their observations and thoughts. In their effort to escape from absolute perplexity they took frank delight in explanations which, to us now, are more of a riddle than the phenomenon they were meant to explain. What, then, did Ricardo attempt? His whole endeavour exhausted itself in trying to show that the philosophical and the empirical theory of Adam Smith,—both of which, indeed, in taking up this position he had to clear and carry further,—did not contradict each other so much as at first sight would appear.  If we limit ourselves to the general rule and the average, value as it is and value as we get it from labour, agree in their amounts—not altogether, indeed, but almost so—with one exception, which is so trifling that it may be quite properly neglected.  Of the two empirical factors in the formation of value which Adam Smith named besides labour, the rent of land—and this was the ultimate gain of Ricardo's famous theory—is entirely eliminated.  Rent does not determine the value of products but is determined by that value.  Interest, of course, remains, but Ricardo thinks he has shown that it increases with the value of products in, approximately, the same ratio as the quantities of labour required for production, so that the quantities of labour do, in the long run, give a fairly true measure of the value relations of all products.  Interest, as treated in this way, forms no hindrance to his system, and Ricardo consequently does not really try to explain it.  He takes it as he finds it—a fact that needs no explanation.  This treatment, which has excited the astonishment of so many later writers, is perfectly intelligible if we remember the impulse which set Ricardo's mind to work.  He had no intention of explaining the whole of economics.  He wished to show only that the value which *is*, is very much the same as the value which can —although only from a certain point of view—be *understood*. Ricardo was the last man in the world to think of reforming economic life.  He never opposed, to the value which is, the value which ought to be.  It never came into his mind to condemn interest, and his system, understood in the sense of its author, does not in the least involve the condemnation of interest.   In this there is nothing illogical, and when the socialists base their crusade against interest on his system, they do not complete it, as they imagine they are doing, but destroy it.   Only if interest is undoubtedly a good thing can one pass over it as Ricardo does.

Since Ricardo's book appeared another half-century has fled, and, since the *Wealth of Nations*, more than a century.  In that time the demands on the social sciences have grown apace. In Adam Smith's day people explained the existing condition of things by the "original" nature of man and the "original" state of things, and were content. We, on the other hand, like to explain reality by reality. Philosophy itself has become empirical. It allows no argument which is not drawn from well-founded experience. The historical state, positive law, the economy of every-day life, are the objects of research, and, at the same time, the ultimate sources of the instruments of research. If Adam Smith and Ricardo were writing to-day, they would be full of the spirit of to-day, and even if they had not command of the abundance of observation and knowledge which the genius of the one and the acuteness of the other have put at our service, their books would be ever so much more perfect than they could have been in their time. Certainly they would avoid the mistakes which the human spirit since their day has outgrown.

Their school, however, still pursues the path they trod, hesitating between uncomprehended empiricism and the purest speculation. And it is a great school. It is strange indeed to find that while, as regards questions of politics and of method, whole sides have renounced the English parent school,—from the socialists to the adherents of the historical school in Germany,—as regards the old economic problem of value many of the newer economists have remained true to its dogmas. As a man's judgment about value, so, in the last resort, must be his judgment about economics. Value is the essence of things in economics. Its laws are to political economy what the law of gravity is to mechanics. Every great system of political economy up till now has formulated its own peculiar view on value as the ultimate foundation in theory of its applications to practical life, and no new effort at reform can have laid an adequate foundation for these applications if it cannot support them on a new and more perfect theory of value.

Of course the ruling theories of value have, in many respects, put themselves in antagonism to the theory of Adam Smith and Ricardo, particularly in Germany—although, indeed, in that country there has of late years been a widening acceptance of the labour theory. The advances which theory has made therefrom can scarcely be overestimated. More particularly may it be noted that Use Value has now been put by the side of Exchange Value, and that, besides the economic life of the individual, we now take cognisance of national and other more general economies. Here, again, the connection between the theory of value and practical politics is strikingly shown. Hostility to the individualist reading of the conception of value took sides with the struggle against the individualist tendency in economics. It seems, however, as if this branch of the ruling doctrine also has exhausted its force, and that this movement also hangs on the "dead centres." As economic research stands to-day, people, on the whole, are investigating, not the phenomenon of value, but the popular conception or conceptions of value. I have said in another place that, for the sciences which deal with human action in any of its departments, the peculiar danger is that of missing their mark. Passing by the act and its motive, they are too ready to investigate the meanings which men take out of their own actions. Thus we get "popular theories," particularly those which can be read out of the ordinary meaning of the terms in which phenomena they deal with are expressed. This remark seems to me peculiarly applicable to the value theories just spoken of.

That the theory of value needs reforming from the very foundation no one will, I think, deny. The imperfection of the prevailing views is confessed even by their own adherents. But while the great majority of economists are still at a loss where to turn, a new theory has come to the front. At first unnoticed, and then for long but little thought of, worked out by men who, for the most part, did not know of each other but yet agreed where so many had doubted and disagreed, came a new theory based on a new foundation—an empirical theory on an empirical foundation.

The new theory starts from the old proposition, that the value of goods comes from the Utility of goods, or—what is the same thing—from the satisfactions of want which goods assure. To find the laws of value, then, one must first know the laws of want. Now, in this pursuit, we come upon the fact that the want for the same things—even in the same person, and in given economic conditions—is of quite different strengths, varying according to the degree in which the want has already been satisfied through the employment of goods. But since the employment of goods depends upon the amount of goods which one possesses, the quantity of goods obtains a decisive influence on the valuation of wants and so on the source of value itself. This observation is the starting-point of the wider investigation. In itself it is of great importance because it ultimately gives the solution of the paradoxical phenomenon that value falls as goods increase. But it is as important through its effects on economic method, because it guides the economist, from the false objects to which speculative methods and ordinary language point, to the empirical heart of the phenomenon of value.

As forerunners of the theory we may name generally all those who have derived value from utility; specially those who were persistent in basing even exchange value altogether on utility, particularly when they did not shrink from their principle in spite of the obvious influence of costs of production. Usually on this point the statement of the theory is either inconsequent or obscure, or retains its logic and its clearness, at the expense of renouncing completeness, by leaving out the question of costs. As forerunners of the new theory in the stricter sense of the term we may name those who take up the question of quantities of goods as well as their utility. Usually, of course, this goes only to the extent of showing the changes in the amount of value which follow from changes in supply and demand. But, in the case of a few writers, it has taken a much more exact form, where "scarcity," "limitation of supply" is recognised as condition under which utility creates value—and that not only, as Ricardo says, as regards certain rare goods, but as regards goods generally. Among writers answering to this description, who may be held the immediate precursors of our theory, are Auguste Walras (*De la Nature de la Richesse et de l'Origine de la Valeur,* Evreux, 1831), and also Condillac, Genovesi, and Senior.[1]

Passing by those numerous pioneer works, we meet with no less than four authors who had worked out the same theory independently of each other, Gossen,[2] Jevons,[3] Menger,[4] and Leon Walras.[5] Gossen's statement, in spite of many quite classical points of superiority, is, on the whole, the most imperfect. That of Walras, though admirable of its kind, suffers, to my mind, from the preponderance of the mathematical element. The laws which govern amounts of value undoubtedly allow of a mathematical expression; nay, the more complicated of these can be expressed exactly only by means of mathematics; and here certainly mathematics has a great task to fulfil. But in the value theory we have to do with something more than the expression of the laws of amounts. The obscure conception of value is to be made clear; all its manifold forms are to be described; the service of value in economic life is to be analysed; the connection of value with so many other economic phenomena is to be shown; in short, we have to give a philosophy of value which needs words, not numbers.

---

[1] Rau, too, with his "concrete *Gebrauchswerth*" may be included. There is a notable treatise of the mathematician Daniel Bernoulli: *Specimen theoriae novae de mensura sortis* (Commentarii Academiae Scientiarum imperialis Petropolitanae, tomus V. Ad annos 1730 et 1731. Petropoli, 1738). Bernoulli maintains that it is *valde probabile, lucrulum quodvis semper emolumentum afferre summae bonorum reciproce proportionale.* He is fully acquainted with the subjective character of value, as well as with the most important law of the change of value. His work is referred to by Jevons in an extract from another of his books. By the kindness of Prof. Menger I have seen the original. Dupuit's *De l'influence des Péages,* 1849, mentioned by Jevons, I have not been able to consult.

[2] *Entwicklung der Gesetze des menschlichen Verkehrs und der daraus fliessenden Regeln für das menschliche Handeln.* Braunschweig, 1854.

[3] First in a paper before the British Association, 1862, then fully in the *Theory of Political Economy,* London, 1871; 2nd edit. 1879.

[4] *Grundsätze der Volkswirthschaftslehre,* Vienna, 1871.

[5] *Éléments d'économie politique pure ou Théorie de la richesse sociale.* Lausanne, 1874-77.—*Théorie mathématique de la richesse sociale.* Lausanne, 1883.—*Théorie de la Monnaie.* Lausanne, 1886.

And, besides all this, the empirical existence of the alleged facts is to be established.

Finally, Jevons's statement, in spite of its amazing wealth of observation and reflection, in spite of its finished expression, in spite of the catholic spirit which speaks from it, must be placed second to that of Menger. Menger goes more deeply into the subject, inasmuch as he starts from a more general conception of value. For this Menger is indebted to the German school of national economists with its patient untiring labour in formulating the general economic conceptions, and pressing forward from concrete phenomena to that height of abstraction from which the phenomena are to be logically arranged. It may be said that, in great part, the German school long ago formulated the conceptions, leaving for us only the task of filling them out by adequate observation. In this it has laid up a treasure from which all succeeding economic effort may draw indefinitely.

Of Jevons's system one part, the "theory of utility," as he calls it, has passed into English literature. Among the works of Continental economists who adopted the new theory, may be mentioned the fine statements of Pierson,[1] and Charles Gide[2]; and in Germany a work of Launhardt[3] on the lines of Jevons and Walras. But it is in Austria, in the lineal succession to Menger, that the development of the new value theory is to be sought. I may be allowed to refer to my own *Ursprung und Hauptgesetze des wirthschaftlichen Werthes*, Vienna, 1884, in which I applied Menger's theory to the phenomena of costs. On this followed a work by Böhm-Bawerk,[4] which, independently of its extremely clear presentation and its careful and fruitful revision of many matters of detail, is particularly valuable from its treatment of the theory of objective value. Finally came a comprehensive work of E. Sax,[5] extending the theory of value

[1] *Leerboek der staathuishoudkunde.* Haarlem, 1884.
[2] *Principes d'économie politique.* Paris, 1884.
[3] *Mathematische Begründung der Volkswirthschaftslehre.* Leipzig, 1885.
[4] *Grundzüge der Theorie des wirthschaftlichen Güterwerths.* Conrad's *Jahrbücher*, N.F. vol. xiii. Jena, 1886.
[5] *Grundlegung der theoretischen Staatswirthschaft.* Vienna, 1887.

over entirely new material to which no previous writer had applied it—to public imposts, and thus giving the theory one of its richest applications.

The ground-plan of the new theory is drawn, but much remains to be done ; not only to widen its reach generally, but to complete it in itself. The following pages are an attempt to supplement what has already been done. In distinction from my earlier work I have not paused to discuss the assumptions of the value theory, but limited myself severely to the subject of value and its direct content. On the other hand I have attempted to exhaust the entire sphere of the phenomena of value without any exception, and, besides that, so far as my ability goes, to think out more exactly the subjects I had already treated of. The present work is on that account in no way a repetition of my former one, but an entirely new book, treating for the most part of entirely new matter, and having nothing more in common with it than the general fundamental propositions. I hope this time to have met the objection urged against the *Ursprung des Werthes* that I had omitted the connections—the "bridges," as one critic called them—between the principles laid down and the concrete phenomena of value with which we are familiar. Whatever may be thought of its truth or correctness, I think I may venture to say that no value theory has ever yet been put forward more complete and exhaustive in external form and treatment.

The very multitude of single matters which I had to touch on has compelled me to pass over almost every critical analysis that differed from mine, and indeed to leave out almost every appeal to economic authorities outside of those authors who belong to the same school, and from whom I directly took the propositions I had put forward. Similarly I have refrained from discussing any of the economic conceptions I had to employ outside of that of value. I shall very willingly put up with the reproach of being incomplete by reason of this if it should succeed in making any clearer the inner connection of the book. At the same time I should not like to be suspected of having done so from any undervaluing of the theoretical work of other economists—least of all, of those of Germany.

I have just said how deeply indebted, in my opinion, every theoretical attempt of to-day is to the labours of German theory. And to it the new value theory stands most nearly related—it is in truth the fulfilment of what German theory had long demanded.

F. WIESER.

PRAG, *September* 1888.

# ANALYTICAL TABLE OF CONTENTS

## BOOK I

### THE ELEMENTARY THEORY OF VALUE

# BOOK II

## EXCHANGE VALUE AND NATURAL VALUE

# BOOK III

## THE NATURAL IMPUTATION OF THE RETURN FROM PRODUCTION

## PART I

### THE GENERAL PRINCIPLES OF IMPUTATION

# BOOK IV

## THE NATURAL VALUE OF LAND, CAPITAL, AND LABOUR

## BOOK V

### THE NATURAL COST VALUE OF PRODUCTS

# BOOK VI

## VALUE IN THE ECONOMY OF THE STATE

# BOOK I

## THE ELEMENTARY THEORY OF VALUE

# CHAPTER I

## THE ORIGIN OF VALUE

WHENCE do things get their value ?  If we put the question
to any intelligent and trained  man of business, who had no
knowledge of  the various attempts of  theorists  towards an
explanation of value, whose  mind was unbiassed  by the forms
of speech  which echo  learned  theories  and have  passed  into
ordinary business use, and who was, therefore, capable of judg-
ing only through  the medium of his own personal  experience,
he would undoubtedly answer, as the first theorists did,—" from
their Utility."  He would be very much surprised to learn that
several considerations made the  truth of this  answer improbable, and  that  many facts—some of them to a certain  extent
generally known, and familiar even to himself—seemed to prove,
with almost  absolute  certainty, that utility could  not  be  the
source of value.   These facts we may state as follows.

First : goods which are to be had in superfluity, and which
any one may appropriate at will, no one will pay anything for,
be they ever so  useful.   In many places water, although indispensable to man, is entirely without value.  Of course this
observation  refers  immediately  only  to  value  in  money, the
so-called " exchange value," and it might  be  thought that it
was  not  true  of value  in the  using of goods, the so-called
" value-in-use."   Closer examination shows, however, that it is
true also of value-in-use.   In the household, as in the market,
the superfluous is regarded  as  the  valueless, and is clearly
separated from those things of which  there is no superfluity.
However frugally we may act with  regard to other things, we
should  never think of economising in things  which we are

always sure of having in over-abundance. No one will ever try to secure possession of them : there is no property in them ; no interest is taken in them. They are used, but we think no more about them.

Second : things which have a great deal of use have often a smaller value than those which have little use. Iron, for instance, has less value than gold. This is true equally of its money value, and of its value-in-use, in the market and in the household. Even in the socialist state—supposing its citizens still to possess the æsthetic sense—it will be considered of less moment to lose an ounce of iron than an ounce of gold.

Third : a large quantity has, under certain circumstances, less value than a smaller quantity of the same thing. It is well known that the Dutch East India Company destroyed a considerable part of their produce and of their plantations, in order to create a more lively demand, and so secure for the remainder a greater value than the whole property had originally possessed. The same thing is observed as regards the returns derived from good and from bad harvests,—the bad harvests showing better than the good. This also, as I hope to show later, applies to value-in-use as well as to exchange value.

Fourth : while the measure of use is in such frequent and striking contradiction with that of value, it happens, as often and as strikingly, that value is in agreement with the exact antithesis of use—namely, with costs. I say "antithesis" because, if goods, by their use, prove themselves the friends of man, they prove his enemy by the costs which they necessarily involve.

A great many of the writers who have occupied themselves in the investigation of value—and, we may add, for a long time many of the best of them—have for this reason refused to consider at all the idea that value may arise from utility ; they assert that the value of goods comes from the difficulty of their attainment, and is proportionate to it. Those again who have based their theory upon utility, have, for the most part, done so in a manifestly unsatisfactory fashion. They have either placed themselves in contradiction to the facts already mentioned without explaining away the contradiction, or laid so much stress on these facts that, in the end, they can scarcely be distinguished from those writers who have rejected the principle of utility, except by their express avowal of that principle.    Only a few authors, the more important of whom are mentioned in the preface, have struck the right road. These have conceived the idea of Use Value in such a way that it is neither confuted nor disturbed by the foregoing considerations, but on the contrary is entirely confirmed by them.

It is as these last-mentioned writers understand it that I mean to state the theory of value.    Before beginning, I may be allowed to make a single introductory remark as to the manner in which I intend to carry out my task, and, particularly, as to the nature of the proofs which will be used.

The economist who undertakes to explain value has to explain the procedure of those who value.    He describes in plain language the meaning of transactions carried on, times without number, by all of us.    He does, on a large scale and with a difficult subject, the same thing as one who accurately describes some trade or some mechanical operation, which every one can do, but which it is not easy, without the assistance of concrete instances, to present and follow up in all its complexity of conditions.    As the poet gives expression to the thought which every one feels but cannot express, or the actor's genius shows the passion which perhaps he may not even feel, so does the man of science describe in words, and apart from their concrete realisation, the actions which every one is accustomed to perform.    He does not require to have any actual case before him, or to accompany his description with any practical working out.

Any layman in economics knows the whole substance of the theory of value from his own experience, and is a layman only in so far as he does not grasp the matter theoretically,— *i.e.* independently, and for and by itself,—but only practically, —that is to say, in some given situation, and in connection with its working out in that situation.    If this be true, how else shall we better prove our scientific statements than by appealing to the recollection which every one must have of his own economic actions and behaviour ?    For this reason, every expression which may be taken as confirming this recollection, is welcome as an aid to our investigation.    For instance, when we find that the unbiassed answer of the layman indicates that he considers usefulness to be the source of value, this judgment is a finger-post which we dare not neglect, unless the most searching and careful examination has proved that it points in a wrong direction. And who else is the final judge of the theory but the public ? The only true theory of the estimate we call " value," will be that to which practical life gives its entire assent. Only, of course, the judge must first himself be educated. He has to judge whether he recognises himself in a description which informs him about his own life and being, and which he himself is incapable of giving.

I trust that what follows may meet the approval of those who not only act economically, but reflect on their actions. I have no other wish than to gain this approval, but I cannot allow the right of judgment to those who protest without having reflected. It costs much trouble to give a clear description of even the simplest and most familiar trade or business, and certainly, in the theoretical study of a matter so many-sided and complicated as that of value—even though it is so familiar to all, perhaps because it is so familiar to all—we cannot do without the most earnest and ample reflection.


## CHAPTER II

### THE VALUE OF SATISFACTIONS OF WANT

IN its ordinary use among economic writers the word Want signifies every human desire, whether great or small, justifiable or unjustifiable, necessary or unnecessary, material or immaterial. Bodily well-being, idle delights, artistic pleasure, moral satisfaction may all be classed together as objects of human want.

In this sense all the " use of goods "—all the utility which goods afford—amounts in the last resort to satisfaction of wants, and the opinion that the value of goods arises from their use may be more exactly stated by saying that it rests upon the satisfaction of wants which they furnish. It is the satisfaction of wants which, in the first instance, has value, or " worth " or " importance to " us. Satisfaction is that which is really desired, and is worthy of desire : and, as we do not desire goods for themselves, but for the satisfaction they give, so do we value them only for that satisfaction. The value of goods is derived from the value of wants.

The theory of value, then, has first of all to do with the value of wants, this being the form in which value first appears.

What it is that gives value to the satisfaction itself we shall not here attempt to explain. It will be enough if we give the symptom by which the degrees of value or importance are recognised. It is the intensity with which the satisfaction is desired. Were we to place the different satisfactions on a graduated scale, it would probably be remarked that those which stand highest are not those which provide the purest pleasure, or which will most serve to beautify our lives. Our most urgent concern is rather with the warding off of extreme want, and with the prevention of care and suffering; the necessaries of life must first be assured " before we can reach the good things of this world." There is a difference between what men might like to have, and what they must first decide to secure ; and it is according to the latter, not the former, that interests are actually ranged above and below one another. The actual ranking of the valuable—no matter how moral judgment or fancy would dictate—is simply that which men recognise by their actions when they are called on to choose between having one thing and another.

In this sense the amount of the value of want depends on the class of want, but, within this class, it depends upon the degree of satisfaction already attained.

This latter point in detail we must now discuss. Here, first, we shall have occasion to remark the influence of *quantity* upon value. And it is not the value of goods alone that is affected by quantity, but the value of wants.

# CHAPTER III

## GOSSEN'S LAW OF THE SATIATION OF WANT

EVERY one knows that the desire for food decreases as the want is gradually satisfied, until, finally, when what we may call the "satiation point" is reached, the desire is for a certain time entirely allayed, and possibly changed into its opposite, surfeit and disgust.  Every one knows that the same happens in the case of numerous other desires; satisfaction diminishes the craving, and in the end fully destroys and transforms it.

There are several authors who have the merit of having, independently of each other, extended this observation scientifically speaking, and made it the starting-point of their theory of value.  These have been mentioned in the preface.  Among them Gossen is worthy of particular notice, owing to the fate of the book in which he gave expression to his discovery and to his ideas on economics generally.  His *Entwicklung der Gesetze des menschlichen Verkehrs und der daraus fliessenden Regeln für das menschliche Handeln,* was published in Brunswick in 1854, but it almost entirely disappeared from sight in Germany, although its author had hoped to win for it a Copernican fame. Any one who reads the book will understand why, as well on account of the peculiarities of its excellences as of its faults,— both of which are great.  Jevons, in the introduction to the second edition of his *Theory of Political Economy,* and also Walras, in an essay which appeared in the *Journal des Economistes* in 1885, have given somewhat detailed accounts of both book and author.  Economics owes a great debt to Gossen, and it is with this feeling that I call the law of the satiation of want Gossen's Law, although my statement of it is not entirely in accordance with his.

It scarcely requires illustration.  Gossen himself added to its clearness by the following addition.  Alongside of the weakening effect which continued satisfaction has upon desire, we find also, in certain circumstances, the opposite tendency; that the desire grows by repetition and exercise, inasmuch as it is thus developed, gets to know itself, its own end and its own means, becomes purified and elevated.  Thus, during the period of development, the law of diminishing desire meets with an opposite tendency, and the law applies unlimitedly only to wants which are entirely developed.  Granting this, however, it applies to every want without exception.

There can be no doubt that it applies to those coarser material wants, which recur periodically, as, for instance, the

desire for food.    Here, however, we must distinguish between
the want as a whole and the several feelings of want which
are included in it.

The want as a whole of course retains its strength so long
as man retains his health ; satisfaction does not weaken but
rather stimulates it, by constantly contributing to its development, and, particularly, by giving rise to a desire for variety.
It is otherwise with the separate sensations of the want.
These are narrowly limited both in point of time and in point
of matter.    Any one who has just taken a certain quantity of
food of a certain kind will not immediately have the same
strength of desire for another similar quantity.    Within any
single period of want every additional act of satisfaction will be
estimated less highly than a preceding one obtained from a
quantity of goods equal in kind and amount.

Many material wants are not intermittent, but require a
continuous satisfaction.    Such for instance is the need of
warmth, the human body requiring to be kept at a certain
temperature.    Here also Gossen's law applies.    That action
which is needed to secure the required minimum temperature,
—that is, the expenditure for clothing, fuel, and so on,
indispensable for keeping the body in sufficient warmth,—will
be most intensely desired, while the multiplication of this
necessary expenditure does not affect our well-being in the
same degree, and will be much less eagerly desired.    In the long
run the prospect of any further increase will be met with
aversion.

With regard to the higher wants,— those which come into
existence whenever the necessaries of life are secured,—the
same law obtains.    It is not, however, so noticeable to ordinary
observation, and, indeed, appearances are rather against it.
The wants of wealth appear to be the very opposite to
those of poverty.    The latter are urgent but narrowly limited ;
the former can be done without, but, when awakened, show
themselves many-sided and extensive.    Many-sided, because
they are from the first rich in varieties, and become always
more so, as one gives rise to another ; and extensive, because
they frequently include objects of great compass, increasing
with the degree of culture attained.    On this account it might
well be thought that such wants were infinite and subject to no

diminution.　But on looking more closely at the matter we shall find that, when the same act of enjoyment is repeated without variation,—the very same, and neither extended nor changed,— ᵛthe result is in this case also weariness and disgust.　The thirst of a collector seems to be insatiable, and his object certainly is one of extraordinary compass, even though it be confined to one article.　The man who collects books or pictures requires a great fortune, and may not even then be able to fully satisfy his wish.　Every new book he acquires serves to stimulate instead of to weaken his desire, and this is not due to morbid extravagance : it is entirely justifiable, as it brings him nearer to his object, the possession of a perfect library or a perfect picture gallery.

But how would it be, if he were offered a duplicate of some work he already had ?　This and this alone, as Gossen re- marked, would be a case of exact repetition,—of the repeated satisfaction of the same impulse ; and here, without doubt, the desire would be much lessened, probably entirely destroyed. And thus we shall ever find it to be if we direct our attention strictly to the proper object.　Even desires such as that of power or of wisdom, even ambition, greed of honour, thirst for knowledge are not exempt from the same rule.　The sum of what these crave, when at their height, is infinite ; no man's life or strength is sufficient to satisfy them wholly even once, not to speak of repeating it.　But the single acts which make up this whole sum, the individual effects, exercises of power, acquisitions of knowledge can be repeated and tired of.　The charm of the whole lies in the power to vary the items. Nothing on earth is of such a nature that man can go on enjoying it over and over again, and lose himself in its con- templation.　This holds of all emotions, from hunger to love.

## CHAPTER IV

### THE SCALES OF SATIATION

IF we were to follow out the course of satisfaction of a want, and mark every separate act of satisfaction with the value that accompanied it, we should obtain a diminishing scale, the zero of which would be reached with full satisfaction or "satiation," while its higher point would correspond with the first act of satisfaction. If we had a common and exact measure for desire and non-desire, we might be able to put into figures the "satiation scale" of every want, and so compare the scales with each other. We are far from having that. But we are able to say quite positively that there are great disparities between the individual scales. It is not only that the higher points of such scales differ, and differ to an extraordinary degree, as the experience of every one sufficiently shows, but that, in the scales, the degrees between one act and the next are very different. There are many wants which almost leap from the point of highest desire to that of full satisfaction—such, for instance, as the coarser needs of daily life. There are others which, although little felt to begin with, continue for long periods without any very perceptible diminution of their strength,—as, for instance, many of the finer wants. Even as regards the individual want the decrease of desire is frequently quite irregular—decreasing more slowly now at the beginning, now at the end of the scale. It must not in the least be expected that every scale will present all the different degrees of desire between which it is possible to distinguish. Assuming the possibility of distinguishing between one hundred different degrees of intensity of desire on the whole, we should certainly find no single scale that would show exactly all the hundred degrees; each would miss one, or another, or even many of the degrees; we should not perhaps find *any* scale which would regularly move, say, ten degrees at a time. Individual scales are, indeed, likely to be formed with considerable irregularity, and we shall find such a series as 100, 90, 80, 10, 0 ; or 20, 14, 5, 3, 2, 1, 0, and so on.

This statement, rude and imperfect as it is, will be found of great use in what follows. We shall have to turn back to it at several important points. Even here, it gives us a first suggestion of how one of the fundamental difficulties of the problem of value may be overcome ; that, namely, arising from observation of the contradiction between value and usefulness. A few words will make this clearer. A sensation of want which belongs to a very important class of wants may nevertheless not possess any great importance. The importance of the *entire class* is measured by the *entire scale* of satiation, especially by its highest degree. But the importance of every separate sensation of desire is measured by some particular and possibly low point upon the scale, according to the condition of satisfaction which has already been reached. The want for food, measured by its *class*, is more important than that for adornment or finery, but none the less may the individual sensations of vanity, in the first stages of their satisfaction, be far stronger than the desire for food, supposing the latter desire to be satisfied for the time being.

Classes of goods correspond to classes of wants, and judgments concerning the importance of classes of wants will correspond with judgments on the usefulness of classes of goods. But the single commodity need no more realise the usefulness of its class than the separate sensation of desire need realise the importance of its class. The last course eaten by one who has almost dined has a comparatively small utility, although it contains in itself the property of saving from the pangs of hunger. Suppose that one has a sufficiently large number of goods of the highest usefulness, some of them can be put only to a very trifling use, and, indeed, if there is a superfluity of them, he will have no use whatever for that part of the supply which is in excess of the demand.

In economic life we have to do not only with classes of wants and classes of goods, but also with the state of subjective satisfaction already reached, or the supply. We cannot, therefore, judge of goods simply by their usefulness; we must judge by the amount of use attainable in the individual case; and, consequently, the value of goods must be kept at least as distinct from their usefulness as the use to which we put them is.

# CHAPTER V

## MARGINAL UTILITY

EVEN where nature is most lavish with her gifts, there are but few kinds of goods with which she provides man in such superfluity that he can satisfy every, even the most insignificant, sensation of want. As a rule the supply of goods of which he can avail himself is so scanty that he must break off his satisfaction at a point on the scale short of complete satiation. This point— the smallest utility obtainable in the circumstances, assuming the most thorough possible utilisation of the goods — is of peculiar importance, both for the act of valuation and for economic life. To it refer the expressions, " *Werth des letzten Atoms*," of Gossen, " Final degree of utility," or " Terminal utility " of Jevons ; and " *Intensité du dernier besoin satisfait* (*rareté*)" of Walras. Menger uses no particular designa-tion. The name " Marginal Utility " was suggested by me (*Ursprung des Werthes*, p. 128), and has since been generally accepted.

Where the supply of goods is too scanty to satisfy every sensation of desire, the necessary break must be so made that it will be felt as little as possible. This will be the case when we begin by satisfying the most intense sensations of want, and go on to extend to its utmost the compass of enjoyment ; or, in other words, when we reach, in unbroken satisfaction, the lowest possible marginal point of enjoyment. Economic con-duct requires that the marginal utility in this sense be placed as low as possible. The means by which to reach this end are, on the one hand, the utmost possible quantitative exploitation of goods, and, on the other hand, the utmost care in choosing how the goods are to be employed where there are several competing ways of employing them. Such a competition of employments may arise from two circumstances—first, where goods are capable of manifold and various uses, and, second, where supplies are accumulated and their consumption should be spread over periods of time. In the first case our concern must be to choose between the separate forms of employment, and to keep the economic balance even ; in the second, to distribute the goods so as best to meet the wants of the whole period.

The difference between the various satiation scales of wants comes into play in the case of goods of many-sided usefulness. Every different kind of employment has its own particular scale of satiation, with a culminating point peculiar to itself and a course of satisfaction peculiar to itself. On account of this the determination of the marginal utility in the given case becomes a very complicated matter. Its principle will be best explained by an example, and we need be at no loss for examples, as goods of manifold utility are numerous enough. The most important are found among the means of production. Who could count up the services which iron, wood, or coal is capable of rendering? Or those for which human labour is fitted? The most many-sided of all goods is, however, money; through exchange it can be turned into almost any other commodity, and thus made serviceable for the satisfaction of almost any want. From no other commodity can we obtain so clear a presentation of the idea of "marginal utility." I therefore take it as example, although money is really useful only as a medium, and presupposes the existence of exchange, a phenomenon of which we shall not treat till the following book.

The money income of the richest man is usually not sufficient to cover every outlay that he might desire. Acting economically therefore, so as to secure what Gossen calls the *Grösste an Genuss*, the greatest possible enjoyment, we shall distribute our expenditure so as to "make it go as far as possible," from the satisfaction of the most urgent wants down to the most insignificant. The larger the income is, the farther it will go, and the longer will it be before we need to break off our satisfaction. But the *Grösste an Genuss* could not be reached if the separate branches of expenditure were not adequately weighed against each other. Nowhere must the boundary-line be overstepped, which is fixed by the general circumstances of our wealth. Every overstepping in one branch will have to be paid for in another, which other, as represented by a higher degree on the scale of wants, will impose a sacrifice greater than the enjoyment got from it. To this extent it is quite possible to speak of a "level

of household expenditure," of a general condition of life pre-
scribed for every household by the peculiar amount of its
demand and the peculiar amount of its means, and necessitating strict adherence to it in all its branches. It would,
however, be a mistake to believe—as almost every writer who
has occupied himself with this question has done, Jevons
more than any other—that it is necessary to keep strictly
in every branch of expenditure to the same degree of satisfaction, the same level, the same marginal utility. That is
quite against the nature of wants, for wants have not each an
equal but each a peculiar satiation scale. Were the "level
of household expenditure" to be understood in this way,
every addition to income would require to be laid out equally
in corresponding enlargement of every branch of expenditure.
As a matter of fact it is usually spent on a few individual
branches, while the others remain as they were; or, if the
additional income be so great as to allow of an improved
condition of things all round, the extra expenditure is distributed in the most irregular manner. The satiation scales
of wants are very diverse; the receptive power of one want is
great, that of another comparatively small; that is to say,
one is susceptible of a degree of intensity which another does
not reach, or which it oversteps. The principle for the
economic employment of goods of manifold usefulness is not,
then, that we must, in every employment, obtain the same
lowest possible marginal utility, but that in all employment as
low a marginal utility be reached as is possible without necessitating the loss, in some other employment, of a higher utility.

What has just been said applies as well to the economic
management of supplies of goods destined to cover periods
of time. Premature and extravagant indulgence should not
impose unnecessary burdens on the future. It would be best
to divide the enjoyment equally over the whole period, but
this is frequently made impossible by the nature of goods,
which does not allow of their being kept, as also by the
uncertainty of providing for changes of value in the economy
in question. The limit of employment should always be of
such a sort as promises the greatest amount of utilisation on
the whole.[1]

[1] See *Ursprung des Werthes*, p. 146, and Sax, p. 371.

A special question is here suggested :—Are present and future satisfactions to be estimated entirely alike ? Is not precedence in time also precedence in degree of importance ? Is it not right that enjoyments should be considered of less value the further they are in the darkness of the future ? Jevons has answered this question in the affirmative, and since him many others, some with great positiveness, though, as I think, wrongly. We cannot avoid going into this matter more closely, even though it detains us a little from the attainment of our present object, the deduction of the elementary law of value.

## CHAPTER VI

### THE VALUE OF FUTURE SATISFACTIONS OF WANT

IF we did not possess the power of providing for future wants, our lives would be but poorly provided for. No new products would be prepared ; those we already possessed would be thoughtlessly dissipated ; only chance and the goodwill of nature would provide for the morrow. And as it is of importance that we should be sensible in advance of the wants of the future, so is it of importance that the degree of that sensibility should be sufficient. Anxiety about future necessaries should be as powerful as the passion with which we give ourselves away before the urgent feelings of the moment. If future satisfactions of want were represented in present valuation, not at their full future value but at only a small fraction of the same, all economic life must in the end fall to pieces, just as though they were not represented at all ; only that the course of economic decay would be less rapid and its end farther off.

It is evident that man possesses the capacity of acting in consideration of future feelings of want, but observation of human nature makes it very obvious that he will act with less energy than when he is under the influence of present feelings. The future want, wherever it comes into the domain of the present, is preceded by a psychical reflection, and this

reflection is of a totally different nature from the want itself.
It is far finer, more *innerlich*, and, even in the case of purely
bodily wants, is always mental.   The hunger of a future day,
*e.g.*, does not act as hunger, but as anxiety for sustenance ; the
object of desire is the same, but the desiring is different.
Instead of a *want* of we have an *interest* in.   Is not, then,
some energy lost in this change from the coarser to the finer ?
Must not the anxiety about a future want always have less
weight than the actual appetite that comes after it ?

If men in civilised societies do possess the degree of
foresight required for a prosperous economic condition, one thing
is certain ;—they have not always possessed it.   It has been
gained through the labour of civilisation, just as, in moral
conflicts, strength to meet the fires of passion has been gained
through the feeling of duty.   At bottom the economic
conflict between the needs of to-day and those of to-morrow
is really of a moral nature ; it is a special case of the struggle
between impulse and reason.   Uncivilised races are only to
a small extent capable of considering in advance the wants
of the future ;—to so small an extent, in fact, that the miserable condition in which they are found can be fully explained
by this alone.   It is not only the foreknowledge that is
wanting, but, quite as much, the previous mental excitation,
the uneasiness which the civilised man experiences in the
consciousness that wants are coming for which there is no
provision.   A heavy numb apathy deadens the sense of the
savage.   He awaits with indifference, or at most with a
feeling of helplessness, the misery from which he does not
suppose it possible to escape, but which he certainly could
escape had he only the energy to will it.

Whether civilised races have reached the high-water
mark of development that is desirable, may easily be ascertained by consideration of their economic actions.   How
do they behave in the majority of cases ?   Do most people
sacrifice their means for the pleasure of the moment, or do
they lay by for future needs ?—There can be no doubt that,
on the whole, the wise householders outnumber the spend-
thrifts.   Certainly there is no one entirely without economical
sin ; no one who has never consumed too soon some thing
which he afterwards bitterly desired and had not.   But, on

the whole, it is an economic principle which is as well obeyed as any of the fundamental economic principles, that wealth and income should be economised with a view to the future and to old age. Every supply of goods should, so far as possible, be distributed over the wants of the period of time which it is intended to cover, in such a way that, whether the time at which they occur be earlier or later, all the more important sensations may be satisfied, and only the less important — those which it is impossible for the supply to cover—be left out. The exceptions to this rule are so few in number, that a theoretical inquiry which regards the principle as invariable, and asks as to its further effects will help to explain our economy, not only as it ought to be, but also as it actually *is*.

To avoid misunderstanding I shall try to explain my meaning more exactly. I have no wish to deny that, in general, the futurity of an event has the effect of weakening its impression. As a rule this is also true in economics. It seems to me, however, that, in a civilised state, every good householder, and, in the main, every average one, has learnt to master this weakness of human nature in one respect;—so far, namely, as to distribute a regularly-acquired income among regularly-expected wants, and, in connection with this again, so far as to try to acquire a regular income, and secure the conditions thereof by exercise of labour power, and main-tenance of the parent stock of wealth. The call for fore-thought in this latter connection is peculiarly strong, and it should not excite wonder that it is more active here than in any other direction.

Moreover a well-regulated and prosperous economic con-dition does not in the least demand that *every* future sensation be fully realised in the present. Only those require to be considered which have to be provided for, and those again only in so far as they require to be provided for. First in import-ance are all those wants which must be covered by the present supply of consumption goods, and by the *income* available at the moment, and which consequently, in economic management, come into conflict with present desires. Alongside of these we may put the far more numerous wants which have to be covered by suitable employment of the present *parent wealth*.

Our conception of both groups of wants, but particularly of the latter, takes a peculiarly simplified form, which easily gives the impression that they are entirely shoved into the background. They are conceived of in the mass, and grouped together in periods of time; and we are generally conscious of them only in so far as they are represented by the goods which are devoted to their satisfaction.    Foresight for the wants of a remote future and of later generations, for instance, is seen in the precept which forbids diminishing of the parent stock of wealth, even although this precept only refers to the goods which form the wealth, while the wants themselves appear to retreat more and more into a darkness which the imagination does not seek and need not seek to illuminate.[1]


# CHAPTER VII

## THE VALUE OF GOODS

ORIGINALLY only the human has importance for man.    Thought for one's self, interest in one's self, comes by nature.    Towards things, on the other hand, man is originally indifferent, and his interest in them only awakens in so far as he finds them connected with human interests and destinies.    This takes various forms; such as pity, when the lower animals are seen to suffer just as man does, or religious or poetic emotion, when observation of the living in nature awakens suspicion of the connection of all life, or, finally, economic valuation, when things are conceived of as instruments to and conditions of human well-being.    This is the coldest form that our interest takes, as it regards things simply as means to human ends; it is, however, at the same time, the most far-reaching, as it embraces most things, and claims not only existence, but property.

Our natural indifference towards things is nevertheless so

---

[1] Many economists would explain interest, particularly the interest on productive capital, by the difference in value between present and future feelings. This seems to me an error.    Interest derived from productive capital is a phenomenon of the very best ordered economic transactions, of those managed with the highest possible degree of foresight.    It is not in the least a sign of a defective economy.    See, however, Book IV.

great that it requires a special compulsion, a peremptory challenge, to make us look upon them as objects of importance, objects possessing value.   Nor does the mere observation that things are "of use" to us, and that the use has for us importance or value exert this compulsion.   Where we employ goods for our own uses, but where at the same time these goods are at our disposal in absolutely assured superfluity, we use them, but concern ourselves no more about them than about the sands of the sea.   Whether they increase or decrease —always supposing that the superfluity remains—we merely think, "What does it matter? we have always enough and more than enough of them!"   In Paradise nothing would have value but satisfactions—neither things nor goods.   Because there one could have everything, one would not be dependent on anything.

On the other hand, where there is not an assured superfluity, interest awakens in the train of self-seeking calculation, and communicates itself to such *goods* as we notice ourselves using and not caring to lose.   Men in general thus lay their account with things, as the egoist with persons.   And here we are not speaking only of cases of real need, of extremest want, where the little that one has is guarded with an Argus eye; nor of objects of great scarceness or rarity, such as a work of art which is quite unique, and whose loss it would be impossible to replace.   We refer also to cases where people are fairly prosperous, but nevertheless require to economise; and even to cases of extreme wealth—always supposing it is not assured natural superfluity—where, in many respects, a man has everything, but where, all the same, the "everything" requires continual guarding, administration, and renewal.   In these circumstances there is not a single change in a man's possessions which is entirely indifferent.   Every addition brings some addition of enjoyment; every loss, even the slightest, disturbs, makes some gap, and breaks the expected line of enjoyments.   Happiness and sorrow are dependent on our possessions; the destinies of goods mean the destinies of men. There is an intimate association of ideas between human interests and goods.   Goods, indifferent in themselves, receive value from that value which their employments have.

Goods which are to be had in an assured and natural

superfluity are called Free goods ; all others are Economic goods. Thus only economic goods can possess value. The value of goods, according to Menger's definition, is "the importance which concrete goods, or quantities of goods, receive for us from the fact that we are conscious of being dependent on our disposal over them for the satisfaction of our wants."

It should be noticed that no part of free goods receives value ; neither that part which is superfluous, and cannot therefore be used, nor yet that part which is used. Of the water which flows abundantly from some spring, neither that portion which fills the jar, nor that which overflows has value. The value of goods, although it has its origin in use, does not all the same reflect the utility : there are cases in which great use is obtained, where nevertheless no value—*i.e.* no value of goods— is created. The theorist, therefore, who would explain value must not content himself with explaining the change in amounts of utility ; he must go further and examine those laws by which amounts of utility are changed into amounts of value. It may be suspected—and we shall find this suspicion confirmed in what follows—that value, owing in many cases so little of its origin to utility, is, even where it has so originated, equally far from always containing the full amount of utility. If the use of a good in the individual case be so far removed from its general usefulness, its value, if our suspicion is indeed confirmed, must be even further removed from that general usefulness—and here is opened up to us a second point of view from which we may explain and make intelligible the contradictions which experience points out between value and usefulness.

# CHAPTER VIII

## THE VALUATION OF A SINGLE COMMODITY

Goods are valued either individually and by themselves, or in connection with other goods. The latter form of valuation takes place chiefly in one of three ways. A good may be valued in connection with other similar goods belonging to one and the same stock or supply; or in connection with goods from which it can be produced; or in connection with goods which can be added to it by purchase.    Of these three cases the first is the elementary one, to which both of the others may be traced back.    It is with this first alone, therefore, that we shall deal in the elementary theory of value.

It is extremely seldom that goods are valued singly. It may be some chance or other which has isolated them, or it may be a consequence of some peculiar character which allows of them being obtained only individually.    In the first case, they are irreplaceable during the period of their isolation; in the second, they are altogether so; and, in both cases, they must, on any reasonable valuation, have ascribed to them the full value of the utility which is expected from them.    The means without which an end cannot be reached must be valued as highly as the end itself.    If the good is by nature fitted for several purposes which, however, mutually exclude each other, so that it can actually serve only one of them, that employment to which the greatest importance belongs decides its value.    Only a barbarian could value the Venus de Milo by the utility of the material of which it is made. A starving man will value his last bite at its full life-saving value,—supposing the saving of his life to be of consequence to him.

Now and then, too, considerable supplies of goods are valued as one indivisible whole, and, consequently, as one good.    A vendor may, for instance, lay down as a condition of selling some large supply of goods, that it be bought entire or not at all.    If circumstances force the buyer to consent to this condition, he on his part must estimate the value of the supply as a whole.    He has to reckon up the whole sum of useful services which he may expect, from the highest utility which the goods composing the stock are capable of rendering, down to the marginal utility fixed by the amount of the stock and of the demand for it; and the sum of all those services gives him the value.    Value here reflects the *whole* utility aimed at in employing the goods.

Suppose a community were forced to buy the grain it requires from some foreign country and in one lot, if the conditions just described were laid down, the government would have to make a valuation which would be almost infinite. It would require to consider that, without the purchase, a great part of the community might die of hunger, and to calculate all that would be gained by the prevention of this most extreme misfortune, and by securing the health and vigour of the people.

Besides that would have to be reckoned all the less important useful results, which really are obtained although their marginal effects are inappreciable. It is obvious that the valuation of the harvest which is actually made stands far behind any such valuation as this. And what is the reason of it, seeing that the actual effects of the harvest are no less important, — that it does in truth keep away hunger and misery, and maintain the strength of the citizens? Why does its full use not enter into the valuation? The reason is, obviously, that we are not forced to obtain and value the harvest in one lot. It comes through thousands of busy hands, by a thousand different means of transport, from thousands of storehouses; and it passes through thousands of purchases to those who need it, and is by them consumed in thousands of different acts. The question as to the effect *on the whole* is never put; the only thing we have ever to do with is the effect of individual parts, which, compared with the whole, are vanishingly small. And this brings us to a law of valuation by which an amount of value is ascribed to the single part, and, therefore, finally, to the sum of all the parts, which is as far removed from the amount of value that would otherwise pertain to the united whole, as the resisting power of all the single rods in a bundle is from that of the whole bundle.

This law we have now to trace. It might be described as the General Law of Value, since it holds in almost every case. Almost all supplies which we possess and employ, which are bought and sold, which are used up and produced, are acquired and used in parts. Seldom only is a supply of goods the object of economic use and valuation as a whole— a whole of which nothing can be lost without everything being lost. As a rule every supply or stock of goods comes to us as a sum of parts, each of which has its separate destiny, and can be individually disposed of.

# CHAPTER IX

## THE VALUATION OF GOODS IN STOCKS. THE LAW OF MARGINAL UTILITY THE GENERAL LAW OF VALUE

SUPPOSE a poor man receives every day two pieces of bread, while one is enough to allay the pangs of positive hunger, what value will one of the two pieces of bread have for him? If for instance a still poorer man, who has nothing whatever, begged of him one piece, what sacrifice would the first make in complying with the request? Or—what comes to the same thing—what use or utility would he retain if he refused to comply with it? The answer is easy enough. If he gives away the piece of bread he will lose, and if he keeps it he will secure, provision for that degree of want which makes itself felt whenever positive hunger is allayed. We may call this the 2nd degree.

One of two entirely similar goods is, therefore, equal in value to the 2nd degree in the scale of utility of that particular class of goods. One of three goods, under the same conditions, will have the value of the 3rd degree; one of four, of the 4th; in short, any one good, in a stock of goods of the same kind, will have in general the value of the final or marginal utility. The larger the supply—the need remaining unaltered—the smaller will be the marginal utility and the value, and *vice versâ*; while, on the other hand, the greater the need the higher will be both marginal utility and value, and *vice versâ*.[1]

This, however, is not enough. Not only has one of two goods the value of the second degree of utility, but either of them has it, whichever one may choose. In our example, neither of the two pieces of bread—so long as the possessor has both—will have that value which belongs to the allaying

---

[1] The amount of supply depends chiefly on the result of production, and thus the elements of production come into relation with value. The nature of this relation we shall first discuss, however, in Book V., under the head of "Costs." Meantime we shall assume that supplies exist without production.

of positive hunger, because, so long as they are both in his possession, he will never be exposed to this extremity. He may give away one of them—whichever he likes, so long as he keeps the other—without losing his provision against starvation. But, if either of the two pieces is equal in value to the second degree of utility, both together have twice this value. And three pieces have together three times the value of the third degree of utility, and four pieces have four times the value of the fourth degree. In a word, the value of a supply of similar goods is equal to the sum of the items multiplied by the marginal utility.

Say that a harvest, consisting of 1,000,000 quarters, is short, and that the community has to be so sparing in its use of it that grain dare not be consumed unless the act of consumption yield a satisfaction equal to the figure 10 : the value of the harvest will be calculated as 1,000,000 × 10. The value of a harvest of 2,000,000 quarters, where the act of consumption need only yield, say, 4, is equal to 2,000,000 × 4. The value of 1,000,000 tons of iron, where the marginal utility is 1, is 1,000,000, and the value of 100,000 oz. of gold, with a marginal utility of 50, is 5,000,000.

As the use obtained from free goods represents no value whatever, so is the use obtained from supplies of economic goods not fully represented in their value, and for the same reason. In the case of free goods we need not concern ourselves at all about their use, that being always assured so long as the goods remain in superfluity ; and in the case of economic goods, our only concern is with the marginal utility, all the higher utilities being assured so long as the amount of the supply remains unaltered. In the former case we need have no anxiety as regards the provision for our wants generally ; in the latter we need have no anxiety as regards the provision for the principal part of our wants—and the larger the supply the less the anxiety—and need only concern ourselves to see that the proper margin of employment is maintained.

The law of value just described owes its existence, on the one side, to the peculiar formation of the scales of want, but, on the other, to the peculiar conditions under which goods are possessed. If goods did not come forward in stocks or supplies consisting of similar items, but only individually and each with

a separate form, the law would not hold.   Where such stocks
do appear, however, it must hold.   How could things entirely
similar be differently valued,—supposing, of course, that they
belong to the same person, and are used to satisfy the same
demand ?   Even if any one in an anxious mood were to set
apart certain items, as a reserve for extreme exigency, and, as
such, might think of putting a special value on them, he would
surely find, on reflection, that the reserved goods were in no
way different from all the rest, and that there would be no
danger of this extreme case arising, even if some accident destroyed the reserve, so long as the other stock held out.

This law of value unites the conceptions of value and of
utility in a way that is fully confirmed by facts.   When experience shows that iron is worth less than gold, and that an
abundant harvest may be of less value than a poor one, our
law can give the explanation.   In the main, it clears up all
the contradictions which appear to separate the conceptions of
value and utility from each other ; and it only remains for us
now to combine the fact of costs with the law of marginal
utility,—a task we shall undertake later.   Meanwhile we
have not yet completely exhausted the elementary theory of
value.   In the first place we have only externally resolved
the contradictions between value and utility.   Under certain
conditions iron *must* be of less value than gold, and the rich
harvest of less value than the poor one—but what hidden
import is contained in this ?   However unconditionally one
adopts our law and is convinced by our logic, he will nevertheless scarcely be able to deny that its inmost content is
veiled in darkness.   In one connection it appears paradoxical ;
in another it even seems to comprehend within itself a complete antinomy.   The final task of the elementary theory of
value will be to clear up this paradox and explain away this
antinomy.   Only when this is done, shall we obtain a clear
idea of the essential nature of the phenomenon of value.[1]

---

[1] We have here reached a decisive point in our examination.   Experience
shows us daily that similar goods obtain similar prices ; and the majority of
theorists (although they may use different names for the same thing) are agreed
that these prices are fixed by a marginal law.   In this is involved that exchange
value, which rests on prices, is the same for all similar goods, and obeys a marginal law.   We, however, have gone still further, and say that Value generally
and in every form, even in that of use, and even where there is no ex-

# CHAPTER X

## THE PARADOX OF VALUE

ASSUME that a man owns one good, and that the employment of it gives a utility equal to 10 ; and suppose that his holding gradually increases up to 11 goods, in the course of which

change—as *e.g.* in a community organised on a socialist basis—must be the same for all similar goods, and must obey a marginal law. Jevons, Gossen, and Walras have not gone so far as to assert this. To these writers the utility of the separate portions or items of one supply is different, according to the amount of use which each actually gives. I can scarcely hope to have brought home to the reader, and still less to have converted him all at once to such an unfamiliar aspect of the question. But I trust that the following presentation of the theory of value, which is founded on the foregoing, and which examines, and—so far as my judgment goes—explains all the different relations of value, will be found convincing.

There is just one more point to which I should like now to draw special attention. Price not only regulates the amount paid by buyers, but also the amount of production by sellers : it gives to the latter its level. All goods produced for the market are produced under a valuation which considers similar goods as equal to one another, and which subjects them to a marginal law, and it is with reference to this valuation that the costs permissible are calculated, that all stocks are inventoried, that all undertakings make up their balance-sheets, and that all profit and loss is reckoned. If a socialist community were to give up exchange—the payment of buyer to seller—it would not on that account require to give up this measuring scale for the valuation of goods. It could continue to value similar goods at the same figure, and to bring them all under a marginal law. And might we not have some right to ask, what reasons it would have to discontinue this ? Certainly it would require weighty ones to justify a change in a method of valuation which has been followed ever since, if not before, human economics began to be enlarged through trade. And, finally, we have still to ask whether it would ever be possible to cease valuing goods in this way. Is it possible to value equal things unequally ? Can we ever regard the useful but unimportant as important ?

Menger's theory of value differs essentially from its rivals on this point. He asserts that the law of equality and the marginal law refer not only to price but to value. In my opinion this places his theory in advance of all the others, and wins for him the fame of being the first to lay a perfect foundation for the theory of value. The other authors we have named examine only the laws of want and the laws of price. Menger alone includes the laws of value. His view of the question is the most wide-reaching, inasmuch as it not only aids us to the clearest comprehension of the present economy, but also enables us to think out possible future forms of economy.

the marginal utility decreases proportionally down to 0. The value of the stock at each point will be as follows :—

| When he has | 1 | 2 | 3 | 4 | 5 | 6 | 7 | 8 | 9 | 10 | 11 | goods, |
|---|---|---|---|---|---|---|---|---|---|---|---|---|
| the value is | 1×10 | 2×9 | 3×8 | 4×7 | 5×6 | 6×5 | 7×4 | 8×3 | 9×2 | 10×1 | 11×0 | units of value. |
| = | 10 | 18 | 24 | 28 | 30 | 30 | 28 | 24 | 18 | 10 | 0 | |

Here a regular decrease of the marginal utility, and, therefore, of the value of the single good, is seen to take place along with an increase of the supply, and further explanation is unnecessary. Each additional good brings with it a diminished increment of utility, and must, therefore, bring only a diminished increment of value. It is otherwise when we consider the value of the whole stock, and follow its development from 10 up to 30, and back again from 30 down to 10 and 0. Judged from the standpoint of that aspect of value with which daily economical life impresses us, this scale seems completely paradoxical. Value is commonly regarded by us as a simple and absolutely desirable characteristic of goods, mathematically expressible as a positive amount. It corresponds with this view when the series shows an increase of value along with the first additions to the stock, but it entirely contradicts it when, towards the end of the series, every further addition to the stock is accompanied by a corresponding decrease in value, until, finally, when the point of superfluity is reached, value completely disappears. Whence comes this contradiction ? How is it to be explained ? The first half of the series appears to confirm the view that value is something desirable, something positive, while the second shows it as a negative quantity, something burdensome or evil. Which then is true ? And how can both ever be brought to agree ?

Very easily, so soon as one gives up the preconceived notion that value is a simple positive amount. Value (as marginal value) arises from a combination of two elements, the one positive, the other negative. It is a complex amount ; or, more exactly, a residual amount. So soon as one distinguishes between these two elements in the formation of value, the series we have just drawn above explains itself in the simplest manner possible ; and the semblance of irregularity, which must have proved insuperable for those who expected and sought a simple progression, disappears.

Both elements in the formation of value have been explained by what has already been said.

The positive element is the enjoyment in the use of goods. Every additional use which is furnished by a newly-acquired good is welcome.  The good which is first acquired brings the largest increment of utility because it satisfies the most urgent stage of desire ; every one that follows has a lesser utility because it meets a desire which has been already comparatively satisfied.  And should the accretion of goods cross the margin of want, there will be no addition to the positive element in the formation of value.  There will now be no employment for additional goods ; they will not bring enjoyment to any one.

Taking the former figures, the increment of the positive element in value will be as follows :—

| With | 1 | 2 | 3 | 4 | 5 | 6 | 7 | 8 | 9 | 10 | 11 | goods, |
|---|---|---|---|---|---|---|---|---|---|---|---|---|
| there will be | 10 | 9 | 8 | 7 | 6 | 5 | 4 | 3 | 2 | 1 | 0 | units of value. |

And the *total* amount of this positive element, calculated for the whole stock, will be as under :—

| With the total enjoyment is | 1 | 2 | 3 | 4 | 5 | 6 | 7 | 8 | 9 | 10 | 11 | goods, |
|---|---|---|---|---|---|---|---|---|---|---|---|---|
| | 10 | 19 | 27 | 34 | 40 | 45 | 49 | 52 | 54 | 55 | 55 | units of value. |
| | | $(10+9)$ | $(19+8)$ | $(27+7)$ | $(34+6)$ | $(40+5)$ | $(45+4)$ | $(49+3)$ | $(52+2)$ | $(54+1)$ | $(55+0)$ | |

The negative element arises from the indifference with which men naturally regard goods.  Only when forced to it, do we transfer our interest from the uses of goods to the goods themselves ; and, in the process of transferring, we have to overcome a natural opposition which varies in strength according to the circumstances.  The greater the need, the more eager will we be to get possession and keep possession of goods ; the smaller in this case will be the opposition.  The opposition will be completely broken down where our need rises to extremity, for here we identify our destiny with that of the goods, and in their loss we see our own calamity.  On the other hand, the opposition will be complete where everything is present in superfluity ; here we can enjoy without any feeling of gratitude for, or interest in, the objects which procure for us the enjoyment.  Between extremest need and superfluity the opposition is a graduated one ; we bestow upon goods an amount of interest derived from the interest we have in the services they render us.  But we do not give them the

whole of this interest; we make a certain reservation. That
is to say, all the single items of a stock are considered only at
the value of their marginal utility. The surplus value, that
which goes beyond their marginal utility, is withheld from the
goods. Here, then, is the numerical expression for the strength
of this opposition : the negative element in the formation of
value is equal to the subtracted surplus value. Making use
once again of the foregoing figures, we find that, so long as we
own only one good, there is no deduction in the formation of
its value; the entire value of the use is transferred, undiminished, to the good. With two goods, on the other hand,
there will be a deduction of 1 from the value, as each of these
is valued only according to its marginal utility 9, while the
utilities of both added together amount to $10+9$. Three
goods have each a value only of 8, and their utility is equal
to $10+9+8$, the surplus value deducted being therefore 3.
Reckoning further in the same way, we shall find the minus
amount in the formation of value as follows :—

| With a stock of | 1 | 2 | 3 | 4 | 5 | 6 | 7 | 8 | 9 | 10 | 11 goods, |
|---|---|---|---|---|---|---|---|---|---|---|---|
| the minus is | 0 | 1 | 3 | 6 | 10 | 15 | 21 | 28 | 36 | 45 | 55 units of value. |

If we put together the plus and minus amounts we shall
obtain the following as result :—

|  | 1 | 2 | 3 | 4 | 5 | 6 | 7 | 8 | 9 | 10 | 11 goods. |
|---|---|---|---|---|---|---|---|---|---|---|---|---|
| Positive (+) | 10 | 19 | 27 | 34 | 40 | 45 | 49 | 52 | 54 | 55 | 55 units of value. |
| Negative (−) | 0 | 1 | 3 | 6 | 10 | 15 | 21 | 28 | 36 | 45 | 55 ,, |
| Residual (+) | 10 | 18 | 24 | 28 | 30 | 30 | 28 | 24 | 18 | 10 | 0 ,, |

Thus we obtain the same scale as that which resulted from the
multiplication of amount by marginal utility.

It is now seen that the apparent irregularity of the scale
is really a consequence of the strict regularity of its conditions.

The value of a supply must increase with the increase of its
items so long as the positive element preponderates; in other
words, so long as the increment of value, furnished by the
utility of the newly-acquired good, is greater than the value
which is lost through the decrement of value which its addition
causes to every good already in the stock. This is the ascending
branch of the movement of value, or, as we might call it, the
" up grade " of value.

On the other hand, the value of a supply must decrease with its augmentation, whenever the negative element gains the ascendency. This is the descending branch of the movement of value, or the "down grade" of value.

Strange though it seems, the value must touch zero twice in the course of its development: in the one case, where we have nothing; in the other, where we have everything. If we possess nothing, there are no objects to value; if we possess everything, there is—just on account of the superfluity—no subjective inducement to an act of valuation. Only if we possess something—be it much or little—does the phenomenon of value appear; and between the two zero points, so different in their importance, it has its existence. It presents itself with the first goods that come into our possession, and increases up to a certain culminating point, from which it decreases, until, when superfluity is reached, interest is again completely withdrawn from the goods.

As a matter of fact, human economies move almost entirely in the ascending branch. In most things we are so far from having a superfluity that almost every multiplication of goods shows a corresponding increase in the total value. The single good certainly falls in value as the stock increases, but as a rule we find that the loss in the items is outweighed by the gain on the whole. On this account we are accustomed to measure wealth and riches by the sum of value of their constituent parts, and regard it as a misfortune if the value of property and revenue goes down. And therefore it appears to us paradoxical when, at times, we are forced to notice that, although the amount of goods and of enjoyments, of wealth and well-being, has been augmented, their value has decreased. It may be that exceptionally favourable weather has resulted in an over-abundant harvest; or it may be the discovery of some new productive stratum of unsuspected fertility; or some sudden and enormous increase of returns through advance in technical processes: or it may be caused by some error on the part of the producer, who has been misled by greed of gain, or a mistaken and exaggerated estimate of demand, into too greatly enlarging his production. But it is always some unusual accident when individual branches of economy are transferred to the descending branch in the movement of value. It is improbable that our whole economic system will ever permanently come under such favourable conditions, and production be brought so near to superfluity, that the ascending movement of value will cease to be the dominant one. The example, however, of those few free goods which nature offers leaves us no room for doubt that value disappears whenever superfluity is reached; and this is really the best proof for our contention that value must begin to decrease whenever superfluity approaches. Even though experience shows the scale of value to have many gaps, yet it gives us sufficient facts to let us trace its ideal course from end to end.

## CHAPTER XI

### THE ANTINOMY OF VALUE AND THE SERVICE OF VALUE

As consequence of the observation that, in the overwhelming majority of cases, the value of possessions increases with economic prosperity, the exceptions have been either entirely forgotten, or put on one side as unessential and unimportant disturbances. The idea has gone abroad that value is the highest principle in economic life, and that all our economic action must be regulated with reference to it. It has been said that people should so act as to obtain on the whole the greatest amount of value.

If this idea were correct, our economic life would be directed by a power which would, in some measure, work against the aims of economic conduct; to the extent, namely, of preventing the realisation of economic ends beyond a certain point; that is, beyond the up grade of value. And one would be justified in speaking of an antinomy in the law of value, which would refer not only to exchange value, as Proudhon has asserted, but to every form of value. It would be expedient for every one, not only from a money-making and selling point of view, but in his own private economy—even for a Robinson

Crusoe who could not sell at all—to convert superfluity into want, and want into greater want, in order to create and increase value. No one, however, would wish to act in this way, and it is therefore untrue that value has the guidance of our economies. The highest principle of all economy is utility. Where value and utility come into conflict utility must conquer; there is nothing in the nature of value which could give it the ascendency. Utility is imperfectly contained in value, with the accompanying peculiarity that the amount of utility which is contained is intimately associated with the very idea of goods. But this latter phenomenon cannot have the effect of preventing any one from entering into transactions which a complete addition of the utilities to be got from the goods acquired would show to be profitable. If I were able, by any method whatever, to secure for myself a constant superfluity of all the services of goods, the idea that my interest need not thereafter be carried over from the services to the goods themselves, would not cause me a moment's hesitation in securing the superfluity. Or suppose that I expected a great amount of utility from some transaction, and the transaction at the same time caused me a certain loss of interest in the goods, this latter circumstance would not deter me in the faintest degree from carrying through the transaction.

Under these conditions, then, what service remains for value to render in economic life? A highly important one. The cases where there is a conflict between value and utility —where increase of the one is decrease of the other— occur but seldom. Experience shows that economic life moves almost always on the " up grade," and here the tendencies of increase or decrease are similar for value and utility. Whenever the utility of a stock increases with the augmentation of the stock, the value also increases, and whenever the utility of a stock decreases with a diminution of the stock, the value also decreases. A greater value almost always corresponds with the greater utility, and a lesser value with the lesser utility, and on this account transactions which commend themselves in consideration of their utility, commend themselves also in consideration of their value. The service of value consists, then, in representing utility wherever both show the same tendency.   We do not calculate utilities; we calculate values.   Value is the form in which utility is calculated, and this renders calculation infinitely more easy.   It is difficult indeed to estimate the utility of a stock; easy to estimate its value.   That is to say, the value of a stock can be expressed as the single product of stock and marginal utility; it is a multiple of the marginal utility: whereas utility can be expressed only by a sum which contains as numerous and as various amounts as the stock contains items.   The utility, for instance, of a harvest of a million quarters can be represented only by an almost inexhaustible description of all the benefits accruing from it, from its greatest effects down to those of the least important employments economically permissible in the circumstances of the case.   The value of this same harvest is easily and shortly ascertained by multiplying the utility of the marginal employments by the whole amount.   Mathematically expressed, the formula for expressing the utility of a stock of 50 items, the most intense use of which—that of the first item—reaches the figure of 100, if we assume a regular decrease in intensity for every successive item, will run:— $100 + 99 + 98 + \ldots 51$.   But the value formula will be simply:—$50 \times 51$.[1]

The simplification of economic calculation by the use of a value instead of a utility measurement is noticeable in pro-

---

[1] The value formula is an abridged utility formula.   Only that part is left out which, on the one hand, renders calculation more difficult, and, on the other hand, is really unnecessary as an adequate motive to economic actions; viz. that surplus utility which is above the marginal utility.   Economic actions which have value (in the up grade) for their motive, are not only approximately, but completely and exactly weighed and limited.   The greater utility is always reached when the greater value is aimed at.

It may be interesting to go more into detail regarding this.   There are two occasions on which economic goods become objects of valuation; first, when we wish to acquire goods, and to measure the amount of the acquisition; and, second, when we wish to part with goods in order to devote them to some given end, and to measure the amount of the service which they thus will render.   On the one side, then, we have to measure results in goods, and, on the other, outlays in goods.   It may be remarked in passing that, without some such end in view, goods are never valued: they are never valued for valuing's sake.   At most, goods are valued in advance to be ready for any contingency; but value never plays the *rôle* so readily ascribed to it by theory;—it never acts simply as the means of valuing wealth.   Wealth may be valued in all sorts of ways, according to the purpose which it is intended to serve.   The rules of valuation which are actually followed have their origin in the fact that they

portion to the economic state of development.    While the utility formula becomes continually more wearisome and less serve towards the ends of economic life, whatever these may be.    Value is adapted to its economic environment, and can only be understood through it.

First, as to the measurement of results in goods.    All acquisitions of goods which increase value are profitable.    Of two acquisitions, between which one may choose, that one will be chosen which gives the greater amount of value, because it also gives the greater utility.    Augmentations of value arising from intentional destruction of goods are unprofitable, and, in consideration of utility—which is the stronger consideration wherever there is a collision between it and value—are forbidden.    Acquisitions of goods which, inasmuch as they follow the "down grade" of value, diminish the amount of value, are nevertheless profitable.

An increase of value occasioned by increased necessity, and unaccompanied by any change in the amount of goods, must not be described as an economical result.    It is not created by any economical act.    Once created, however, it naturally influences economic action, etc., through the fact that it changes the value of goods used as outlay.

Second, as to the measurement of "outlay" in goods—whether in purchase of other goods, or in production, or in mere satisfaction of personal want.    In every appropriation of goods to a particular purpose the value of the sacrifice involved must be estimated and compared with the expected result.    The greater the sacrifice of value,—if we disregard the circumstances of the "down grade,"—the greater the sacrifice of utility, and it must be justified and made good by the obtaining of a higher result.    It is difficult to show this as regards consumption. The employment of goods towards the satisfaction of personal wants must also be guided by the value of goods.    But how can marginal value serve this end ? Would not that require that only marginal wants be satisfied ?    The difficulty solves itself whenever we give up the old and deep-rooted but erroneous belief that consumption as such is an economical act.    Consumption as such does not arise from any economical considerations.    It is only economising in consumption that is economical (see *Ursprung des Werthes*, p. 133).    The demands of economising are, however, exactly met when we keep to the marginal utility. In other words, value does not control consumption : it only forbids uneconomical consumption ; that, namely, which would not assure uninterrupted satisfaction down to the lowest attainable utility.    This prohibition and nothing else is expressed in marginal value ; no employment of goods which goes below the margin drawn can be allowed.    Through the fact that want on its side is active and demands satisfaction, economic satisfaction is reached by a combination of claims and refusals.    Whoever possesses 1000 items of the value of 10, may permit himself every enjoyment which has an intensity of 10 or more.    Whoever possesses 2000 items of the value of 8 may go further, and allow himself all enjoyments which have at least the intensity of 8.    The first may have his enjoyment, at an intensity of at least 10 degrees, a thousand times ; the second, at the intensity of 8, two thousand times.    This is the true meaning of that estimate of the value of supplies of consumption goods, to which we generally give the more material formulation, that the first possesses $1000 \times 10 = 10,000$, and the second possesses $2000 \times 8 = 16,000$ units of value.

See, upon the calculation of value, my *Ursprung des Werthes*, p. 180, and Böhm-Bawerk's *Werth*, p. 46 ; further, on the service of value, Book II. chaps. iv. and v. and Book V. chap. xiii. below.

clear, the value formula becomes more comprehensive and uniform, particularly through the entrance of costs,—which we shall discuss later.    Where money is the medium of exchange everything is measured equally, for purposes of trade, according to its money value; all utility in its illimitable variety is reckoned by the value of coin, the separate items of which are all equal to each other, and the amounts of which appear in the calculations as multiples of one and the same unit.

It is the possibility of calculating utility in terms of value which first puts us in a position to draw out exact economic plans and foresee their necessary limitation.    Thus value comes to be the controlling power in economic life.

# BOOK II

## EXCHANGE VALUE AND NATURAL VALUE

### CHAPTER I

#### PRICE

EXCHANGE gives rise to a phenomenon which, originating from value, reacts upon it in the most powerful manner; this phenomenon is price. It is not our task here to deal either with price or with the forms of value depending on it. Our concern — as will be shown clearly enough later on —is rather to describe natural value; *i.e.* value as we should find it in a community at a high stage of development carrying on its economic life without price or exchange. Nevertheless it will not do simply to disregard exchange and the forms of value connected with it. A description of social conditions whose actual or possible realisation is extremely doubtful, would be somewhat purposeless, if the description did not admit of some applications to life as we know it. Now to make these applications we must understand price and exchange value to the extent of rendering a comparison possible. At the least their general outlines must be indicated, so as to serve as background against which the clearer picture of natural value, which we intend to draw, will stand out in relief. In this way we shall be able to judge whether the fundamental features in both contrast or agree.

For this purpose it will be sufficient to describe that particular case of the formation of price in which its peculiar principle can be most clearly discerned. This is at the same time the normal formation of price under the organised division of labour. On the one side, we have numerous sellers, whose aim is the sale of stocks which they have produced for the market, and which they could not possibly use themselves ; on the other side, we have numerous buyers who compete with each other in buying, just as the others compete in selling. Menger's theory of price, and that contained in Böhm - Bawerk's *Werth*, which goes considerably farther, may be used as starting-points for our own statement. Into any further consideration of the abundant literature existing on the subject of price our present task will not permit us to enter.

Suppose a person wishes to acquire an object, no matter what, he will not, however strong his desire, agree to pay *any* price that may be asked. There is a certain maximum at which he would rather withdraw from the market than raise his offer further. This maximum is determined by two valuations : first, the value in use of the good that is to be acquired (which will be determined according to the laws laid down in the previous chapters), and, second, the exchange value of the sum of money that will have to be paid (the estimate of which will be considered in the next chapter). The sum of money whose exchange value is equal to the value in use of the desired good, determines the maximum offer. To offer more would involve a loss, as more value would be given than received. This rule holds equally for all would - be buyers without exception. Every one who thinks of making a purchase puts both these valuations before him ; establishes in his own mind this equation or equivalence ; and comes to the market resolved not to go beyond it. But although the rule is the same for all concerned, the results of its application in the individual case are very unequal, inasmuch as the amounts that enter into the calculation differ greatly from each other. The value in use of the good that one buys will vary according to the different degree of individual need — which may depend on natural inclination, on accidental circumstances, or on the degree of satisfaction already reached—and according to the amount of supply one already has. The exchange value of the money, on the other hand, will vary principally according to the amount of the person's wealth (see on this subject the following chapter). When one considers the very great variety of possible economic situations, it will be seen that the equation or equivalence of both values cannot fail to be very different

from buyer to buyer.    The highest offer can be made by
the person who is actuated by the strongest desire, and is
at the same time the richest, because for him the highest
real value is expressed in the greatest sum of money.    What
a contrast from the offers of poor men, in whose case the same
degrees of desire are represented only by a most trifling sum
of money, or from the bids of those whose desire, in the
particular case, is so slight that they do not care to set apart
anything but a small sum towards its satisfaction !

If we begin with the highest equivalent, that of the man
who is the richest and the most anxious to obtain the goods,
and come down gradually to the lowest, we shall obtain a
descending scale of maximum offers.    By way of example
we shall assume that these range, in the hands of a hundred
purchasers, from £5 down to 1s.; and we shall assume,
first, for simplicity's sake, that each purchaser is desirous to
buy only one single good or one single item.

Here we can see clearly what is the power that must decide
the competition of prices.    A skilled seller may at times succeed
in inducing an inexperienced buyer to pay a price which goes
beyond his maximum; but, as a rule, the sellers will not be
able to do more than drive the buyers to their maximum.
The endeavour of a seller, who is honest but looks to his
own advantage and acts purely according to his own interest, will be to find out those, among all the buyers, who
can pay most, and to drive them, if possible, to the margin
of their purchasing power.    On the other hand, the would-be
buyers will try to buy as much below that as is possible.
The inter-competition of buyers, therefore, is to the advantage
of sellers, and the inter-competition of sellers is to the advantage of buyers.    We shall now see how far it is possible for
each side to achieve its object.    We assume as before that
the sellers are forced to get rid of the entire quantity of
goods they have brought to market, and have no wish to
reserve any part of it for their own use; the goods having
been produced for sale and being of no personal use to the
sellers.

Supposing one single good is put upon the market, it
will obviously—if all are equally alive to their own advantage
—fall to that buyer who has the highest purchasing power,

viz. that one whose money equivalent we put down at
£5. He is in a position which enables him to exclude
all competing buyers, and he will do so if he understands
his own interest. He must, of course, make up his mind
to go the length of 99/, as this is the price to which his
most dangerous competitor may go,—that one whose purchasing power stands next to his own. And as he, for his own
part, is unable to give more than 100/, the price settles
between 99/ and 100/.

Suppose, again, that two goods are put on the market;
the one must fall to the first, the other to the second in the
series of competing buyers. The price paid by the latter,
if rightly determined, must lie between 99/ and 98/; that
is, between his own equivalent and that of the next competitor,—the buyer whom he must outbid if he would not have
his acquisition of the desired good disputed. But that buyer,
again, whom we called the first, will not, under these circumstances, pay any higher price. There is now no necessity
for him to offer more than 99/; it will suffice if he, along
with the second buyer, outbid the third buyer's offer of 98/.
Whoever buys in an open market, and from competing sellers,
pays for the same article the same price as is paid by every
one else. However great may be his own purchasing power,
he need not use it to its full extent; there will always be a
seller willing to let him have the good at that same lowest
price which has to be conceded on the market to buyers
generally.

If there are three goods, they will fall to the first
three purchasers, and the price will be fixed equally for
all three goods between 98/ and 97/, — between the money
equivalent of the third and fourth purchasers. Where there
are ten goods the one price is fixed, for all buyers, between
91/ and 90/; in order to dispose of all their goods the sellers
must keep the price below 91/, and, in order to exclude the
other competitors, the buyers must keep it over 90/. For
fifty goods the price will stand between .51/ and 50/, corresponding to the equivalent of the 50th and 51st purchasers; for seventy goods it will be between 31/ and 30/,
corresponding to the equivalents of the 70th and 71st
purchasers. In short, the larger the stock which has to be

sold, the lower will fall the price, as this permits of the entrance of more numerous and less capable purchasers, and the market price established is one and the same for the whole market.  If we give the name of Marginal Buyer (following an expression of Böhm-Bawerk's) to the weakest buyer, who, all the same, must be allowed to purchase if the whole stock is to be sold, the law of price will run thus : Price must at all times settle between the equivalents of the marginal buyer and that of the buyer who stands next under him ; viz. that one among the excluded competitors who has the greatest purchasing power.  Where commodities come forward in great quantities and have a large sale, the degrees of difference between the equivalents of various buyers,—whom we should more correctly consider as classes of buyers, —are not great.  And for such cases the law of price may, quite correctly, be still more simply stated as follows : Price is determined by the money equivalent of the current marginal buyer, or marginal class of buyers.  It settles at a figure very near it, and indeed a little under it.

The very first glance shows us that the law of price is nearly related to the law of value.  The value of a stock consisting of separate items is determined as a marginal value, according to the marginal utility of the single good ; the price of a stock which is sold in separate items is also determined as a marginal amount, according to the purchasing power of the marginal buyer of the single good.  In both cases what decides, is, on the one side, the amount of the stock,—addition to which shifts the margin and lessens the determining amount, while diminution enlarges it—and, on the other side, the want with its varying gradations.  In the case of price, however, there is, along with the degree of want, another determining fact which does not exist in the case of value.  This fact is the valuation of money from the side of the buyer ; that is to say, his wealth and income.  Before however proceeding to examine the exceedingly important effects of this fact, we must assure ourselves that the law of price just explained holds also in the case where buyers, instead of desiring to purchase one single good, desire to purchase several or more than one. Only if this is the case can the law have any real interest for us.

We need not waste much time over this point. Such a buyer will have in his mind a maximum offer determined in the manner just described. The collective value in use of the goods to be acquired, estimated in a sum of money whose exchange value, according to the subjective valuation of the would-be purchaser, is equal to this value in use, gives the maximum. The more items there are to calculate, the greater will be the maximum, reckoned as a whole, but the smaller will be the maximum of the single item, because in this case the value in use of the unit will be proportionally less (and the higher also will rise the exchange value of the money as consequence of the increased expenditure on the whole). If *e.g.* a person were willing to buy 10 goods at a shilling each, but were made by the seller to buy 20 instead, he would be able to give only a smaller price per item, as the larger purchase would bring with it a smaller utility, and at the same time the larger expenditure would be more heavily felt. At no time, however, will any purchaser—and this is our most weighty proposition—consent to pay anything but one and the same price for one and the same article, and that price will be the equivalent of the current "marginal item," say the 10th good in the case of 10 items, or the 20th in that of 20 items—always assuming that the market is an open one, and the buyer at liberty to purchase more or less according to his pleasure. If in any open market a price were demanded for any particular good which was in excess of the money estimate of the marginal good, the buyer would do better to abstain from purchasing this particular good, for which he would have to pay more than its value. The same considerations which—in estimating the value in use of a stock that may be divided up at pleasure —lead to every good, without exception, being valued at its marginal utility, also necessitate that, in the purchase of a stock which may be greater or less according to desire, for every good without exception only the equivalent of the marginal utility shall be paid. And here we see that the laws of value which we have already explained have a direct influence on the laws of price, and that the latter could not be understood without the former.[1]

---

[1] Here we have a proof from experience for our statement in Book I. chap. ix. that (for the same owner) the separate items of a stock, so far as they are equal to

If this is once established there is little more to say. At
every extension of his purchases the buyer will calculate his
maximum.   If we were to add together the calculations of all
buyers we should obtain the quantities of goods which might be
placed against every conceivable price.   Where goods are held
for high figures only small quantities will be sold, and that to
the most " capable " buyers for the satisfaction of their most
urgent demand.   Where prices are low larger quantities will be
sold, partly to the richest buyers to meet their less urgent
demand, partly to others who are less " capable."   But, at a
fixed price, only a fixed amount will be demanded and may be
sold.   If now sellers, on their side, come to market with a
fixed quantity of goods which must be entirely got rid of, they
will find the price already determined.   It is that price at
which just this amount is demanded.

Here again we have the same determinant facts;—the amount
of supply already owned, the degree of want or desire, and the
purchasing power of the buyers.   The two latter have, however,
the peculiarity that what decides is not simply the money
equivalent of the marginal purchaser, or the marginal class of
purchasers, but the money equivalent of the marginal purchaser,
or class of purchasers, *for the marginal good* or goods.

Where sellers do not wish to part with their whole supply,
but to retain a portion, either for their own use or for future
sale in some altered condition of the market; where, instead of
free competition on both sides, some monopoly exists, or the
sale, instead of being public and open to all, takes place
privately and in small groups or quite in isolation ;—in such
cases our law of price can act only imperfectly or in a greatly
weakened manner.   At the same time the characteristic element
in the formation of price—that the purchasing power of the
buyers is put in the scale—will always, excepting, at most,
the case of monopoly on the side of the buyers, be present and

each other, have the same use value, and are all valued according to the amount
of the marginal utility.   One and the same buyer will not consent to pay other
than one price for the similar items which are all bought at the same time : he
will not pay more for one than for another, and for none will he pay a higher
sum than the marginal equivalent.   This shows that he values them all equally,
and all according to the same marginal amount.   Otherwise there would be
nothing to prevent his paying different prices for them, and possibly paying more
than the marginal equivalent for a great many of them—indeed for all except
one, the marginal item.

retain its importance. Goods are not paid for simply according to the amount of utility (*i.e.* of marginal utility) which they render to the buyers, but also according to the amount of purchasing power which the marginal buyers put on that utility.

Of the many weighty consequences arising from this proposition, I shall at present refer only to one. " The highest prices therefore," (to quote from the *Ursprung des Werthes*, p. 26) " are obtainable for those goods which are to be had only in small quantity and are objects of desire to the richest classes ; the prices of such goods rise till all but the wealthiest classes—even those groups of the middle classes who are in most comfortable circumstances—are excluded from the circle of purchasers. Goods which, owing to their inferior quality, are desired only by the poorer classes obtain extremely low prices, as also do those goods of better quality which are so plentiful that the poorer classes must be admitted, to a considerable degree, within the circle of purchasers. Medium prices are reached by those goods of which the middle classes form the majority of the purchasers, those who have small means either being entirely excluded from purchase, or entering the struggle of competition only in so far as will satisfy their intensest sensation of desire for such goods. Changes in the economic possibilities of great classes in a community will naturally induce changes in the prices of goods. The greater the inequalities of wealth, the greater will be the differences in price. Luxuries will rise in price when great fortunes increase, and will fall when they decrease." [1]

[1] It is as result of the recognition of this principle that we first arrive at a complete understanding of the remarkable phenomenon which has occupied the attention of so many theorists ; that the value of goods which can quite well be done without, such as diamonds, may be so much greater than that of the indispensable necessaries of life ; the value of gold, for instance, so much higher than that of iron. It has already been shown, in the elementary theory of value, that the value in use of an entirely insignificant good must be greater than that of a much more useful one when the marginal utility of the former is, owing to its scarcity, comparatively high, while that of the latter, by reason of its superfluity, has fallen very low down on the scale. Even greater differences are found, under certain circumstances, in prices, and consequently in the estimates of exchange value, than are shown in the different estimates of use value. Diamonds and gold stand exceptionally high in price because they are luxuries, valued and paid for according to the purchasing power of the richest classes ; while the coarser food stuffs and iron are low in price, because they are common goods,

# CHAPTER II

## EXCHANGE VALUE IN THE SUBJECTIVE SENSE

THE fact that goods can be bought and sold gives a new and powerful impulse to the estimating of values in all individual economies which exchange with one another. In the housekeeping of a Crusoe only the value in use of things obtains; whereas, in all individual economies which trade with each other, exchange value also has to be considered. The best explanation of the nature of exchange value, of its relation to value in use, and of the services which it renders to the individual economy, will be got if we examine separately the different cases of its occurrence.

Money is always, and by all who possess it, estimated according to its exchange value. Its use consists in the spending of it,—in the parting with it in purchase of other goods [1] that are expected to satisfy those sensations of want which would otherwise have no provision. The exchange value of money is the anticipated use value of the things which can be obtained for it. The law, therefore, which obtains for the latter obtains for the former; it is demand and supply, according as these express themselves in marginal utility, that decide the exchange value. The various things which determine money value to the individual are the following :—the amount of money which is at his disposal; the nature and quantity of the goods which can be obtained under the existing market conditions and prices; the utility which those goods are able to give, as also the utility already secured by possessions otherwise acquired; and, lastly, the amount and urgency of demand.[2]

in regard to which the decisive factor is the purchasing power and the valuation of the poor.

[1] Or, as we say simply, in purchase of *goods*—money and goods being generally thought of as in opposition to each other.

[2] For instance, the value of a shilling to me depends (1) on the number of shillings I have to spend ; (2) on what and how much I can buy in the shops for a shilling ; (3) on what use I can make of the shilling's worth of goods when I get them—which, again, depends (*a*) on how much I have of similar goods

The unit of money always receives its value from the least important expenditure which, in the circumstances of the possessor, it serves economically to defray ; every larger sum of money, and the entire amount of money owned, contains this marginal unit value as often as there are units. It is inevitable that different persons give very various estimates of value to the same sum of money. The circumstance which most largely influences these estimates is amount of wealth and income.[1] The penny is more to the poor man than the shilling to the rich. Every one must be conscious how very important it is, for the proper ordering of his own economic affairs, that he should have an exact idea of the value which money has for him. No one is utterly ignorant of this, and with every good householder the knowledge is almost a part of himself.

Besides money, all goods which are made or held for sale are estimated by their possessors according to this exchange value,—whether it be that the owner cannot himself make use of them, because they are unsuited to his personal needs, or that, although he might be able to use them, the utility they would furnish seems too trifling to be weighed against the proceeds of a sale.[2] The proximate basis of valuation is the expected money proceeds, or the exchange value of that money ; the ultimate basis is that use value which is anticipated from the exchange value of the money proceeds. Again the estimate of value leads us back to use value, and again the law of marginal utility obtains. The same good on the same market obtains for all sellers the same price, but how different are the valuations of that good on the part of those whose whole yearly income is dependent on their sale, as compared with those whose enjoyment would scarcely suffer were they to do without selling them from one year's end to the other !

already ; and (*b*) on my natural or acquired capacity of consuming or employing such goods.—*W. S.*

[1] See Jevons, p. 152.

[2] Of course the author does not mean that the consideration of possible personal use of his goods ever comes into the mind of the maker or merchant who supplies the market. Their "use" to him *is* their "exchange." Wieser is only making out the logical point that even goods made for sale would not be estimated at their exchange value if it were not that the personal use is less than the exchange use.—*W. S.*

Finally, numerous goods which their owners have not the smallest intention of selling, are estimated by their exchange value.   In illustration we may make use of the example which Böhm-Bawerk, who was the first to examine this particular instance, gives in his *Werth* (p. 37).   A poor man values his overcoat on account of the use he expects from it as a defence against cold, knowing well that, should he lose the coat, he will be exposed to all the severity of the winter weather, as he does not possess sufficient means to purchase another. Even to a man in better circumstances the loss of his over-coat would be a loss ; but in this case it could and would be replaced at the price of making another.   The rich man, there-fore, will not value his coat according to its utility, but accord-ing to the cost of procuring it ; in his estimation this cost will stand lower than the utility, and to that cost he can always reduce the injury he suffers from its loss.   Cases of this kind of valuation by exchange value are innumerable.   All house-hold goods which, when lost or stolen, can be replaced by purchase are thus valued.   Here we see that the proximate basis for valuation is the market price at which the purchase can be made, while the ultimate basis is again a use value ; that, namely, which is anticipated in the valuation of the purchase price.[1]

To sum up.   The exchange value which we have here explained is that value which is ascribed to goods, either by reason of the owners' intention to sell them, or because of the possibility of replacing them by purchase.   More briefly stated, it is that value which attaches to goods on account of an anticipated act of exchange.   Exchange value in this sense and use value are of the same nature ; the former is derived from the latter, and is one of its forms of development.   Both forms of value follow the same general laws ; both are subjective ; and the amount of both varies according to personal circum-stances.   The price of an article never completely expresses the exchange value it has for its owner.   This depends further upon the " personal equation " of money to him.

Subjective exchange value cannot be absent in any indi-

---

[1] On the change of motive which results from this in the conflict of price, see Böhm-Bawerk's *Werth* (p. 515).   I may perhaps be allowed to point out that in my *Ursprung des Werthes* (p. 185) I alluded briefly to the case described above.

vidual economy without causing the greatest confusion in all
its exchange relations.   The "personal equation" of money is
indispensable in every economy, in order that we may weigh
against each other goods estimated according to their use value,
and goods estimated according to their exchange value.   Without it no expenditure, no purchase, no sale could be logically
made.   The poor man could not enter the market as a poor
man, nor the rich man as a rich.   Every separate act of
exchange depends upon it, and thus not only the regulation
of individual economies, but the whole of exchange depends
upon it.

It is most wonderful that a fact of such universal practice,
and of so great importance, has, until quite lately, been almost
entirely neglected by theory.   Menger was the first to give it
a clear theoretical explanation, and to adopt it in his system ;—
and it is not the least of his many services to economics.


## CHAPTER III

### EXCHANGE VALUE IN THE OBJECTIVE SENSE

No one can take his own personal valuation of money, and of
the money value of goods, outside of himself, and apply it to
other people.   No one will persuade a business man to let him
have a commodity at half-price simply by proving that it is
more difficult for him to procure the half-price than for some
other person to procure double the price.   And no business
man could sell an article at twice the market price, simply
because he could prove that the double gain was necessary to
enable him to satisfy his most urgent wants.   Every one needs
to have an exact subjective estimate of the value of money to
himself, as a private individual economising his own resources,
in order to decide for himself what attitude he may take up
with regard to things outside of him.   But this personal
attitude can have no effect on the movement of goods in the
great economic exchange between one economy and another,
or in the end between any economy and his own, except
in so far as he may succeed in influencing the prices of

goods. It is the prices that absolutely decide in exchange. Goods fall to those who pay the highest prices, and—what is most important—the amount expended upon production is regulated by the prices expected from the sale of the goods. Those goods which will be sold at the highest prices attract the most means of production. The rank of goods in economic exchange—their external economic power—is absolutely decided by their prices, however individuals may judge as to their intrinsic importance.

When we speak generally of the value of goods we mean the economic rank given them by their prices. A good whose market price is £100 has, in the common usage of speech, absolutely, and for every one, ten times more value than one whose price is only £10. The dearest good is, in the ordinary use of words, also the most valuable. But we must make one single limitation : goods have ascribed to them as value only those prices which are paid for them in the usual run of cases. Exceptional prices, usurious prices, and "cut" prices form no foundation for value ; and accordingly goods whose prices fluctuate greatly have, in common usage, no fixed "intrinsic" value.

As a matter of fact some particular designation is indispensable for the ranking of goods in economic exchange, and it is impossible to find any other designation than that of value. And this not simply because we are forced to it from the outside as it were, by ordinary usage of speech, but because it essentially justifies itself. What subjective value does for the individual economy,—measuring every outlay and every return, and deciding the amount of consumption that is permissible and the extent to which production may be extended,—is done for economy generally by this ranking of goods as it is determined by relation to the objective prices. It is the measure for outlay and returns, and upon it distribution and production are dependent. But it must be emphasised that the word value alters its original sense somewhat, when transferred from the subjective relation to wants to the objective relation to price. Subjective value represents a distinct feeling ; that of being dependent upon the possession of a good for the satisfaction of a want,—a distinct degree of personal interest in goods. Objective value, on the other hand, merely represents a definite price; a definite amount of payment which is expected or required in buying and selling. The former has its measure in the different gradations of desire, the latter in the quantities of coin,—in the figures of the price.

Of course internal valuations of personal interest do, always and without exception, attach to objective value also, but these valuations are only subjective, being greater for one and smaller for another. Objective value or price is not in the least the expression of the economic valuation of goods, even when it is the result of economic competition, and of the individual valuations of all the different members of the economic community. Price is a social fact, but it does not denote the estimate put upon goods by society.[1] Luxuries are paid for more highly than necessaries, but who would affirm that they are therefore of greater social importance? Those very persons

---

[1] The ordinary conception, which makes price the social estimate put upon goods, has to the superficial judgment the attraction of simplicity. A good A whose market price is £100 is not only ten times as dear as B whose market price is £10, but it is also absolutely and for every one ten times as valuable. In our conception the matter is much more complicated, and according to it we obtain the following propositions. 1. A is paid for with ten times as much money as B: its price is ten times greater. 2. Its objective exchange value is also ten times greater—the weightiest consequence of which is that ten times the cost may, and, if practicable, will be expended upon its production. 3. But these relations of price and of objective value do not in the least degree correspond with the relative position of the two goods in regard to their economic *importance* or *subjective* valuation. Price alone forms no basis whatever for an estimate of the economic importance of the goods. We must go further and find out their relation to wants. But this relation to want can only be realised and measured individually. Suppose both goods are owned by the same person (or by people under exactly similar conditions of want and provision), A will, of course, have ten times the importance of B. But it may just as well happen that A has exactly the same importance for one owner as B has for another; it may indeed happen that A, in spite of its greater exchange value, has for its owner, supposing him to be a rich man, even less value than B has to its owner, supposing him to be a poor man. If there are many goods of the class A and many of the class B, the individual valuations of the various owners will be widely diverse, and a unanimous judgment is not to be expected. And the question how it is possible to unite those divergent individual valuations into one social valuation, is one that cannot be answered quite so easily as those imagine who are rash enough to conclude that price represents the social estimate of value.

See further, on the relation of objective to subjective exchange value, my *Ursprung des Werthes* (pp. 10 and 21 ; also Böhm-Bawerk's *Werth*, introd., etc.), and Sax (chapters xlviii. and xlix.).

who, on the market, come to an agreement regarding the price of goods—compelled thereto by the power of circumstances—will each reserve his own judgment upon the importance of the goods to him personally; and that authority which is earliest called upon to deliver the social judgment, the government, is universally considered to be the furthest removed from recognising the prices of goods as a measure of their social importance. A government, indeed, is, for the most part, concerned with the carrying through of just such economic tasks as could not be justified by their money return, if they were not justified by their utility.

In what follows, when the word " exchange value" occurs, I shall always mean "exchange value in the objective sense." There is no need to formulate the law of "exchange value"; we know it already, if only in a general way. It is the law of price.[1]

---

[1] Exchange value is, so far as concerns its application, without doubt the most important form of value, inasmuch as it governs the largest sphere ;—that of industrial economy generally. Political economy, outside that chapter where the theory of value is given, is almost exclusively concerned with it. No wonder, then, that theoretical treatises have taken it as their end. But application is one thing and explanation another. To explanation subjective value is chief in importance, for only through it can exchange value be reached. Subjective value is the original and perfect form of value ; exchange value taken by itself and unrelated to subjective value is imperfect and unintelligible. What does it signify to say that one article costs this and another that price in money, if we cannot say how money and prices are themselves valued ? Theorists who have confined themselves to the examination of exchange value, or, what comes to the same thing, of price, may have succeeded in discovering certain empirical laws of changes in amounts of value, but they could never unfold the real nature of value, and discover its true measure. As regards these questions, so long as examination was confined to exchange value, it was impossible to get beyond the formula that value lies in the relation of exchange ;—that everything is so much more valuable the more of other things it can be exchanged for. Why the exchanged things had value ; why things generally were worth anything to us ; and how this value was to be measured ;—these theories could never explain nor hope to explain. Value was conceived of relatively, by referring one thing to another ;—as the ratio of valuable things. Absolutely and by itself value was not to be understood. It is significant of this conception to state that one thing cannot be an object of value in itself; that a second must be present before the first can be valued.

Theory has only very gradually shaken itself free from this misconception, this circle. Where an absolute theory was attempted—such as the labour theory, or that which explained value as usefulness—some logical leap generally reconnected it with the relative conception. It was forced into this by the over-estimate of exchange value from which it seemed impossible to get free. A

# CHAPTER IV

### THE ANTINOMY OF EXCHANGE VALUE

EXCHANGE value—that is, as just explained, objective exchange value — shows the same movement as subjective value. With every addition to the amount to be sold (demand remaining constant), goes a fall in the return got for the single item, while the total return rises : this is the " up grade " of value. But, when a certain point is reached, the total return also falls : this is the "down grade " of value. And where, finally, there is universal superfluity, no price whatever can be obtained.

The causes of this movement are even stronger in the case of exchange value. It is induced not only by the natural limitation of wants, inasmuch as these cannot reach beyond the point of satiation, but also by the actual limitation of the purchasing power of many buyers, who have not means enough to satisfy their wants to the point of satiation. Goods which would still find purchasers, so far as wants are concerned, often find no sale in the market, and consequently the upper limit of price is often reached sooner than that of subjective value.

There would, nevertheless, be just as little reason to speak

striking example of this is Ricardo's theory of value. As a matter of fact value is still chiefly regarded relatively. German literature has for long had the great advantage of much penetrating criticism of exchange value, and of manifold attempts to supplement it, but it has nevertheless failed in any final solution. Among the later reformers of the theory of value, Jevons is distinguished for the strictness and accuracy with which he separates the two conceptions of value from one another, but he fails to construct a theory of subjective value (see second note to Book I. chap. ix.), and to determine the functions of both kinds of value. Menger, on the other hand, has a complete theory of subjective value, but makes no attempt to develop objective value.

My own investigations in the *Ursprung des Werthes* are almost entirely occupied with subjective value. And even favourable critics have concluded from this that I do not recognise objective value. The reproach is the less merited that (on page 38) I have especially acknowledged the necessity for an objective conception of value. The relation of subjective and objective value has been best described by Böhm-Bawerk, and—particularly as regards the distinction of their separate functions in economic life—by Sax.

of an antinomy of exchange value as of an antinomy of subjective value, were it not that the economic order, under
which society exists, gives to exchange value an efficiency in
the general business economy, which goes far beyond that of
subjective value in the individual economy.    In every self-
contained private economy utility is the highest principle; but,
in the business world, wherever the providing of society with
goods is in the hands of undertakers who desire to make a
gain out of it, and to obtain a remuneration for their services,
exchange value takes its place.    The private undertaker is
not concerned to provide the greatest utility for society
generally; his aim is rather to obtain the highest value for
himself:—which is at the same time his highest utility.    Utility
approves itself as the first principle in the undertaker's economy ;
but, just because of this, in the conflict between exchange
value and social utility, it is exchange value which is
victorious,—so far at least as the undertaker has power to act
according to his own interest.

Proudhon, therefore, is right—although he may not have
formulated his contention quite correctly—when he affirms
the antinomy of exchange value.    Every undertaker finds it
to his advantage when he succeeds in turning free goods which
he cannot sell, into economically scarce goods which he can
sell.    And it is to his advantage when he is successful in
reducing the amount to be sold, and raising the returns, just
as it is to his disadvantage to increase the amount that is
to be sold, and thereby diminish the returns.

The conclusion which Proudhon draws from this—that
the discord can only be resolved by a socialist organisation
of society—is nevertheless incorrect.

In the main the antinomy does not exist in the "up
grade" of the movement of value.    And in this up grade
is found by far the greater number of the actual forms of
value.    Further, the antinomy only holds in so far as the
undertaker is able to rule society.    But where there is really
free competition no undertaker has this power.    Under free
competition, social utility will be—as it ought to be—the
first principle of economic life.    Here each of the competing
undertakers is bound to strive to widen to the utmost the
compass of his undertaking.    The increase of supply which

the individual producer causes is, in relation to supply as a whole, too trifling to have any material effect in lowering prices, while it materially increases the amount which the individuals have to sell.    Thus every one calculates, and, on the strength of this calculation, production is stretched to the utmost possible extent.    The economic history of our own time is rich in examples which prove that competition can press prices far on the down grade of exchange value.

In any remaining cases, society—if it is to escape injury —will, of course, require to carry on production, or have it carried on by individuals, on common account; but such cases are too few to call for the socialist organisation of society. From the first, governments have undertaken such responsibilities.    The antinomy of exchange value does not necessitate a complete overturn of the free economic order of society; it merely requires that it be supplemented by suitable interference on the part of governments.


# CHAPTER V

### THE SERVICE OF EXCHANGE VALUE IN GENERAL ECONOMY

If we consider the elements which go to form exchange value, we are forced to the conclusion that the charge of antinomy is not the heaviest that may be raised against it. Entirely apart from this, the law of its formation remains such that, even in the most favourable circumstances—say when there is no disturbing element, no suspicion of force, dishonesty, or error, and when the transaction is one we are accustomed to call free and just,—exchange value is calculated to render its service in economic life only in an imperfect manner, and with consequences which society feels to be serious evils.

It must be premised that the service rendered by exchange value to general or industrial economy, as compared with the service rendered by subjective value to the self-contained economy, is greater by one additional task.    In the latter, value has only to measure outlay and return materially against each other; in the former, it must also do so personally. The material or economic-technical service of exchange value relates chiefly to production. Here it has the function of control. It gives the measure for production and for expenditure of costs. Goods should be produced according to the rank of their value, and other goods should be sacrificed for them as costs only in so far as the comparison between the value of amount produced and the value of costs allows. The personal service of exchange value, on the other hand, comes in, principally, in the distribution of the products acquired among the separate individuals taking part in the exchange; in this case value is the measure of the personal acquisition. To every participator in the great economic process must be assigned a return equal in value to the amount of his outlay—whether it be outlay of wealth or expenditure of labour.

The exchange value of all goods which are brought upon the market in stocks or quantities, is measured as a marginal value. That is to say, each unit of the stock is valued at the same as the marginal equivalent, and the whole stock is estimated as a multiple of the unit,—as product of the amount into the unit value. So far exchange value gives the same appropriate and faultless assistance in the economic calculation as marginal value generally does. Its applicability to this kind of calculation is indisputable. It is, then, unnecessary to repeat in detail what has already been said on the subject in general in Book I. chapter xi.

In order, however, properly to appraise the service of exchange value in economic life, it must be remembered that it does not contain exactly the same elements as does value in use in the self-contained economy. The latter simply depends upon utility: the former is besides dependent upon purchasing power (see Book II. chap. i.). Value in use measures utility; exchange value measures a combination of utility and pur- chasing power. The stock which is greater in use value (in the "up grade") is also always the richer in utility; the stock which is greater in exchange value is not necessarily so. In the latter case the higher value may arise from higher utility, but it may also arise from the greater wealth of the buyers, and the strong inducement held out to them to throw their riches into the balance in the war of competition.

In the material service of exchange value, as well as in the personal, this peculiar method of its formation obtains importance. As a consequence of it, production is ordered not only according to simple want, but also according to wealth. Instead of things which would have the greatest utility, those things are produced for which the most will be paid. The greater the differences in wealth, the more striking will be the anomalies of production. It will furnish luxuries for the wanton and the glutton, while it is deaf to the wants of the miserable and the poor. It is therefore the distribution of wealth which decides how production is set to work, and induces consumption of the most uneconomic kind: a consumption which wastes upon unnecessary and culpable enjoyment what might have served to heal the wounds of poverty.[1]

It may be of interest to follow somewhat more particularly the law of distribution, in so far as it is conditioned by the law of exchange value. The favouring of the rich, and with it the perverted employment of goods, really goes much further than the mere fact of wealth would allow one to suspect. The rich have not only the advantage over the poor of possessing more means wherewith to purchase goods; they have the further advantage of being for the most part in a more favourable position to utilise their means. In the battle of price the decision lies with the weakest buyers, who are, as a rule, also the poorest; and price is adapted to their valuation. They must, therefore, pay for the goods exactly as highly as they value them, while their stronger competitors, who pay the same price, pay *under* their personal valuation. The beggar and the millionaire eat the same bread and pay the same price for it; the beggar according to the measure of his hunger, and the millionaire according to the same measure—that is, according to the beggar's hunger. The price which the millionaire might be willing to pay for the bread, supposing he were hungry and driven to offer his maximum, never comes into the question. It is only where the rich compete among themselves for luxuries which they mean to reserve for their own enjoyment, that they pay according to

---

[1] On the effect of exchange value on distribution see Böhm-Bawerk's *Werth*, p. 510.

their own ability, and are measured according to their own personal standard.

But the more the ability of the rich is spared in the purchasing of necessaries, the greater are the means which they have over, wherewith to extend and increase the prices they offer for luxuries, and the more defective is the impulse given by consumption to production.

The law of value in the individual economy is strict, but its strictness is undoubtedly necessary and salutary. It forbids satisfaction to go beyond a certain marginal point, namely, the point beyond which, when everything, including the future, is carefully weighed, the means possessed at the moment will not suffice. Any violation of this prohibition brings its own punishment, when, to make up for the trifling want that has been rashly satisfied at the moment, a far more urgent desire later on has to go unsatisfied. The law of price follows the law of value in demanding a marginal point beyond which purchase must not go, but it does not present the same unquestionable and material necessity; and the natural and reasonable strictness of the prohibition is thereby changed into what seems personal and inconsistent severity. The man who cannot furnish the price paid by the marginal buyer is excluded from competition within the economic circle, just as, in the individual household, the quite trifling desires are excluded from satisfaction. As in the household there are marginal wants, so in economic life are there marginal entities, and anything below that level is permitted to exist only by way of charity. But while, in the individual household, the marginal line is drawn naturally, in economic life generally it is influenced also by the manner of the distribution of wealth. In the midst of the comfort and luxury of the opulent classes, law condemns the poor to a restriction, as though there was no affluence, and nature herself forbade the greater satisfaction.

These are the charges which may be brought against the law of exchange value. They would soon make short work of it could we not answer them. The examination of these charges and their answer does not, however, belong to the theory of value, but to the greater theory of economics and economical laws; and this book does not propose even to exhaust the theory of value. I only wished to explain the elements in the formation of exchange value so far as is necessary to show clearly what I should like to be understood by the term "Natural Value." We have now arrived at this point, and need hesitate no longer in presenting to the reader my explanation of the expression. The thing itself is not new to us; the value which we looked at in the first book, under the elementary theory, is natural value.

## CHAPTER VI

### NATURAL VALUE

EVEN in a community or state whose economic affairs were ordered on communistic principles, goods would not cease to have value. Wants there would still be, there as elsewhere; the available means would still be insufficient for their full satisfaction; and the human heart would still cling to its possessions. All goods which were not free would be recognised as not only useful but valuable; they would rank in value according to the relation in which the available stocks stood to the demand; and that relation would express itself finally in the marginal utility. Social supply and demand, or amount of goods and utility socially compared with one another, would decide value. The elementary laws of valuation, as we have explained them, would be entirely and unlimitedly effective for the whole community.

That value which arises from the social relation between amount of goods and utility, or value as it would exist in the communist state, we shall henceforth call " Natural Value." [1] I choose the name in full consciousness of the double sense which an appeal to the "natural" has in the disposition of human

---

[1] What I propose to call " Natural Value" has been hitherto called social use value. With the word " value in use " (*Gebrauchswerth*) are connected too many misunderstandings to permit of our using it without danger. Use value is commonly understood as usefulness, or something closely related to that, and not as actual value. It is, moreover, rarely used in connection with production, and I wish to speak as much of the value of production goods and of costs, as of the direct use value of consumption goods.

affairs. In its simplicity, purity, and originality it is so attractive, and at the same time so contradictory to all experience, that it is doubtful whether it can ever be more than a dream. So too we shall think of the communistic state as the perfect state. Everything will be ordered in the best possible way; there will be no misuse of power on the part of its officials, or selfish isolation on the part of its individual citizens; no error or any other kind of friction will ever occur. Natural value shall be that which would be recognised by a completely organic and most highly rational community.[1]

The laws which we found in the elementary theory of value are its natural laws, as those would take shape under the simplified assumption that goods come into men's disposal without requiring to be first produced. If we do away with this assumption we obtain the natural laws of value in production. It will now be our task to find out these laws. We shall ask ourselves what productive instruments would be likely to obtain value in a communistic state, whether labour alone, or also land and capital; in what measure they would obtain value; whether there is a natural rent from land and a natural interest on capital—and so on through all the circumstances of production, till we arrive at the question of cost value and its natural measurement.

The relation of natural value to exchange value is clear. Natural value is one element in the formation of exchange value. It does not, however, enter simply and thoroughly into exchange value. On the one side, it is disturbed by human imperfection, by error, fraud, force, chance; and on the other, by the present order of society, by the existence of private

---

[1] The question whether such a community can or ever will exist is one which does not in the least concern us. We shall content ourselves with imagining it, and it will be an excellent aid in realising what would remain of our present economy if we could think away private property, as well as all the troubles which are a consequence of human imperfection. Most theorists, particularly those of the classical school, have tacitly made similar abstractions. In particular, that point of view from which price becomes a social judgment of value, really amounts to a disregard of all the individual differences which emerge in purchasing power, and which separate price from natural value. A great many theorists have thus written the value theory of communism without being aware of it, and in doing so have omitted to give the value theory of the present state. By making our assumptions quite clear, and guarding against a similar error, we may do more for value as we find it than they have.

property, and by the differences between rich and poor,—as a consequence of which latter a second element mingles itself in the formation of exchange value, namely, purchasing power. In natural value goods are estimated simply according to their marginal utility ; in exchange value, according to a combination of marginal utility and purchasing power. In the former, luxuries are estimated far lower, and necessaries, comparatively, much higher than in the latter. Exchange value, even when considered as perfect, is, if we may so call it, a caricature of natural value ; it disturbs its economic symmetry, magnifying the small and reducing the great.

The fact that natural value forms an element in the formation of exchange value, puts our investigation in touch with reality, and gives it its empirical importance. The value which would be recognised by an extremely rational and completely united commonwealth is not entirely foreign to that value which is recognised by the society of to-day. Every individual desires for his own part to form a rational judgment about value, but it is not always within his power to do so ; and, in the coming into connection with others in exchange, the final effect becomes altered, as I said, into caricature. There are innumerable more or less correct approximations to natural value. Every one finds them within his own economic circle ; and even when the single circles come together these individual valuations are not entirely lost, but only somewhat altered. It will be of interest to investigate closely to what extent the phenomena of exchange value are of natural origin, and how great, accordingly, is the formative power of natural value in existing conditions of society. I believe the sequel will show that it is enormously greater than is usually supposed. Land rent is, perhaps, the formation of value that is most frequently attacked in our present economy. Now I believe our examination will show that, even in the communistic state, there must be land rent. Such a state must, under certain circumstances, calculate the return from land, and must, from certain portions of land, calculate a greater return than from others : the circumstances upon which such a calculation is dependent are essentially the same as those which to-day determine the existence of rent, and the height of rent. The only difference lies in this, that, as things now

are, rent goes to the private owner of the land, whereas, in a
communistic state, it would fall to the entire united community.
In such a state it would not form personal property, but it
would be calculated separately in the total income of the
community, and that on essential grounds;—namely, in order to
find out what is the quota which individual lands contribute
to the total return, and to judge therefrom what outlay may
and ought to be expended to obtain this quota. In other
words, the economic-technical service, that of controlling production, would remain, while the personal part it plays, as a
source of private income, would fall away. Should our examination succeed in establishing this and similar facts, no one will
be able to deny that it helps us to a clearer understanding of
existing economic conditions. It would show what part of the
present forms of value not only exists for the satisfaction of
self-interest, but renders at the same time a technical service
to social economy; it would show therefore what part must
never be given up, on pain of leaving the economy without
power of calculation and without control.

On this account the examination of natural value will be
useful, as well for those who wish to understand the economy
of the present, as for those who wish to evolve a new one.
Defenders of the existing order of things, equally with those
who are fighting to prepare the way for a new and ideal state,
may, without prejudice and without going against their principles, unite in this study. Natural value is a neutral phenomenon, the examination of which, whatever may come of it,
can prove nothing for and nothing against socialism. If land
rent and interest on capital are natural phenomena of value,
they will have their place in the socialistic state also, without
necessarily breaking it up and leaving the way clear again for
capitalists and landowners. Every natural form of value may
be left its material office, without connecting with it any
personal privilege of income.

So little is natural value a weapon against socialism, that
socialists could scarcely make use of a better witness in favour
of it. Exchange value can have no severer criticism than that
which exposes its divergences from the natural measurement,
although, indeed, this forms no particular proof for the essence
of socialism. As is well known, however, the socialists have

another theory of value. This we shall find again and again in contradiction with the claims that rest on natural value, and although we say nothing against socialism, but wish to remain throughout within the neutral sphere of natural value, we shall be obliged again and again to speak against the socialists.

It will be of advantage to the statement which follows if we first try to make a general survey of the socialist theory of value.

# CHAPTER VII

## THE SOCIALIST THEORY OF VALUE

SOCIALIST writers, however much they find to object to in value as it is in the present day, have little enough to say concerning its future. They give us very scanty information as to the part it would have to play in the socialist state. Karl Marx, in explanation of this reserve, says that " the social relations of man to his labour and to the products of his labour are here transparently simple." It would appear that value, in the socialist sense, resembles those organs of the human body of whose existence, when diseased, we are painfully conscious, while in health they are scarcely noticed. Physicians even, who know their pathology thoroughly, are not able to say what vital functions they serve.

The socialists teach that the one and only source of value is labour. In the socialist state there are to be only two objects of value,—labour, and consumption goods produced by labour. Land and capital will not be objects of value. Value presupposes utility, but does not originate in it. It is created by labour, and the expenditure of labour naturally attracts to itself the interest of man. Its measure is labour-time, or even the exertion involved in labour. Of the social services rendered by value only that of the distribution of goods is retained, and even this only to a limited extent; the produced consumption goods, estimated according to their labour-value, are distributed among the labourers according to the amount of labour service they have rendered. Productive land and capital are the exclusive property of the state, and are neither objects nor standards of the distribution. The other service rendered by value, that of being the controlling power of social economy, and, in particular, of production, is not claimed at all. The only claims allowed are those of utility or of use value, but by "use value" is not to be understood value in the sense we give to it, but utility pure and simple, and therefore utility without that peculiar measuring power which arises from comparison of want and provision.

This, in outline, is the socialist programme of the future for the valuation of goods,—although, of course, not expressed in the original language of its authors. In my opinion there has never been, in the whole course of history, a more important change contemplated in the social order than that now desired in economic life ; and never has plan of alteration been more imperfectly thought out. To change a feudal kingdom into a modern administration, or a monarchy into a republic, or an aristocracy into a democracy, would be nothing to this ; for it is the attempt at an economic revolution which would affect not only those few who are interested in political matters, but the whole body of the people, — affect them, too, just where they are most strongly conscious of their own interests. Dreams of political freedom, of equality, of brotherhood, even the religious dreams of a kingdom of God on the earth, however fantastically tricked out, have never betrayed so imperfect a knowledge of their object, as does the socialist theory of value. These have at least the excuse that they appeal to feelings of human nature which may soar to unknown heights, and which, of their very nature, give nourishment to the most extravagant expectations. But value is a thing for the most unimpassioned thought. Here it is wrong for any one to let imagination speak instead of reason,—wrong for the academic writer, and ever so much more wrong for the social reformer and agitator. Not for one day could the economic state of the future be administered according to any such reading of value ; indeed the first preliminary arrangements for its introduction would show its utter uselessness.

To a certain extent, however, the socialists are justified by their very opponents. The idea of labour value, and many other ideas of socialist theory, originated among the bourgeois economists, and were found by the leaders of the labour party to be, theoretically, perfectly developed : it only remained to make a practical application of them for the benefit of the socialist party.    It was hard not to make use of the advantage thus put into their hands.    If it be acknowledged that labour alone creates value, it seems impossible to deny the claim that the labourer alone should enjoy the value.    In the academic struggle the socialists undoubtedly got an important tactical advantage through the unqualified acceptance of that theory—the theory held by a large section of their opponents, and a section which, under the circumstances, might be considered the most formidable.    If all the tremendous conflict of interests could have been ended by the arguments used by the spokesmen of the socialist party in their wordy warfare, at a certain period of the literary development the victory of socialism would probably have been complete.    But, of course, what was good enough in argument would have broken down in face of facts,— for no amount of plausibility can impose on them,—and, after vanquishing their opponents with one theory, the socialists would have required to make up another to support their position.

In the socialist theory of value pretty nearly everything is wrong.    The origin of value, which lies in utility and not in labour, is mistaken.    The relation of supply to demand— that fact which impels us to attribute utility to goods, and upon whose fluctuations depend, in the last resort, the fluctuations in amount of value—is overlooked.    The objects to which value attaches are not all embraced, for among those must be included productive land and capital, both as elements in the calculation of costs, and also *per se*.    And the service rendered by value in economic life is only half understood, inasmuch as the most essential part of it, the material control of economy, is neglected.

All of this we shall require,—now that we have made acquaintance with the elementary phenomena,—to demonstrate in the circumstances of production.    In particular we shall have to show that, in the natural order of economy, labour is valued according to its utility, value attaches to land and capital, and land rent, as well as interest on capital, is calculated among costs.    If this were to be neglected production would become chaos.

# BOOK III

## THE NATURAL IMPUTATION OF THE RETURN FROM PRODUCTION

# PART I

## THE GENERAL PRINCIPLES OF IMPUTATION

### CHAPTER I

#### RETURN VALUE

PRODUCTION goods, as well as consumption goods, afford utility. Land, capital, and labour afford utility inasmuch as they produce useful objects of consumption. As the latter serve directly, so do the former indirectly, toward the satisfaction of wants. The seed, the tree, the soil, the yarn, the coal, the machine :—these are not indeed ripe or finished goods, like the fruit and the garment, but they are just as really goods. They contain prospective or potential utility.

And the production goods, land, labour, and capital, must receive value on account of their utility, so far as they are not available in superfluity. The atom of air, which floats above the field in company with the countless others that throng space, is useful but valueless, because its place is at any time taken and filled by another. On the other hand, in the judgment of economic men, all those elements of production must receive value on account of their useful effect, which, however numerous they be, are yet not numerous enough to prevent even a small loss in them being perceptible and bringing harm in its train. Production does not despise free goods; it does not disdain the fruitful land although it should stretch away in excess of all requirements, or the wood in the primeval forest, or free water power: on the contrary, it seeks them out and prefers to use them wherever it can, because their services are the most perfect possible, and present no break in the rendering. None the less it must be said that production pays little attention to free goods,—indeed less than little. It does not consider them at all. It merely uses them; it ascribes to them no value. It does not even reckon to them the services they render. Utility alone gives no value; there must be limitation of supply as well, before value emerges from utility. Utility is and remains the source of value, but in order to set the source flowing there must be a peculiar motive power, which will direct the atten-tion of man to the necessity of watching and attending to it.

It is, however, not usual to follow the value of production goods to its source in utility. To estimate the value of a field I do not consider what satisfactions of want can be had from its crop. I content myself with calculating what and how much crop it will probably yield; this crop then I estimate according to the value which attaches to it in virtue of its utility; and this value is to me the basis from which I ascertain the value of the field. The act of valuation of production goods, which ought to reach right back to wants, is, therefore, usually carried only to that point at which the relation of these goods to the value of their products is clearly established, for in the value of products the calculation of the wants is already represented. To this extent it is possible to say that the value of production goods is determined by the value of their products or by the value of the return. Productive value is return-value. The consideration that, from production goods, one can obtain a return in goods which possess not only utility but value, gives pro-duction goods their value.

According to the manner in which production is planned and carried out, it is possible to obtain from the same goods widely diverse kinds and amounts of return. Economic prin-ciples demand the obtaining of the greatest possible return; that is, the return possessing the greatest value which it is possible to obtain under the circumstances. It is this "greatest possible return" whose value should serve as basis for the valuation of production goods.[1] Probably it never is possible to decide this beforehand with absolute accuracy, but

[1] The value of the productive unit again is decided according to the marginal law—*i.e.* by the least among these returns. See below, Book III. chap. viii.

some anticipatory estimate there must be.   It is not therefore
actually the value of the return which forms the ground of
production value,—but the expectation which is formed of it.
It is the anticipated value of the anticipated return.

The greater the return reckoned on, the greater will be
the productive value.   The greater the dividend expected
from a stock, the higher will be the value put upon the
stock.   This illustration of stocks and dividends is, on the
whole, the best that could be given to explain productive
value.   Every means of production, every tool, every piece of
land or raw material, every service of labour, represents, if one
may say so, a share in an undertaking.   This share contributes
to the result cf the undertaking, and consequently gets ascribed
to it a quota of the result, and upon the amount of this result
its value must depend.[1]

---

[1] The classical political economy really examines only the value of products,
or, more exactly, of produced consumption goods.   So far as the factors of production are concerned, it looks upon them, on the one side, as sources of income
(rent, interest, wage, and, perhaps, also undertaker's income) ; on the other side,
as the elements which go to form the costs of production, and are considered to
decide, principally, the value of the products.

But when one compares with this the endeavours which, explicitly or im-
plicitly, guide the new writers on the theory of value, we find the circle of the
phenomena to which the idea of value is applied extraordinarily widened.
Factors of production—better expressed by the later writers as "production
goods"—are conceived of all through as objects of value ; costs are directly
phenomena of value ; and even income must be so conceived.   Further than this,
the relations between the value of utilities and the value of production goods is
turned just the other way about—the former being considered as determining,
the latter as determined.   On the present occasion we have first to do with the
proposition which may serve as starting-point for the whole theory ;—that production goods receive their value from the value of the products which they
serve to create.   Gossen, Jevons, Menger, and Walras are all agreed on this
point.   In my opinion it is again Menger who gives the most clear and comprehensive statement of the matter.   He divides (as does also Gossen, though
much less perfectly) the entire goods which stand in the productive nexus into
Ranks, and value is conducted from rank to rank.   The first and lowest rank is
formed by those utilities which receive their value direct from wants.   The value
thus received passes over first to goods of the second rank, those, namely, which
serve directly towards the producing of goods of the first rank ; as *e.g.* the meal
and the labour of the baker in the preparation of bread.   From these value
passes on to goods of the third rank (*e.g.* wheat and the labour of the miller) ;
and so on, step by step, till it reaches the highest, or, as Böhm-Bawerk calls them,
the most remote ranks.

## CHAPTER II

### THE PROBLEM OF IMPUTATION

No productive instrument, be it ever so efficient, yields a return by its unaided agency; it always requires the assistance of others. And the more the art of production is developed, the more numerous will be the productive instruments which co-operate. The very simplest products often require the most complicated methods of production, because they, more than any others, allow of the application of machinery and, therefore, of power in the mass. The proposition that production goods obtain their value from the value of their returns, suffices only for the valuation of the co-operating productive factors as a whole ; not for their valuation individually. To obtain this also, we need a rule which will make it possible to divide up the whole return into single parts.

When land, capital, and labour work together, we must be able to separate out the quota of land, the quota of capital, and the quota of labour from the joint product. More than that, we must be able to measure the services of each separate piece of land, of each separate quantity of capital, and of each separate labourer. Of what use is it to know the return which falls to machinery, coal, and raw material *together ?* It is necessary to distinguish what each has contributed to the total result, just as the contribution of the stone-cutter who hews the block must be distinguished from that of the artist who chisels it into the statue.

If we may form a judgment from economic practice, we should say there *is* such a rule of division. No one, practically, is limited to saying that return is due to all the producing factors together ; every one understands and practises, more or less perfectly, the art of division of return. A good business man must know, and does know, what a day labourer and what a skilled worker would yield him ; what

profit a machine will bring in; how much has to be ascribed
to the raw material; what return this and what return that
piece of land will produce. If he did not know this; if he
could only compare his outlay and his results as a whole
and in the lump, he would not know what to do in case the
return proved less than the outlay. Must he give up the
production altogether ?   Must he alter the management ?
Must he be more saving with labour or capital, with machinery or raw material; or, on the contrary, must he employ
more of these ?   Only if there is some adequate means of
following out individually the working of each productive
element, can he judge clearly upon these points. That there
is such a means is testified by the fact that economic decisions
of the nature we have just mentioned *are* made, and made
with as much confidence and as favourable results as are any
other decisions in matters of value generally. The existence
of this means of calculation is still more certainly proved by
the fact that decisions of this nature are so often made in
the same way by many people,—in fact, by all persons who
find themselves in the same circumstances. Why at a certain
point of time does the entire body of undertakers, in some
particular branch of manufacture, suddenly replace hand labour
by machinery, when previously they had not found machinery
profitable ?   Why is agriculture in one country so much
more " intensive " than in another ?   Chance and caprice are
here out of the question. It is calculations of production that effect these alterations. They give arithmetical
proof that it is advantageous to eliminate the one element of
production, with its accompanying share in the return, and
substitute for it the other. The more perfect the production,
the more exact will be its calculations, and the more highly
will the art of distributing the return be developed. A
" model economy " calculates everything. But the rudest
peasant, and the wildest savage, make calculations, inexact and
hasty though they be. They, too, make use of their experience, though very imperfectly of course, in regard to matters
where the impulse and the confidence are given by nature.
The peasant, dwelling in some cleft of the mountain, says to
himself that this field is more valuable than that; and. this he
could not do unless he understood the art of separating the

return of the field from the return of the co-operating labourers, tools, and materials.    These are rules which arise naturally, from the very nature of man, when he finds himself confronted with the problems of economic life.    In applying them, the attempt would undoubtedly be made even by a communistic state, to calculate the result of each individual productive element.    And in a highly cultivated state these calculations would be made with great exactitude, in order to lay down that plan of production which, for the time being, was most effective.

It is singular how few of those writers who have attempted to grasp economic procedures into the unity of theory have tried to discover this rule,—which is certainly one of the most important followed in practical economic dealings.    Of the many difficulties which have to be overcome if we are to get, apart from actual transactions, a purely theoretical and scientific account of what people actually do when impelled by circumstances, probably the first and most difficult of all is to put before ourselves what *are* the problems really put in business transactions.    Every theory begins with the least important of the things it has to do, and only in the end arrives at its true vocation.

The second difficulty is to state the problem correctly. The few writers who have managed to get over the first obstacle mentioned have almost all come to grief at the second. For the most part they pitch the question too high, and thus change, what to the simple man is a simple and natural thing, into a subtle and sophistical riddle, of which they then say, rightly enough, that no solution is possible.    They try to discover which portion of the joint product, *physically considered*, each factor has produced, or of which part of the result each factor is the *physical cause*.    This, however, is not to be discovered. At the most it could be possible only in cases where the product is a complex of materials externally bound together ; and even that only so far as regards the materials, and not as regards the power which makes them a complex—a power whose effects inhere in all the constituent parts of the mass, without being incorporated in any one of them.    Looked at in this way, we cannot get beyond the proposition that the result is the joint product of all its factors and causes ; that those factors must work in combination or they cannot work at all,—like the four brothers in the tale who saved the princess only by their united endeavours. If we wish to find the principle for division of return which is applied in practical life, the question must be put quite differently; it must be put as practical life puts it, and it must be put simply.

The causes of any phenomenon, whatever it may be, can be interpreted in very various ways. The philosopher looks at them in one light, the peasant in quite another; and yet both may judge rightly, and, so far as their judgment is correct, may apply rightly their conception. The difference in their opinions rests on the fact that they judge from different points of view. The former searches after the final causes that may be grasped by human reason ; the latter limits his attention to the proximate and immediate causes, taking for granted the agency of all those which are further removed. Each would fail were he to make use of the other's knowledge; the peasant's maxim does not answer the purpose of philosophy, and the philosophic conception has no place in the economy of the peasant; yet each is serviceable enough in its own place. In whatever industrial situation men come to a judgment as to the causes of the phenomena which they encounter, the horizon of the judgment is always strictly limited by the point of view they take. Whatever lies beyond that cannot properly be taken into consideration, or the judgment would never come to anything. It would only end in needless critical reflection, which would be of no help as regards the objects aimed at. If we wish to obtain a practical judgment the object must be kept in view, and the matter looked at from the point of view of those concerned. A theory which proposes to explain the *idea* in business life, must, of all things, not be above its business ; it must limit itself, so as not to give too deep a meaning to, and thereby really distort, the limited subject.

A science nearly related to our own as regards its subject, that of jurisprudence, may give us admirable instruction on this point. For an act of murder there must necessarily be a perpetrator, a victim, an instrument, and an opportunity. Besides these, the act is influenced by innumerable circumstances, which can often be shown to reach back to a far distant past in the previous history of the murderer, and even in the history of the community among which he came into existence and grew into manhood. The sociologist, the historian, the philanthropist, and the lawgiver will have much to consider that has but an indirect connection with the committing of the murder. But, however far back they may carry their consideration, some idle brain can always go still further, and follow *ad infinitum* the series of causes which led to the deed,—as, for instance, the history of the tool with which it was done, as well as the history of the doer. The judge, on the other hand, who, in his narrowly-defined task, is only concerned about the *legal imputation*, confines himself to the discovery of the legally responsible factor,—that person, in fact, who is threatened with the legal punishment. On him will rightly be laid the whole burden of the consequences, although he could never by himself alone—without instruments and all the other conditions—have committed the crime. The imputation takes for granted physical causality. It cannot fall upon any one who stands outside the series of causes which led to the result, and any proof that the accused does stand outside exempts him from condemnation. But if the causal nexus is once established, far more is laid to the account of the doer than was or could be physically done by him. Only a foolish interpretation of the judgment could take exception to this. The expression " this man has done it " does not mean " this man alone has done it," but " this man alone, among all the active causes and factors, is legally responsible for the deed."

In the division of the return from production, we have to deal similarly not with a complete causal explanation, but with an adequately limiting imputation,—save that it is from the economic, not the judicial point of view. Observation of the fruits of the earth suggests to a religious mind the Creator of all things. A scientific investigator is directed by the same observation towards the pursuit of the cognisable causes of their creation. A Faust pines after knowledge regarding the hidden forces of their life. The farmer, as farmer, thinks differently from all of these. He ascribes his crops, soberly and unsentimentally, to a very limited and small circle of all the causes which have actually produced them. He asks—"Towards what things must I direct my economic attention in order to receive this return?" —and reckons the result accordingly. He therefore sets apart from the total active causes all those which lie behind in the past. From the present causes he then sets apart all those which can be of no use, or are not recognised as having any use. From the recognised and useful, again, he divides off all those which are not under economic command. From these last he, finally, separates out all those causes which need not be cared for, because they are present in superfluity. As we can readily understand, he does not in the least believe that the remainder is the sole originating cause of his return. At the same time he rightly attributes or imputes the return to it alone, taking the working of all the other elements as assured. His judgment, though limited, is neither false nor even inexact. It embraces *all* the causes which have to be considered by him if his labour is to be attended by good results.

If, in the economic working out, parts of the total result should be traced back to individual instruments of production, it is that we continue the reasoning with which we started : we trace back the total result not to its numerous wider causes, but simply to the *economic* instruments of its production. In regard to the part we limit ourselves still more than we did in regard to the whole ; we seek out that one among the economic elements to which the part is practically to be imputed, although, certainly, it could have produced it only in combination with the other elements. Here, again, there is neither fallacy, nor even inaccuracy. On the contrary, so far as this method succeeds in founding, upon the imputation of the return, a valuation of goods and a plan of production which insures the most successful employment of each single element, it is the height of practical wisdom.

To show that imputation in this sense is both allowable and practicable take one single case. Suppose that two fields, the one fertile, the other poor, but both worked with similar amounts of capital and labour, give different returns. To which account is the surplus return of the better field to be attributed—to that of the seed, or the manure, or the plough, or the labour ? But these were the same in both fields. Is it not rather to be attributed to the land itself and its greater fertility ? No one can be in doubt as to that, nor can one raise the objection that, without seed, manure, plough, and labour, there could have been no surplus return. Taking things as they are, *more* depends upon the possession of the better soil—just as much more, in fact, as the surplus return amounts to.

It is of great importance that we should try to formulate theoretically the rules for the imputation of productive return, not only as regards land but as regards all productive instruments. If we do not succeed in doing so, the valuation of production goods will remain an enigma; and the existing order of things, under which the actual imputation of returns forms the basis for the distribution of national income among the citizens, will lie under the accusation of arbitrariness, if not the worse accusation of force and injustice. It would not even be possible to justify the difference in wages paid to some labourers as compared with others. If there is no rule by which to adjust the quarrel between owners and workers, neither is there any by which to measure the rank of the inventor against that of the day-labourer who carries out the invention. It would be purely arbitrary if one tried, even approximately and by way of valuation, to show respect to genius, devotion, art, power, skill—in short all the virtues and excellences which, from time immemorial, have been held in respect in economic matters as well as in others, and which society has to thank for the most beneficent and useful services of its members.

## CHAPTER III

### THE SOCIALIST READING OF THE PROBLEM.    THE CLAIM OF THE LABOURER TO THE ENTIRE RETURN

THE socialist theory so greatly limits the circle of those things which may be counted as means of production that the problem of imputation is also sensibly narrowed.

Socialists do not recognise three productive factors, land, capital, and labour: they acknowledge only a single productive power, Labour. Only human labour, they say, is creative; it alone can really produce. Of course, to be effective, it requires land and capital, but these hold a subordinate position to labour, and act merely as auxiliary means of production.

But in the existing order of things, landowners and capitalists —as having exclusive possession of the material auxiliary means of production—are placed in a position to force the labourer to give up to them a great part of the product of labour, as it is only on this condition that they will lend their property and allow labour to use it. By reason of this, land and capital have become sources of personal income for the idle classes, but unjustly so; and it would be a great error to infer the fact of productive power from that of income. When the owners refuse to grant to labour the use of these auxiliaries, they place obstacles in the way of labour, as Rodbertus says; when they do grant this use, they do nothing more than merely remove the obstruction they have themselves created; they simply withdraw their own arbitrary fiat. It is always the labourer who must produce. Land and capital are only conditions, not causes of production. All return is exclusively labour-return.

As a matter of fact Rodbertus is perfectly right when he says that no conclusion can be drawn from personal income to material return. The problem of distribution of return must be entirely separated from that of distribution of income, if it is to be judged of correctly. But if the problem is to be entirely separated, it must also be so in its application. Let us then leave the personal quarrel entirely out of consideration. Let us completely disregard the question as to what persons should have the products; and, without regard to consequences, simply apply ourselves to find out which factors are to thank for their production, and to which factors they should be imputed. Let us imagine to ourselves the communistic state as seeking for the natural laws of imputation. Here the entire product falls to the enjoyment of the labouring commonwealth. The question then is :—Does *it* therefore consider the whole product as a result of its labour, or does it also impute the product to its possession of land and capital?

Clearly this will depend on the standpoint from which the imputation is calculated. If it is the moral imputation that is in question, then certainly no one but the labourer could be named. Land and capital have no merit that they bring forth fruit; they are dead tools in the hand of man; and the man is responsible for the use he makes of them. Evidently all those who, in any sort of way, have assisted in bringing about the result, are counted among the labourers,—those who direct as well as those who carry out. Indeed, there is no possible doubt that the greatest thanks are not due to mechanical exertions, if we are speaking of imputation in the highest sense of the word. Above these must stand the services of those who direct the executant labourer; who not only supply him with ideas, organisation, and energy, but also procure for him the materials for labour, contrive the machinery, and bring together the labourers who are to work with him. Compared with potencies such as these, the executant labourer himself takes the same position as the material means of production do as compared with himself. Morally considered, things are auxiliaries to him, but he himself is the auxiliary of his leader.

This moral imputation may be important for the personal disposition of income; for the material division of return, of which alone we are now speaking, it is of no consequence. The question here is: On what factors are we practically dependent if the return is to be obtained? Every one who knows economic life as it is, will answer quite plainly: Upon labour *and* productive wealth. Increase of possession raises the return just as surely as does additional industry. No one feels that the return is dependent upon those production goods of nature which are as abundant as the atom of air floating above the field, or the trees in a primeval forest. But every one feels that the return *is* dependent upon all goods which, however abundant they may be, are yet scarce; those goods which one economises and tries to multiply. Where would not such possessions have value? And if they have value why is it, if not on account of the return, and according to the amount of the return, which they secure? So long as men consider themselves rich in possessing land and capital, so long do they prove that they impute to them a portion of the fruits which they assist in bringing forth, and so long do they attribute to labour only the remainder of the total return. The socialist who wishes to see his state as rich in property as possible, confutes thereby as completely as possible his own theory, that labour alone makes rich.[1]

[1] We shall find further on (Book V. chap. x.), in the socialist theory itself, a much clearer confession that labour is not the only factor in the formation of value. See also Book III. chap. xvii.

All means of production in which value is recognised, are recognised thereby as practically influential causes of production. To these means of production land and capital will belong, so long as they are not available in ever-assured superfluity. No one can seriously doubt this. The only thing that can be doubted is whether it be just and advantageous for society to permit the existence of private and individual property in land and capital, whereby the return from land and capital is transferred exclusively to single individuals. On this question it is not so easy to come to a decision, and so far as we have gone we have not made any, nor even tried to do so. We have only explained the material relation between products and means of production, without in any way anticipating the ranking of personal claims.

# CHAPTER IV

## PREVIOUS ATTEMPTS AT SOLUTION

THE only writer who has made any attempt at an exhaustive treatment of the problem now occupying our attention is Menger. In this Menger starts from the fundamental idea of his theory of value. Supposing that I possess a stock of consumption goods, the clearest way of finding the value of one single item of the stock is by assuming that I lose it. In this way I find what enjoyment depends upon this item —the marginal enjoyment already described,—and find at once the source and amount of its value. This method of determining value Menger now applies to the more complicated case in which one has to decide the value of a single item, among several co-operating production goods. Here also he asks what would be the consequence of losing a single item, or a definite portion of any such item, from among the entire group of available goods (land, seed, agricultural implements, labour, cattle, manure, and so on)—*e.g.* a cart-horse or quantity of manure. The decrease in the total return which would take place, gives him the amount of return which the owner feels to be dependent upon the possession of the item in question, and gives him at the same time the foundation of its value.

In applying this Menger has arrived at some very remarkable and important results. No production good can work by itself: to accomplish anything every good requires the co-operation of others; and, in so far as production goods mutually demand and supplement each other, they are, to use Menger's expression, "complementary goods." At the same time the combinations which they enter into are less strict than might be expected. If a single good falls out of a productive group of goods, the efficiency of the remaining goods is not, as a rule, completely destroyed thereby. It happens frequently that the group may still remain a group, and still be effectively employed, although with somewhat diminished return, without the lost good being replaced at all. Land, *e.g.*, yields some return even without manure, or without the whole amount of manure demanded by good farming. Or the loss may be made up, if not with quite the same effect, by the substitution of a good taken from some other group, in which latter group, naturally, the return must equally sink a little. Or it may happen that the goods left over become ineffective, or too little effective, when grouped as was originally intended, but allow of being annexed to other groups, whose return is thereby raised, although, perhaps, not by the entire amount of what was lost originally. Take, as example, agricultural capital and labour, which have lost their original employment through laying waste of the ground for which they were intended, and are turned to industrial purposes.

It will be seen that the complementary nature of goods does not reach so far as at first sight might be supposed. Every single good requires the co-operation of others in order to be really of use, but the connection of the goods is not a very strict one. Only a portion of the return from the combination ever depends upon any one single element of production; never (except in a few cases which scarcely require to be considered) the entire return.

What Menger has done is distinguished, as well by the logical sequence of his argument as by his skill in observation, and the lifelike interpretation of that observation. It brings light into the darkness of a subject which no other theorist could have faced, much less illumined. At the same time even Menger has not given the entire solution quite perfectly. An example will make this clear.

Suppose three productive elements, employed in the most rational plan of production possible, promise in combination a product whose value amounts to 10 units of value. If the three elements were to be employed otherwise, in combination with other groups, they would certainly raise the return of these groups, but it is against our hypothesis—which is that of the most rational plan of production,—that the return can be raised by 10 units; otherwise the first combination chosen would not after all have been the best. There is always an infinite number of ways in which the elements in question can be grouped, but there is always one plan, and that the best, which should be carried out : if this be given up in favour of another, the result must be smaller, even if only to a trifling extent.

Suppose, again, that the three elements are employed in some plan other than the best—which, be it remembered, demanded their being combined with one another in a distinct group. Say that, by being each separately employed in some other group, the return of each of these three groups is raised by 3 units, and the three elements accordingly now produce a return amounting to 9 units of value.

How in this case will the value of each single item be reckoned according to Menger's principle ? By the decrease in return which ensues in the case of loss. In this case the decrease amounts to 10 units — the full return of the best combination now broken up—of which, however, 6 can be recovered by the new employment of the two remaining elements. The loss, therefore, amounts finally to 4, and this is true indifferently of any of the three goods. 12, then, is the value of the three taken together. But this is impossible, since, when most profitably employed, they can give only a return of 10.

This mistake in the result proceeds from a mistake in the method. The normal and determining assumption on which one calculates the value of a good, is not that of its loss, but that of its undisturbed possession, and of the use it gives in fulfilling its end. The assumption of loss serves,

in certain circumstances, to show more clearly the advantage
of possession.   I see more clearly what I have by possessing
a thing when I imagine what would be the consequence if I
ceased to have it.   But this holds only under certain circumstances, namely, as regards a stock of goods of the same kind,
where if, in imagination, I take away one good from the
others, it is this one good alone and nothing else that is
taken away.   It does not hold in the case of a stock of
heterogeneous and co-operating production goods, where if, in
imagination, I remove one, I deprive the others also of a
portion of their effect.

The full effect of all the elements in any productive
combination can only be realised when these elements remain
together undisturbed ; it is therefore impossible to discover
what value I receive and enjoy from this undisturbed possession, if I begin by assuming the dissolution of the combination, and then ask what still remains.   The question must
be put positively :  What do I actually obtain from the goods
as they stand at my disposal ?   Those productive employments which stand first,—the employments which are most
desirable and would be first chosen—decide the value; not
those which stand second, and would be taken up only in
the exceptional case of some disturbance of the original combination.   Two persons who are both in exactly the same
circumstances, and whose judgment agrees as to the best
arrangements for production, must obviously ascribe precisely
the same value to their productive possessions, although one
of them should have something better to fall back upon in
case the first plan falls through.   According to Menger, however, the values, in this latter case, would require to be
assessed differently, and indeed the higher valuation would
be that of the person who had the least to fall back upon,
because to him it would be much more important that the
first plan should not fall through.

The assumption of loss is sufficient if what is required
is the dividing up of the return which the elements of one
combination guarantee when put into other combinations ;
but it is of no use when what is wanted is to calculate as
well the surplus by which the first-chosen combination excels
all others.   This surplus is left an undivided remainder of

the return, and as regards it the problem of imputation is not solved, but comes up again for solution.[1]

It needs only a very slight turn to correct the error in Menger's theory. Every well-thought-out train of reasoning teaches by its very faults, as these faults also possess the first requisite of scientific insight, that is, clearness ; and Menger's theory contains in itself the indication as to how the error may be corrected. The deciding element is not that portion of the return which is lost through the loss of a good, but that which is secured by its possession.[2]

[1] Menger reckons this undivided residue to each separate factor instead of charging it to the entire amount, and thus the value comes out too high. In our example the surplus equals 1 (10-9). Menger calculates it three times instead of only once ; thus calculating two units too many, and showing a value of 12 where there is only a return of 10.

[2] The other attempts at solution of the problem do not go beyond suggestions. In Böhm - Bawerk alone (*Werth*, p. 56) is there a more detailed statement,—and it professes only to point out the direction in which probably the solution of the problem might be sought—"To measure the share which each one of several co-operating factors takes in producing the common product." Böhm - Bawerk, speaking first of some less important cases of "complementariness," establishes firmly the fundamental maxim that no element in a group which admits, firstly, of a separate employment outside the group, and which, secondly, may be replaced at the same time in the group by other goods of the same nature—obtained from some outside source—can receive a value higher than its "substitution value." By substitution value he means " that which is derived from the decrease of utility in those branches of production from which the substituted goods are procured." Of such a nature are, *e.g.*, the bricks destined for housebuilding. If some cartloads of these are destroyed, it will not hinder the building, as they are simply replaced by others. This proposition Böhm-Bawerk applies to the cases of productive complementariness, dividing the total amount of complementary production goods into two categories. Of these, one—which includes the overwhelming majority—contains those goods which, as marketable wares, are "replaceable at will"; *e.g.*, "the services of hired labourers, raw materials, fuel, tools, and so on." The other category — which contains the minority — includes those productive elements which "cannot be replaced, or are difficult to replace ; *e.g.* the piece of land which the peasant cultivates, mines, railway plant, factories, the activity of the undertaker himself with his high personal qualities." The value of those goods which belong to the first group is decided, in every case, through the other employments possible to them ; it is, so far, fixed. This value is first deducted from the total return, and the residue then falls "to the member or members which cannot be replaced"; thus the "peasant ascribes it to his land, the mine-owner to his mine, the manufacturer to his factory, the merchant to his capacity."

Similar ideas may be found more or less clearly stated by various writers ; in the *Ursprung des Werthes* I have myself pointed to a similar solution. Probably we should not be far wrong were we to assume that the reason why so

## CHAPTER V

### THE PRINCIPLE OF SOLUTION.　THE PRODUCTIVE CONTRIBUTION

SUPPOSE that a hunter's life depends on his last cartridge killing the tiger about to spring on him. If he misses, all is lost. Rifle and cartridge together have here an exact calculable value. Taken together, the value equals that of the success of the shot, neither more nor less. Taken singly, on the other hand, there is no means of calculating the value of each. They are two unknown quantities for which there is only one equation. Let us call them $x$ and $y$, and put the successful result at $100$; all that can be said as to their value lies in the equation $x + y = 100$.

Again, suppose an artist were to fashion a pewter vessel which commanded great admiration on account of its perfect form. Suppose, further, that this were the only artist who could do really artistic work, and that his was the only artistic work known. And suppose that, besides the piece of pewter which he had employed, no other material of similar suitability were to be had, neither gold, silver, wood, clay, nor even another piece of pewter. It would be absolutely impossible to distinguish in the value of the vessel between the value of the labour and that of the material. The skill of the artist who conceived and executed, and the suitability of

many writers have neglected to take up this problem of distribution, is that they supposed distribution in this sense to be as easily solved in theory as it is in practice. How is it, however, when several "unreplaceable" goods come together? Do not the mine and the activity of its owner, as employer, go together? And are not many—indeed very many—replaceable goods often combined? The value of these, which, *practically*, can always be ascertained by referring to their secondary employment and valuation, must, *theoretically*, be first separated from the combination, as again the secondary employment itself always requires combination with complementary goods,—but how can this be done unless the rules of distribution are known?

If these observations of Böhm-Bawerk can give no solution of the problem of imputation, they none the less contain an important and notable contribution towards its theory, for that could never be complete without recognising the distinction to which he has drawn attention. On this point see, in Book III. chap. xii., the examination of "cost goods and monopoly goods."

the material which yielded to his hand and retained the form
he gave, would be regarded as equally irreplaceable conditions
of success.   If we, under existing economic conditions, do
understand how to value the artist, and how to value the
material, we have to thank the circumstance which distinguishes
every act done under the influence of exchange from the ad-
venture of the lonely hunter ;—the circumstance, namely, that
these acts are not isolated, but take place along with many
others of the same kind, and can be compared with them.
This very pewter, out of which the artist creates a vessel of
great artistic value, serves at the same time to furnish articles
for ordinary use of very trifling value.   We conclude from this
that the pewter itself can have but a trifling value, and that only
a small portion of the high value of the artistic product falls
to it, while by far the greater share must be the property of the
artist.   We should be confirmed in this opinion were we to
observe that every work of the artist was highly valued.   But
if, at the same time, we observe that he also works with such
materials as gold and precious stones, and that these, on their
side, equally lend a high value to all products of which they
form part, we are forced to the conclusion that, in spite of his
talent, the greater part of the value of his products does not
always belong to the artist, and that, when he employs these
materials, a highly important, if not very much the more
important, part of the value must be ascribed to them.   Certainly
we can never succeed in considering either the artistic power
or the material by itself alone, and thus we cannot succeed in
measuring the effects of which they are independently capable.
Every productive factor, if it is to be effective, must be combined with others and join its action with theirs ; but the
elements that are bound up with it may alter, and this fact
makes it possible for us to distinguish the specific effect of each
single element, just as though it alone were active.

It is possible not only to separate these effects approximately, but to put them into exact figures, so soon as we collect
and measure all the important circumstances of the matter ;
such as the amount of the products, their value, and the amount
of the means of production employed at the time.   If we take
these circumstances accurately into account, we obtain a
number of equations, and we are in a position to make a

reliable calculation of what each single instrument of production
does.    To put in the shortest typical formula the full range of
expressions which offer themselves, we have, for instance,
instead of the one equation $x + y = 100$, the following :—

$$x + y = 100.$$
$$2x + 3z = 290.$$
$$4y + 5z = 590.$$

Here $x = 40$, $y = 60$, and $z = 70$.

According to the number of individual productive combinations carried out within the entire field of production, will
be the individual equations.    In these equations the combined
factors of production on the one side, and the value of the
jointly acquired (or anticipated) returns on the other, are set
against each other as equivalent amounts.    If we add together
all the equations, the total amount of productive wealth will
stand as equivalent against the total value of the return.    This
sum must be ascribed, entirely and without remainder, to the
individual productive elements, according to the standard of
the equation value.    To every element there thus falls a
definite share in the total performance, and this share could
not be figured out either higher or lower, without overthrowing
the equivalence between productive wealth and return.

It is the share in the return, thus credited to the individual
productive factor, which is usually called shortly the "return"
of the factor in question ;—the return of labour, return of land,
return of capital.    I shall describe it as the "Productive
Contribution" (see *Ursprung des Werthes*, p. 177), in order
that it may always be clear whether we are speaking of the
return as a whole, or of the share of the single factor in the
return.    The productive contribution, then, is that portion of
return in which is contained the work of the individual productive element in the total return of production.    The sum
of all the productive contributions exactly exhausts the value
of the total return.

It need scarcely be said that, as a matter of fact, calculation
can rarely be made so exactly, and never so comprehensively.
The equations indeed are all set down, and in every case the
productive outlay is estimated according to the standard of the
greatest attainable return.    But the stating of the equations is

frequently made with only a trifling degree of exactitude ; and the sum of all the equations is never fully taken, and thus cannot be divided out among the individual elements.   None the less we are constantly trying to ascertain the result of the addition and division; only that, instead of calculating directly, we try to attain our end, in a somewhat circumstantial way, by a method of testing.   The values obtained in the individual case are applied, so far as they appear suitable, to other cases, and corrected, the one by the other, till in the end the right division is attained.   And this is rendered immeasurably easier by the fact that we already possess, in the familiar and authenticated productive values, a key to the division which only requires to be adapted to the changes which emerge from time to time. At no time has the whole mass of production goods to be calculated all at once; it is only the contributions of individual members among these which require to be calculated anew, and even for them a good basis is found in the old values.   New calculations require to be made only in those branches of production where the attainable returns and their values either rise or fall.   This gives rise to new equations for the factors in question, either with more favourable or less favourable total values.   According as it is one or the other, will production be extended or limited, and productive elements attracted from other branches of production, or attracted to them, until the most favourable plan of production is again discovered.   The experience obtained while transferring now one, now another productive element, and watching the effect of each combination upon the value of the return, gives us sufficient information as to the amount with which the individual elements are bound up in the total return.[1]

[1] If we are to succeed in our calculation of the productive contributions there must be a sufficiently large number of equations.   There must be at least as many equations as there are unknown quantities.   Now this condition is certainly fulfilled.   How many unknown quantities are there ?   Just as many as there are classes of production goods distinguishable in exchange.   Without doubt these are very numerous.   When theorists speak simply of land, capital, and labour, they include within each of these groups an enormous number of classes of goods which in exchange are as far as possible from being homogeneous. The value of labour is not to be calculated as one thing ; there must be separate calculations for every kind and quality of labour between which one can distinguish.   In calculating the value of agricultural land there will be, in one and the same district, as many different and distinguishable types of land, as would

## CHAPTER VI

THE PRINCIPLE OF SOLUTION (*continued*).   CONTRIBUTION
AND CO-OPERATION

THE difference between our solution and that of Menger is as follows.

Menger assumes an economic course of events different from that which actually regulates economic life. To discover what return is obtained from the production goods which we possess, he tries to show what would happen should we cease to possess them. According to Menger, for example, the value to a farmer of a cart-horse is calculated by the diminution of return which would ensue were the farmer to lose the horse, and be forced to go on without it. That portion of return calculated by Menger to the single production good we may designate "the share dependent upon its co-operation."

We, on the other hand, start by assuming an economic course of events such as owners of production goods would

be distinguished in the register of a perfectly exact land tax imposed both on the cultivating and propertied agricultural classes. As to capital and its incalculable variety of forms we need not speak. But however far exchange may be specialised, the classes of productive *combinations* are undoubtedly even more numerous than the classes of production goods. The classes of combinations into which a good like iron or coal (even of one distinct origin or quality) may be introduced, are incalculable, and the same may be said of unskilled or day's labour. One and the same field is planted in rotation with the most various crops. And thus it comes that a mere change in the quantity of the same kind of goods in a group is sufficient to produce a new equation. Among all the many kinds of goods employed in production, it would be difficult to find one which, either as regards quantity or kind, would always be combined with others according to the same unalterably fixed formula. Different degrees of wealth, of knowledge, of skill, of local conditions, involve that even those kinds of goods which only admit of one single kind of employment,—that is to say, which are only suited to produce one single kind of product—must, at the same time and for the same purpose, go into a manifold variety of combinations. If there are exceptions to this rule they are only isolated ones. The contribution of such goods can, however, still be calculated—always supposing that there are not two such elements in one and the same group. In this case, indeed, the principle we have established would not work, because we should have two unknown quantities and only one equation.

expect.  We trace the effects that will ensue if all the production goods which we possess are actually employed as we wish and plan.   In this way we calculate what we have called the " productive contribution " of each factor.

The sum of all the " productive contributions " is exactly the same as the sum of value of all the products ; the sum of all the " shares dependent upon co-operation " is, on the other hand, as we have already shown, greater.   In other words, the " productive contribution " is essentially smaller than the " share dependent upon co-operation."   We reckon for instance the return which the cart-horse gives to the farm lower than Menger does, as we only estimate it at a portion of the decrease that would ensue were the owner obliged to farm without it.   According to Menger, consequently, the farmer who loses his cart-horse loses only the value of the animal, whereas, according to our conception—which calculates differently the same numerical loss — not only does he lose the value of the animal, but he suffers, beyond this, some disturbance in the value of his remaining productive wealth.

Menger's is undoubtedly the simpler and clearer method. The distinction which we find it necessary to make between the " contribution " and the " co-operation " of a factor, appears contradictory and artificial.   As a matter of fact, we introduce into the question no more difficulties than are actually contained in it.   " Contribution " and " Co-operation," under whatever names they may be known, are everywhere distinguished, and must be distinguished, from each other in practical economic life.   It is a generally-accepted fact that every productive factor furnishes the basis, not only for its own value, but also for that of all the other factors in the production.   If any essential element is removed from any undertaking whatever, the whole undertaking must sensibly suffer.   If there be a scarcity of raw material, human labour and machinery will lose some of their capacity of service, and *vice versâ ;* experience can show thousands of such cases.   In innumerable ways experience shows that means of production mutually demand and mutually hamper each other.   Increased activity on the part of labour raises the return to productive wealth, and extended exploitation of productive wealth raises the return to labour.   What does this prove but that the share of return which furnishes the basis of value for its factor—the "return" imputed to it which we have called its "contribution"—does not exhaust the entire share contributed by it to the success of the production ? Thus we find that the distinctions mentioned really exist, and are not introduced by us into economic life for the purpose of aiding our solution ; we find that, by means of this solution, we explain an otherwise inexplicable economic contradiction, and our theory receives thereby no small degree of support and credibility. Or does it appear no contradiction to say that labour, besides affecting "its own" return, makes the "return to capital" rise or fall, or that capital, besides "its own," also affects the "return to labour"?

## CHAPTER VII

THE PRINCIPLE OF SOLUTION (*continued*).     THE ECONOMIC
SERVICE OF IMPUTATION

THANKS to the imputation of the "productive contribution," every production good, without exception, has ascribed to it a *greater* effect than it could obtain through its own powers. No production good, not even the most powerful of all, labour, could by itself produce anything ; every such good requires the co-operation of others, and is nothing by itself. On the other hand, again, every production good without exception, has, thanks to this imputation, a *lesser* effect ascribed to it than might be expected from the degree of dependence in which the complementary goods stand to it. If we take from a group any element, however unimportant, so long as it is a necessary and economic element, not only is its own return lost, but the other elements also are robbed of a portion of their effect. This holds of labour in its relation to capital, as well as of capital in its relation to labour. The well-worn argument, then, that without labour nothing would bring forth fruit, and that to labour conse-quently must be imputed the entire return, is false. Only those who misunderstand the rules of imputation in every-

day use, could employ it.   Nothing is easier than to reduce it
to an absurdity by supposing labour obliged to work without
land or capital.

The imputation of the productive contribution assigns in
this way to every production good a medium share.[1]   To calculate the productive contribution, and therefore also the value,
at this medium amount, is sound common sense.   It is the
only practical and useful kind of calculation; it justifies its
logic by its utility.   The value of production goods should be
the controlling power of production.   Now it will be so, most
perfectly, if it is based, according to our standard, on the productive contribution of these goods.   On the other hand, it
will be so only imperfectly or not at all, if we depart from the
principle.   The sum of all the contributions is, as we have seen,
equal to the value of the greatest possible total return, and
this return will be actually reached if we demand from each
factor a service equal to the contribution imputed to it.   If
we do not impute anything to the means of production, we
deprive ourselves of all possibility of controlling their employment by reference to their value.   If we impute to them
either more or less than their actual " contribution," our
control will be at fault, as it will induce us either to a too
limited or a too extensive employment.

Perhaps I may be allowed to pursue these ideas still
further into detail.

If we did not ascribe any share in the return to labour,
nor yet to land and capital, we should have to use all these
without being in any way guided by their value.   If again
the whole return were imputed to labour and none of it to the
material instruments, production would be misled by productive value.   Land and capital would be declared valueless;
there would be no need to consider them at all; whereas
labour would be overestimated, and would, consequently, be far
too greatly withheld.   The most overestimated would be that
labour which got the most intensive material assistance, and so

---

[1] Medium, that is, between the greater and the lesser shares just mentioned.
The share of labour, for instance, is not determined by the (socialist) consideration that capital without labour is dead, nor by the (opposite) consideration that
labour without capital is crippled.   In becoming organic every element gains
in importance by becoming arbiter of others, but loses as it puts itself into the
same position of dependence upon others.— *W. S.*

gave the absolutely largest returns. Labour which, in co-operation with a large amount of capital, gave a total return of 100, would be estimated more highly than labour of equal amount, but different quality, which, with a tenth part of the capital, gave a return of 99. Artistic labour, working without much outside assistance, would have a low valuation, while plentifully assisted labour, even although unskilled and mechanical, would have a high valuation. With the former extravagance might be allowable, while with the latter we should have to economise. The whole sphere of production would be dominated at every point by confusion and per-versity.

The imputation of return to land, capital, and labour, according to the measure of their respective productive con-tributions, is a natural economic dictate; it holds in all forms of economic life—in the communistic state as well as in the present one. It may—possibly—be a just demand that the whole product be given over to the labourers as personal income; but in any case, and even should this come to pass, it is an economic demand that the products be credited to the sources of the return, according to the contributions which they afford, in order that we may have a standard for the further employment of the means of production.

It need scarcely be said that there is a limit to the appli-cation of this law. When too large a number of production goods are grouped together as one unit—as when theorists talk of all kinds of labour as "labour," all kinds of capital as "capital," and all varieties of ground as "land"—there is no longer the number of equations necessary for any solu-tion. Of "land, capital, and labour" there is nothing to be said except that, together, they bring forth everything; alone, nothing. In practical life, we have often occasion to look at things in this wholesale way. But, even if these occasions were more frequent than they actually are, the individual imputation would not be any the less necessary. Although production is carried on under these wholesale modes and conditions required for preparation, introduction, and security, still, in the conduct of production it necessarily comes, in the long run, to detailed calculation. The man who calculates the result most exactly, who measures and makes a difference as regards even the smallest amounts, will, so far as it depends on the working out, get the largest total result; while the poorest will fall to him who estimates things only in the gross, and in an outward and superficial way.   If it be everywhere a sign and a principle of human advance that we make more and more minute division and classification of causes, it must also be so in the great sphere of economic life.   If socialism means to do away with the productive imputation, it will induce a condition of things worse than that experienced in the deepest barbarism.   The savage knows what he owes to his net, and what to his bow and arrow, and would be badly off if he did not know.   Happily the same instinct which directs him is possessed by all men, and no amount of theories will ever make people neglect to measure the effects of the productive powers in the way that practical self-interest demands.

On the other hand, again, the individual imputation does not do away with the necessity of considering production as a whole.   The preparation for and introduction of productive labour often requires, as has been said, very large and whole-sale standards, where it is not sufficient merely to reckon up the productive contributions.   These contributions correspond to the individual results which emerge where production succeeds.   But how if it does not succeed ?   How if certain goods are wanting, and the want retards production, limits it, or even makes it quite impossible ?   Then, indeed, we get results from the single good which go far beyond the amount of its contribution.   Then it becomes evident that the in-dividual good not merely creates " its own return," but, besides this, conditions the returns of other goods.   The disturbing power of a want or loss of goods—the difference between " contribution " and " co-operation "—is larger, the larger the quantity of goods lost.   Where, then, there is any danger of a loss, and especially a loss of wide extent, individual imputation is not sufficient; it reckons the damage too low; its only standards have too small a range.   In this case it is necessary to be fully informed concerning the whole circle of conditions upon which the production depends, and the whole importance of the co-operation of all the factors.

Individual imputation and observation of production as a whole, although they may lead to different valuations of the same goods, do not on that account contradict each other, nor cancel each other. Each valuation can be employed only for its own purposes. Individual imputation serves, *in* the carrying out of production, to measure the economic employment of each portion of a nation's resources; consideration of production as a whole serves to guarantee that the production *is* carried through. The labour powers of a nation, for instance, must be individually valued and employed according to the exact amount of their contributions, while, at the same time, particular care must be taken to meet the perils which so often all at once threaten the labour power of individual groups, and indeed of great classes. Again, the various forms of a nation's capital must be individually valued and employed according to the measure of their contributions. At the same time care must be taken that capital as a whole, and capital in the chief branches of production, remains and increases in the face of possible danger and attack. The consideration of production as a whole must thus aim at securing against all disturbance the essential foundations of production, and the harmonious relation of its elements.

In the economic life of to-day individual imputation devolves chiefly upon the individual citizen, while consideration of production as a whole is mainly undertaken by the government. The former belongs peculiarly to the sphere of private economic valuation, the latter peculiarly to that of public economic valuation. Here we only indicate the distinction, leaving more exact consideration to the last book.

## CHAPTER VIII

### THE PRINCIPLE OF SOLUTION (*continued*). IMPUTATION AND THE MARGINAL LAW

IN the case of production goods which are available, not individually but in stocks, imputation of the productive contribution follows the marginal law. To each single item or quantity is imputed the smallest contribution which, under the circumstances, can be economically aimed at by the employment of this particular item or quantity—the "Marginal Contribution" as I have already called it (*Ursprung des Werthes*, p. 177), or, looking at it from a different point of view, the "Marginal Product." Böhm-Bawerk has drawn attention (*Werth*, p. 502) to the fact that this law of exchange value has long been recognised in the case of certain production goods :—" Thünen, and all the body of economic doctrine after him, have taught that the rate of interest is decided by the productiveness of the last applied dose of capital, and the rate of wages by the return of the last labourer employed in the undertaking." Now what is here conceded to a limited extent holds generally of all production goods, and for every form of value, as a law of natural valuation.

It is self-evident that the marginal law which holds as regards produced consumption goods, holds also as regards the goods which produce them. We know that, in every stock of consumption goods, every unit receives its value from the marginal utility ; thus the value which the products are expected to have is already adjusted to the marginal level, and the value of the production goods, as derived from this, is consequently placed, from the beginning, on the basis of the marginal value. If the communistic state wish to produce a million new rifles to one pattern, it will, in the calculations previous to production, reckon every individual rifle as equal in value ; and thus it is, from the first, impossible that one quantity of metal destined to make these rifles should obtain a value different from any other quantity of like amount and quality. If from 1000 productive units 10,000 units of product are produced, each with a marginal value of 5 (the total value being expressed by the formula 10,000 $\times 5 = 50,000$), the entire productive stock receives a value of 50,000, and each individual unit will be valued equally at 50.

While this application of the marginal law to production goods results indirectly, through the medium of products, we have to consider a second and direct application. Production goods which are capable of being employed in many different ways, are used to create products of various kinds. In each kind, taken by itself, the value of the product is adjusted to the

level of its particular marginal utility, but we need not expect
—and, in fact, it would be essentially a mere chance—that the
marginal amounts of all the different kinds should, when compared with each other, entirely agree.    We have already shown
(in Book I. chap. iv.) that only in a limited sense can one speak
of a common level of household economy ; and it is only in the
same limited sense that we can speak of a common level of
production.    Production stocks must always be employed in
such a way as to bring forward those products which will
secure the greatest possible satisfaction of want.    In particular, the destination of production goods to individual
branches of production,—or, what is the same thing, the choice
of the kind and amount of goods to be produced, and the in-
vestment of labour and capital in the individual classes and
branches of production,—must always be weighed and decided
with a view to providing the greatest possible satisfaction of
wants.    This does not, however, in the least imply that products must everywhere have the same marginal utility.    Many
products satisfy wants of trifling extent, where the satiation
point is reached very speedily: others again satisfy wants
whose receptive capacity is very great, and where the scale of
satisfaction shows the finest shades of transition from the
stronger intensities of desire downwards.    To take as drastic
an example as possible, compare the employment of gold in
the filling of teeth with its employment for purposes of
luxury.    The two scales of satisfaction do not in the least
correspond with each other, and it is quite impossible in the
two kinds of employments to keep always exactly to the same
marginal amount.    All economic demands are fulfilled when
care is taken that goods of less marginal utility are never produced from production goods which, if employed in producing
other things, might have brought a higher marginal utility.    It
may, therefore, very well happen, and, in the case of all means of
production which are capable of numerous and varied employments, it will always happen, that the marginal amounts in the
different classes of production will differ from each other.

Suppose, for example, that from one stock of iron are produced three kinds of products, which we may designate as A,
B, and C ; that, in kind A, the unit of iron receives a value of
10—corresponding with the economically-attainable marginal

utility of 10 ;—that in kind B the unit receives a value of 9—
corresponding with the marginal utility 9 ; in kind C, a value
of 8—corresponding with the marginal utility 8.   Here we
have a case where utility, at the stage of the products, is not
yet completely adjusted to the marginal level, and where the
equalisation must first take place directly and at the stage of
the production goods.   That the equalisation must ultimately
take place cannot be doubted.   It is quite impossible to estimate one-third of the iron higher than another third ; indeed,
assuming it to be all of one quality, there would be no possible way of deciding which concrete portion of the stock
should have the preference over the rest.   So long as any
appreciable quantity of the iron is destined to turn out products with a marginal utility of 8, no unit of the entire stock
can be valued at a higher return.   To every unit in such a
case must be imputed the marginal return of 8, and the value
of the entire stock is found by multiplying the number of
units which it contains by the marginal value 8.[1]

The fact that the marginal law applies, partly directly
partly indirectly, to production goods also, first renders it possible for value actively to fulfil its peculiar economic service,
as the form in which we calculate utility and the means by
which we control it.   Compared with stocks of consumption
goods, stocks of production goods are larger, more concentrated,
and more homogeneous.   In the household of an individual
there are not many stocks of anything, but the elements
which produce almost all he possesses are accumulated in
stocks—in the hands of producers sometimes in enormous
stocks,—and thus become subject to the simplified calculation
of value, where the economic amount of each stock is expressed
by a multiple of its amount and marginal value.   And thus,
through the law of costs (see note below), products also
are subjected, in great numbers, to this simplified form of
calculation.

---

[1] This is one of the most pregnant applications of the marginal law ; we shall
return to it again and again later on, particularly in the fifth book, where we
consider the subject of costs.   To assist our comprehension of the law of costs,
we may here anticipate so much as to say, that the productive marginal value on
its part has a levelling effect upon the value of products.   In the above example
the value of the marginal utilities 10 and 9, in kinds A and B respectively, will
be alike pressed down to the productive marginal amount of 8.

We constantly see producers making calculations as to their warehouses, materials, plants, and stocks in this simple way; namely, by taking the amount and the price of the unit, and putting down as the total value the amount obtained by multiplying the one into the other. This observation by itself is sufficient proof of the wide extent to which the marginal law obtains in the economy of to-day. Not only are prices decided by a marginal law, but, by means of prices, the whole sphere of production, which makes its calculations throughout in terms of price, is based all through on a marginal valuation. Is it not worth while to discover what is meant by the application of a marginal valuation such as this ? And is it not satisfactory to know that the naive form of estimating goods, pursued from time immemorial in virtue of the original prompting of man's nature, is a wonder of simplicity and appropriateness ?

## CHAPTER IX

### THE INDIVIDUAL FACTORS OF IMPUTATION.   I.—SUPPLY

THOSE things which are always adduced as causing the changes in the value of production goods, effect this change, in the first instance, by altering the amount of contribution imputed to the production goods. We shall now discuss these in turn, and this may possibly prove the most wearisome part of our task.

In the first place we have to notice the available supply. The larger the available supply of any definite kind of productive instruments, the less important may and must be the goods produced—always supposing that in other respects no disturbing change of circumstance takes place. If more iron be raised, iron products of smaller marginal utility may and must be made. It is inevitable that this result should be attributed to the material, the iron, and expressed in a lower valuation of its marginal productive service. It cannot be imputed to any other factor, such as the labour that co-operates in the production, as no change has taken place in

the circumstances of any other factor. Of all the equations of
return, only those in which iron occurs have been reduced,
those in which labour occurs, expended on other materials,
remaining unaltered ; consequently the calculation is lower
for the former, not for the latter. To iron, therefore, and not
to labour, is imputed a smaller share of the return. If one
were to calculate everything as before, or were to impute to
labour the diminished return, the calculation would defeat its
own purpose ; one would be calculating as if everything could
be spent as before, or as if labour could be employed with greater
freedom. Neither of these could be allowed.

Of all production goods, the smallest contributions must be
imputed to those the supplies of which are most abundant in
comparison with the demand for them. These may be spent
most freely, down to their most insignificant uses. So far as
productive exploitation is concerned, it is desirable that those
goods which are most needed should also be the most abundant, and should have the smallest contributions imputed
to them.[1]

# CHAPTER X

### THE INDIVIDUAL FACTORS OF IMPUTATION (*continued*).
### II.——DEMAND AND COMPLEMENTARY GOODS

In the case of goods for immediate consumption, demand
and want coincide : the amount of agricultural produce required for the full satisfaction of personal want forms the
demand for agricultural produce. It is otherwise with pro-

---

[1] It may be of use to the English reader to note how our representative
English economist expresses similar ideas :—"Other things being equal, the
larger the supply of any agent of production, the farther will it have to push its
way into uses for which it is not specially fitted, and the lower will be the
demand price with which it will have to be contented in those uses in which its
employment is on the verge or margin of not being found profitable ; and, in so
far as competition equalises the price which it gets in all uses, this price will be
its price for all uses. The extra production resulting from the increase in that
agent of production will go to swell the national dividend, and other agents of
production will benefit thereby ; but that agent itself will have to submit to a
lower rate of pay."—Marshall, *Principles of Economics*, 2nd edit., p. 565.—*W. S.*

duction goods; here personal want does not always create a demand. If land, of its own accord and without cultivation, were to bring forth fruits in superfluity, there would be no demand for agricultural implements. And likewise, on the other hand, if land refused to make any return, if all land were waste and barren, there would be no demand for agricultural implements; there could be no use for them. A demand for means of production arises only when, on the one hand, we are *obliged* to employ them or else go without what they produce; and when, on the other hand, we *can* employ them, inasmuch as we have at our disposal the necessary complementary goods. So long as the complementary goods are wanting, we can, at best, speak of a *latent* demand; the demand is *effective* only when we have also acquired the complementary goods.[1]

It follows from this that the effective demand for means of production must vary, not only when there is a variation in personal want, but also when there is a variation in the quantity of complementary goods.[2] In both directions we must examine the effect upon the imputation, and thus, in looking at demand in the case of production goods, we have a far more complicated causal connection than in the case of consumption goods. We shall find, however, that the law remains the same for both. The contribution imputable to production goods always varies with the demand, just as does the value of consumption goods. If demand increases, from whatever cause, so does the contribution, and, as demand sinks, the contribution sinks with it. To prove this in the shortest manner possible.

First: it may be granted that the effective demand rises when the abundance of complementary goods increases, personal want remaining the same. Suppose *e.g.* that the amount of agricultural capital and available agricultural labour power increase, and that the effective demand for land also increases

---

[1] See on this point Menger, p. 39.

[2] Compare with this Marshall's *Principles*, p. 563 :—" In the account given of the demand for the several agents of production, it was indicated that the ultimate demand for each depended on the co-operation of the others in raising the joint product of their labour ; or, to state the case even more broadly, that the demand for each is in a great measure governed by the supply of the others."—*W. S.*

thereby, inasmuch as latent demand becomes active; suppose, that is to say, that it is now and henceforth possible,—so far as depends on complementary goods,—to cultivate more land and more completely satisfy want.   How will this affect the calculation of agricultural return?   Evidently there are again several cases which must be distinguished from each other. It may be that the ground will not permit of any further cultivation, so that, in spite of increased facilities in capital and labour, production cannot be extended,—as might readily happen with vine-growing land in a specially favourable situation.   Or the return may increase in perfect proportion with the increase of capital and labour, as we may assume to be possible on the slightly cultivated land of a new colony.   Or, finally—and this is the general rule in old countries—the return may indeed be increased, but not entirely in proportion to the increase of complementary goods; here indeed all the new capital and labour find employment, but with diminished results.

Different as these cases are, the final result is the same in all, although it comes about in a variety of ways.   In every case a larger share of the return will be imputed to the land.

(*a*) If production cannot be extended, the value of the products remains the same as before, as no reason for change has emerged.   What does change is the distribution of the imputation.   The equation on which, in the above example, is to be calculated the return of the vine land, of the capital employed upon it, and of the labour employed upon it, all taken together, remains as it was.   But the added capital and labour must now find employment elsewhere; must enter into new combinations, either on other land, or in some trade or industry where they give a smaller return.   Their equations are, therefore, on the whole less favourable, and the consequence is that the equation, which the wine production presents, is now solved in a way less favourable for them.   Their marginal productive contribution sinks, and, less being deducted for capital and labour, the value of the wine leaves a greater share to the credit of land.   Land obtains a greater share, as it were, by *absorption* of the effects which can now no longer be attributed to the complementary goods, inasmuch as the marginal law requires that these should everywhere be estimated at the same value, and inasmuch as the common margin of their possibility of employment has fallen.

(*b*) Where production admits of being extended indefinitely the total value of the products rises (in the "up grade" of the movement of value), although the single product may lose in value. The equations of return are more favourable equally for all factors concerned, and the greater total return gives, equally to land, capital and labour, an absolutely greater share.

(*c*) Where production can be only partially extended we have a combination of both results. The contribution credited to land experiences a double augmentation, one due to increased utilisation, and the other to the reduced valuation of the auxiliary means employed.

Second : the effective demand rises when personal want increases, complementary wealth remaining the same. Here the matter is very simple. The figures of the ratio which decide the distribution of return remain unaltered, but the value of the return has risen. The consequence is that the same quota has an absolutely greater value.

Every-day experience makes the changes of relation, which we have just pointed out between the co-operating factors of production, sufficiently familiar to every one who knows about exchange value. Every undertaker knows that it is to his advantage when the auxiliary means he employs come upon the market in larger quantities, whether it be because they are being more largely produced, or because there is less use for them in other directions. He can now extend his business, or make more out of it, by spending less upon the auxiliary means of production he requires, while the return remains unaltered. Every undertaker, on the other hand, knows that it is to his disadvantage when the auxiliary means he employs become scarcer in the market, or, what amounts to the same thing, are drawn off in larger quantities by other branches of production. In the communistic state entirely similar calculations will require to be made, in order to estimate correctly the mutual effects of the complementary goods on each other. Assuming the circumstances just mentioned, a vineyard, even in the communistic state, would inevitably be more highly valued wherever the auxiliaries towards its cultivation came forward in greater quantity, or were less freely employed in other directions: and it would certainly be estimated at a lower figure wherever the auxiliaries towards its cultivation were more highly valued, either on account of a diminished amount of them coming forward, or of their increased employment in other directions. Further, its share in the return would sink to zero whenever the auxiliary means of its cultivation were so highly valued that their contributions equalled the whole return of wine; and its cultivation would have to be given up entirely whenever it became impossible to meet these contributions out of the return of wine.

Should any one factor of production, be it land, capital, or labour, come more freely into our disposal, the natural rules of imputation require that all the others obtain a higher valuation; as they also require that all the factors be more highly valued if there should be an all-round increase of personal want.

## CHAPTER XI

### THE INDIVIDUAL FACTORS OF IMPUTATION (*continued*).
### III.—TECHNIQUE

TECHNIQUE is the art of making the best use of productive instruments. Every advance in technique improves either the quantity or the quality of products. Even a so-called "labour-saving" machine acts in the long run like an intensified utilisation. By dispensing with another productive instrument at a certain point or for the present, it preserves it for other or later employments.

Improvement in the quality of products raises their value. Multiplication of their quantity certainly diminishes the value of the individual product, but at the same time (in the "up grade" of value, which, for the sake of brevity, we shall alone consider at present) increases the sum of value of all the products taken together. Technical improvements have, therefore, this result, that the known quantities, in the equations of return by which the contributions of the production goods are to be calculated, are put higher, while the unknown quantities remain the same. Thus, according to circumstances, the contributions of all the factors, or simply of individual factors in the production in question, will be raised ; it frequently happens, however, that the circumstances are such that the contributions of certain factors must be calculated at less.

What happens, for example, when some expedient to reduce cost is introduced into a kind of production incapable of further extension — say, the production of wine in a limited area already cultivated to the utmost extent ? The return of wine remains the same, and its value remains the same, but to the vineyard must be imputed a larger share of the return than formerly, because it has to share it with a smaller number of productive factors. The elements of production thus saved can and will find another employment ; they increase the supply available for other purposes while the demand for such purposes remains the same. The final result is consequently a reduction of their productive contribution. The same is true of all means of production which have been driven from their former employments by reason of technical improvements. The familiar effect of labour-saving machinery is that it makes *wages* fall ; and this arises from the fact that, in the first instance, it reduces the *contribution* of labour. Even in the communistic state this part of the effect would emerge. The more labour could be replaced by machinery, the more labour power would there be left to dispose of ; and the less remunerative the employments to which it would be devoted. If formerly it had been a mistake to devote it to such employments, it would now be a mistake not to do so. The *rôle* of labour in production would have altered ; it would take another position ; and other effects would have to be imputed to it, if the imputation is to be based on natural principles,—that is, principles which promote the most advantageous employment possible.

In all cases where production is limited by certain specific elements, the chief advantage obtained by improvement of technique is ascribed to these elements. Means of production

which have a more extensive employment are but little affected
by changes in individual branches of production ; only those
technical improvements which affect all, or a greater part of
their employments, are of much importance to them, since it is
only in these cases that the equations of return are noticeably
altered in their favour.     The improvement in means of
transport, which brought with it the increased utilisation of
an enormous number of industries, is an example of a comprehensive technical improvement which actually had the
power to raise the returns of almost all means of production.

Every change in technical art naturally calls for a certain
change in the plan of production, a certain rearrangement in
the disposal and destination of our productive resources.
Other results seem now the more attractive ; other products
are now the marginal products.     The rapid development of
industry in the course of the present century has attracted
many labourers from agricultural to industrial pursuits.     This
transference, which was a very serious matter to the landowners since, among other things, it compelled them to pay the
labourers they had left at the higher rate given by the manufacturers, was entirely beneficial for production generally.     It
removed the labourers from occupations which brought them
little, but were, however, in the absence of anything more remunerative, permissible up till that time, into others in which
they could assess their powers at a higher contribution.     If in
the communistic state a similar phenomenon should ever come
in the train of technical development, it also would require to
be met by a similar transference of capital and labour, the
measure for which would be obtained by observation of the
marginal productive contributions.

# CHAPTER XII

### THE INDIVIDUAL FACTORS OF IMPUTATION (*continued*).
IV.—THE IMPUTATION TO COST GOODS AND TO MONOPOLY GOODS

WHAT has been said as to the influence of supply, of demand,
and of technique, gives sufficient evidence that, in the im-

putation of return, there is a certain category ·of production goods particularly favoured, and another peculiarly prejudiced. The line of division, however, which separates these two categories cannot be drawn with any great strictness; the transferences from one group to the other are imperceptible; the grouping changes with the change of circumstances; and, even within the separate groups, there is the same division. Goods which are favoured above many others may nevertheless be quite the reverse in comparison with just as many more.

The first group is composed of those goods to which attaches a natural monopoly (as opposed to a legal monopoly). Characteristic of this group is the comparative rarity of such goods as compared with the demand for them, or, it may be, the comparatively small quantity that can be produced. As examples of goods which have pronouncedly the character of monopoly may be mentioned the following;—scarce raw materials, land exceptionally situated, the work of one peculiarly gifted, —particularly an artist or scientific worker of the highest rank,—a secret and at the same time successful process (or, more exactly, the exclusive knowledge of such a process, whereby the persons who have it obtain a preference over others), and, finally, works of human hands, which, on account of their size, or on account of technical difficulties, cannot be repeated.

Goods which belong to the second group may be called " Cost Goods," inasmuch as they are the elements in the calculations of cost.[1] They are goods easily accessible and abundant, or goods whose production can be indefinitely increased. The following goods have markedly this character; —unskilled labour, coal, wood, the common metals, and also land devoted to industrial undertakings where there is no question of any particular advantage in situation. Things which are to be had in superfluity are not counted among cost goods; indeed they are not reckoned among economic goods at all. While monopoly goods are *specific* elements of individual industries, cost goods are the common cosmopolitan and indispensable powers and materials of production.

Articles whose making requires no monopoly goods may be produced, comparatively to others, in the largest

[1] See below, Book V.

quantities; on the other hand, those will be produced in the smallest quantities which demand productive factors of a peculiarly marked monopoly character, even although cost goods, subject to very little limitation, should be employed along with them. Assuming equal wants, then, the value of goods produced under monopoly must, by reason of their small available quantity, stand comparatively high; and consequently, to monopoly goods, as compared with cost goods, must generally be imputed a contribution of higher value. This is the first advantage which monopoly goods enjoy. In the course of economic development, however, many other advantages accrue to them, as the development itself accentuates the gulf which naturally exists between them.

In the ordinary course of economic history the available supply of many monopoly goods increases but slowly, or not at all,—in many cases, indeed, it becomes smaller; whereas the available supply of many cost goods increases rapidly and uninterruptedly. We have here two causes which widen the difference between the two imputations, inasmuch as the contribution imputed varies for every good in inverse ratio to the change in its supply, and in direct˜ratio to the change in complementary wealth. Now in the ordinary course of economic history, wants are continually increasing, and the numbers of those who want are continually increasing, while, at the same time, technique is always becoming more perfect. Both of these facts create a tendency towards raising the value of production goods. This tendency affects monopoly goods unreservedly, but, in the case of cost goods, on the other hand, it is frequently outweighed,—either immediately or after a certain lapse of time,—by the opposing tendency which comes from their increase. Generally speaking, cost goods gain only by such rises in the value of return as are wide-reaching enough to extend beyond the sphere of one single industry. Rises in value which are confined to individual branches of production are completely absorbed, as we have shown (Book III. chapters x. and xi.) by the specific elements in that branch, by the monopoly goods. And even should there be no such elements—as sometimes happens—an increase of value in one particular industry has comparatively little effect upon elements which are simultaneously employed in a great many.

Although cost goods are thus prejudiced in the calculation of the return, they have nevertheless the strongest influence on the result of production and its regulation, and, consequently also, on the basis of imputation.   They are the goods of universal diffusion—the goods which are to be found in every market; they form the majority of goods, and build up generally the body economic.   Monopoly goods must conform more to circumstances made for them; the using of them changes constantly with the change in the general economic conditions, for it rises and falls with them, just as the level of a stream when it runs below ground rises and falls with the level above.   Thus, practically, it would seem to come to this; that the imputation of the share due to the monopoly goods is made only after that due to the cost goods is finished.   The shares due to cost goods are always first deducted from the total return of production, and the residue then falls to the monopoly goods.   But closer consideration shows the matter to be somewhat different.   It is only in the individual case that such a calculation can be made.   In the totality of cases it is impossible to overlook the influence of monopoly goods upon the ordinary formation and imputation of return.   This influence is in part an indirect one, inasmuch as great quantities of cost goods are employed in monopoly productions, whereby the marginal productive return of the monopoly goods must be indirectly affected; and it is in part direct, inasmuch as through the results of monopoly productions, value equations are furnished, which are indispensable to the total valuation.

Monopoly goods have often received a quite peculiar position in theory.   Ricardo, for example, teaches that they owe their value altogether to their scarcity, while all other goods receive their value from the labour of producing them. A sufficiently wide consideration, however, shows that monopoly goods come altogether under the ordinary conditions of valuation, and differ from other economic goods only in that they display much more strikingly the character common to all.[1]

[1] In the second note to Book III. chap. iv. reference was made to the present chapter, stating that it would there be shown that, without taking into account the distinction to which Böhm - Bawerk has drawn special attention, and which deals with the opposition between monopoly goods and cost goods, the subject could not be finally settled.   The importance of the distinction ought by this time to have become clear.   The reader will remember that, in

# CHAPTER XIII

THE INDIVIDUAL FACTORS OF IMPUTATION (*continued*).  V.—
THE IMPUTATION TO PRODUCTIVE FACTORS OF PREFERABLE
QUALITY

OF two production goods of the same kind, that one possesses
the better quality which shows the greater " rentability "—to
use a clumsy but convenient German expression.  In other

distribution as Menger would have it, there is an " undivided residue." Now,
in every combination, this "undivided residue" falls, for the greater part, to
that good which possesses most strongly the character of a monopoly.  Consequently, where a pronounced monopoly good is combined with pronounced cost
goods, the "undivided residue" is imputed to the monopoly good ; where cost
goods alone are combined it is imputed to that good which most nearly resembles
the monopoly goods ; and, lastly, where several monopoly goods are combined it
is imputed to that one which most distinctly bears the monopoly character.

It must be noted, however, that only the greater part, not the whole, of the
" undivided residue " is to be imputed to the good in question.  Some part of it
—although often a most trifling and indeed practically indistinguishable part—
must always be ascribed to the other co-operating goods, as all of these experience
a certain increased utility from the maintenance of the combination, while the
dispersing of it would destroy that plan of production which is regarded as best.
The share to be ascribed to the other co-operating goods will be the greater, the
more the maintenance of the above-mentioned combination is dependent upon
them—*i.e.* the more they themselves possess the character of monopoly goods,
and the less they possess that of cost goods.  A scarce good will, as a rule, be
more seriously affected by a trifling change of productive destination than one
that is less scarce ; as was explained in the text, there must be considerable
alterations in demand and supply before the value of goods which are most
distinctively cost goods, shows a corresponding change.

The difference, therefore, between "contribution" and "co-operation"
remains fundamentally clear for all cases, although practically it does not come
to much, and, so long as only units of goods are concerned, need for the most
part scarcely be taken into account.  So much the more important is it when we
are examining the influence that larger quantities of production goods have upon
the amount of productive return.

In this sense I had, in the *Ursprung des Werthes*, although only by way of
suggestion, already disposed of the problem of "complementarity."  There I
stated that to production goods must be imputed their "marginal productive
contribution," while, to the "specific productive factors belonging to individual
productions" falls the residue of return, after deducting the quotas of all
supplementary goods.  The only matters omitted were : what would happen
were several monopoly goods combined together, and an exact formulation of
the law for calculating the contributions.

words, it is that good which, when co-operating with the same
amount of complementary goods, gives a return of higher value ;
—whether it be that the higher value of the return arises from
more being produced, or from what is produced being of a
better or preferable quality.   In what follows, for brevity's
sake, we shall consider only the former case.

If we possessed several production goods which, in this
specially limited sense, were of different qualities, we should
undoubtedly, in the production, employ the goods of poorer
quality only when the supply of better ones was not sufficient
for the demand ; and the share of return which fell to the
better goods would, of course, be higher than that which fell to
the poorer ones, by an exactly ascertainable quota.   According
as the better means of production, when working along with
an equal addition of complementary goods, produce a greater
total return, the value equation becomes more favourable to
them by the whole amount of the surplus return.   Their productive contribution is equal to that of the poorer quality plus
this surplus return.   Should the poorer goods be present in
superfluous amount and so have no contribution imputed to
them, the contribution of the better goods alone will be
credited with the surplus return.   Experience confirms these
propositions in thousands of ways ; they answer to the economic
observation of everybody.

Some economists who have paid very little attention to the
laws of complementarity in general, have shown extraordinary
earnestness in discussing this particular case.   Ricardo, in his
theory of land rent, deals with the advantage obtained from
greater natural fertility in the case of agricultural lands, or the
greater productiveness of mines.   Then he goes on to the
advantage, as regards return, which industrial capital first expended has, as against the increments of capital which follow.
His theory of land rent was amplified by pointing out that
rent of land is influenced also by its situation, *i.e.* by its
distance from the market for its product.   Finally it has been
shown that the " rentability " of land in towns, and also that
of capital and labour, is graduated in the same way as that of
agricultural land, and that the opportunity of obtaining for the
better quality a greater rent—a surplus return and a surplus
value—occurs as often in the one case as in the other.

These theoretic statements all relate to price, but they hold equally as regards the theory of value. The more fertile land, the land which lies nearer to the sphere of demand, the more skilled labourer, the more capable machine, are not only more highly paid, but have imputed to them as well, on account of their better quality, a comparatively greater share in the return —which, indeed, is the cause of their being more highly paid. In the communistic state, too, calculation will be made in the same way. The more fertile or more conveniently situated land will be cultivated before any other land, and, should other and poorer land require to be cultivated, the better qualities will be more highly valued in exact proportion to their surplus return.

# PART II

## NATURAL LAND RENT

### CHAPTER XIV

#### RICARDO'S DIFFERENTIAL RENT: THE FIRST PART

RICARDO, in his famous *Principles*, takes up what we may
call Contract rent, the rent which emerges when an owner
lets his land.  It is generally granted that the law of this
kind of rent is true also, in all essential respects, of that
income which the owner of the land could obtain without
letting it, by selling its products.  What has been said as to
imputation has probably shown that the analogy must be
carried still further.  The personal income which land yields
is, in the last resort, dependent upon the fact that the land
in question yields a return such that, after the shares of
capital and labour are deducted, there remains a share which
must, on natural laws, be imputed to the land.  The problem
of land rent, conceived of primarily as a problem of division
of income, in the last resort contains also a problem of distribution of return.  As a problem of distribution of return
it will emerge in the communistic state just as it does under
existing social conditions, and in both cases the solution is
fundamentally the same.

Ricardo begins his statement with a disquisition upon
primitive historical conditions.  So long as population is thin,
and it is unnecessary to cultivate even all its rich and fertile
land in order to provide food, no single piece of land can
obtain a rent.  Who " would pay for the use of land when

there was an abundant quantity not yet appropriated, and, therefore, at the disposal of whosoever might choose to cultivate it"? Should, however, population increase to a degree which necessitates the cultivation of land of the second quality, rent immediately commences on that of the first quality. Land of the second quality would require a greater expenditure of costs, in order to produce the same return as that of the first quality; it can therefore be cultivated only when the increased demand has raised the price of agricultural produce enough to cover the necessary costs. But this price leaves a surplus to land of the first quality, according to the saving of costs which it allows. If, further, land of the third quality requires to be cultivated, a rent emerges for that of the second quality, while the rent for land of the first quality is increased; and thus every new and poorer quality which is pressed into use creates a rent for those above it, measured by the difference in quality.

To put it into exact figures. Suppose the value of wheat is 40s. per quarter, and that, with an expenditure of £200, the cultivation of a piece of land

of the 1st quality produce a return of 120 qrs. with a value of £240,
of the 2nd     ,,          ,,        ,,       100  ,,        ,,         ,,    200,
of the 3rd     ,,          ,,        ,,        80  ,,        ,,         ,,    160,

a private owner will confine himself to the cultivation of the two better classes of land, and will calculate to himself from the first class a rent of £40.

In the communistic state the result will be the same, granting the same assumptions. So long as land of the first class is to be had in superfluity, or is " free," no share in the return which it helps to produce will be imputed to it. And why? Because people have still the choice as to which of the many lands of equal quality they will cultivate, and because they are dependent upon no single one of these. Land of the second quality is cultivated only when that of the first is all under cultivation, and when, at the same time, the demand for land produce has risen sufficiently to meet the increased cost. When, by the higher value of the return, however, the increased cost on the second class of land has been thus covered, there remains to the first class a surplus which must be attributed to the land as rent. The land and its better quality are indeed the "cause" of the surplus return. It is impossible to derive the surplus from the cost goods, seeing that similar amounts and qualities of costs have been spent on both classes of land. A very simple negative proof will confirm the propriety of this method of imputation. Suppose a piece of first-class land be left uncultivated, the surplus return will immediately disappear; the cost goods will be incapable of reproducing it elsewhere, because there is no other piece of land of the same quality to take its place. There is no lack of practical opportunity to establish this conclusion. In every question as to the utilising of such lands we have to be fully apprised that they guarantee such and such rent if properly cultivated, and that this rent will have to be given up if they are left entirely uncultivated or used in some other way. If *e.g.* we have to make a road, we shall soon know that it leads through lands of the first quality by its costing extra the whole amount of the rent. But why multiply examples? If we are to calculate at all in production, it must be in this way. Were we to refrain from reckoning the differential rent, it would mean that we disregarded the circumstance that land, as a matter of fact, is of different degrees of fertility; it would mean that we were quite indifferent whether we got much return or little.

In the inventory of the communistic state the lands of better quality will be entered at an amount corresponding to the capitalisation of their rents. The agricultural officials will require to be made responsible for the return of a rent from these better lands corresponding to their quality. In fact, in all those connections it will be impossible for the communistic state to act differently from any large landowner of the present day, who tries to manage his property economically, and to have an effectual control over his servants.

## CHAPTER XV

### RICARDO'S DIFFERENTIAL RENT : THE SECOND PART

THERE is a second part to Ricardo's theory which is frequently overlooked, although it is really the more important. From

the very nature of land every piece of it has powers of
different quality. Just as only the best lands are at first
taken up, so are only the best powers in each piece of land.
Of these powers the poorest class—so long as this class is in
excess of the demand—gives no rent, and the better classes
give a net differential rent.

In this second part of Ricardo's theory also, the natural
principles of imputation are found to be in perfect agreement
with the rules he has laid down for the formation of contract
rent. This may be best shown by an example. Say, as before,
that the quarter of wheat brings 40s. Then a certain piece of
land, according as it is cultivated at a greater or smaller
outlay in capital and labour, will produce the following
returns :—

| | | | | | |
|---|---|---|---|---|---|
| to a first £200 of expenses the return is | 120 qrs., | and the value | £240. |
| to a second £200 | ,, | ,, | 100 ,, | ,, | 200. |
| ∴ to £400 | ,, | ,, | 220 ,, | ,, | 440. |
| to a third £200 | ,, | ,, | 80 ,, | ,, | 160. |
| ∴ to £600 | ,, | ,, | 300 ,, | ,, | 600. |

Under these circumstances a private owner will find it
advantageous to expend only £400. He gains thereby a
return of £40 ; and, instead of sinking the third £200 in his
land and gaining a return of only £160, he will do better to
employ it in some other direction, where it may give its full
possible return of £200. From the £440 return thus
obtained, he reckons £400 as the costs; the remaining £40
he can claim, and the tenant can pay, as rent. Just so must
the communistic state make its calculations according to these
natural principles of valuation. There, too, natural principles
will demand that only £400 be sunk in the land, and that
the surplus of £40 thus earned be imputed to the land as
rent.[1]

---

[1] If £600 were sunk a total of £600 would indeed be received in return, but
none the less would there be a loss of £40 on the third two hundred. If only
£400 were sunk, and the surplus of £40 were imputed not to the land, but to the
capital or to the labour, we should make two mistakes, each contradicting the
other. Firstly, the land, as such, would be declared to yield no return. The
practical conclusion would be that it ought not to be cultivated, and that the
capital and labour should be otherwise employed, in which case the whole £40
would be lost. Secondly, this application of capital and labour would be shown
to be peculiarly profitable—the practical conclusion of which would be that it
would appear permissible to sink even more capital in the land. But this

The differential rent received from preferable powers of the soil may be called the "Intensity Rent," because it emerges and rises according as the land is cultivated intensively. This "intensity rent," according as Ricardo conceives of it, might quite well be a universal rent for all the lands of a country, or of the whole world, supposing them to be all cultivated with sufficient intensity. Ricardo's differential theory in no way requires—as is often said—the existence of no rent land. It is sufficient if there are no rent *powers* in the soil.

It need scarcely be said that "intensity rents" must receive as exact consideration from the economist as the rent of better lands. It is perhaps unnecessary to say anything further on this point.


# CHAPTER XVI

## CRITICISM OF RICARDO'S THEORY

ACCORDING to what is certainly the most usual opinion, the differential rent of better lands, or of better powers of land, is to be explained simply by the fact that there are not sufficient of such to meet the demand; that, in fact, as is frequently said, they "have a monopoly." But it may easily be seen that this is not sufficient for an explanation. We must add two other assumptions.

First, the lands or powers of land last taken into cultivation must be available in superfluous amount. In order *e.g.* that first quality lands may bear a differential rent, not only must these lands be insufficient to meet the demand, but there must be besides them "free" lands of the second quality. The limitation or "monopoly" of first-class lands is the proximate occasion of rent, and rent would emerge in any case, even if there should be no other qualities of land. Then the interposition of second-class lands, which are more than enough to

ought not to be done, as £400 is the highest expenditure economically permissible. The land rent of £40 is, therefore, the rational expression of the most advantageous disposition of production.

meet the demand, and are consequently rentless, has the effect of keeping down the rent of first-class lands—which might otherwise rise indefinitely—to the amount of difference existing between the qualities of the two.  If second-class lands were not " free," they also would bear rent; and this rent, again, could only be kept down to the differential rent through the intervention of a third class.  In short, if there is to be a net differential rent, there must be a last, rentless, and therefore " free " category of lands (or powers of land) alongside the better and limited ones.  There must be both limitation and superfluity of land.

Second, there must also be "monopoly" of capital and labour.  Why does any one prefer the better classes of land?  Because on them capital and labour prove more productive.  But why should it be of consequence that capital and labour prove more productive?  Because, as a general rule, we do not have enough of either.  If it were quite a matter of indifference what return was obtained from definite amounts of capital and labour, because it was always possible to make up any deficiency by employing other quantities of the same, it would also be a matter of indifference from which class of land they got their return—assuming, of course, that there was never any scarcity of at any rate the poorest quality of land.  And if, in face of such superfluity of the poorest class of land, the better and best classes are marked out and preferred, it is because man has to economise his labour and capital.  The differential rent measures exactly the advantage which the better and best classes of land secure in the accomplishment of that task.

Thus we see that, wherever a net differential rent exists, land is partially limited (in the better and best classes), partially over-abundant (in the poorer classes), while capital and labour are always limited.[1]  To have overlooked this circum-

---

[1] Among the trees of a primeval forest which have, as a rule, no value, because they are available in superfluity, there are nevertheless some which may receive value ; all those, namely, which have peculiar advantages as regards felling and carrying to market—say, *e.g.*, that they stand in the near neighbourhood of a natural watercourse.  Their value is exactly represented by the saving in costs—saving of labour and transit—which they assure as compared with the trees less favourably situated, to which no value is attached.  Here is a capital which bears a perfect analogy to Ricardo's differential rent from lands of prefer-

stance is the first defect in Ricardo's theory. He states positively that the amount of labour (and under this he includes capital), which may be expended in production can be had, as a rule, for the asking—may be increased at will; while the rent-bearing classes of land are to be had only in limited amounts. This defect is connected with another and still greater one—and one that applies not to Ricardo alone; he has no general theory of economy, of value, and of imputation. All his ingenuity is expended upon details, such, for example, as the explanation of land rent, and this in itself shows that these details can only have been looked at and conceived of in a one-sided fashion.

A further defect of the differential theory is that it does not suffice for all cases. It sometimes happens that even the last cultivated lands, or powers of land, return a rent, and for this Ricardo has no explanation, or, to speak more exactly, no law. Whenever the demand for land products has increased to such an extent that the class of land last taken into cultivation is not sufficient to meet it, while, at the same time, the value of the land products has not risen sufficiently to permit of a new and still lower class being put under the plough, the last cultivated land returns a rent, although it becomes differential only when the next class of land has actually been put under cultivation. And when all the classes of land have been exhausted, and cultivation in general cannot be further extended, there emerges a universal land rent,—universal not only for all lands (for in this sense the " intensity rent " might be a universal one), but even for all powers of land. This case—of the impossibility of extending cultivation—occurs more frequently than one would think. It is not, as would seem at first sight, a thing to be expected at the very end of the historical development of economic life, when the whole earth is over-populated. It belongs rather to the normal

---

able quality. Even to the pure "intensity" rent there are analogies in capital. The sheep on the plains of South America do not receive value in their entire useful content—I mean a value corresponding to the entire usefulness of similar sheep in Europe, or any other district of great demand—but only in that portion of the same—say, perhaps, the hides—which repays the costs of transport to the sphere of the greater demand. The remaining part is meantime valueless, but may also receive value through an increase in demand. It is easy to infer from these examples the conditions for a purely differential rent.

phenomena which occur in the course of this development. Indeed it is just as regards the past that it can be established with perfect certainty; while prophecies of what is to come must always be uncertain, and can never be made with scientific exactitude. A slight consideration will suffice to make this clear.[1]

Land and capital, so far as regards the conditions under which they are acquired, appear to stand in complete opposition to each other. All capital, with trifling exceptions, has been worked for by human hands, and the sum of capital is always increasing and is capable of indefinite increase. All land, on the other hand (with exceptions which are quite insignificant as compared with the whole) has been in existence from the beginning, and it is practically impossible for human power to extend its compass—so at least a geographer or physicist would have to say. But can we say so economically? Certainly not. Economically speaking, man has not from the first had command over the whole solid surface of the earth and its treasures. Starting with a very insignificant portion of it, the sphere of his control has extended at a rate which scarcely comes behind the increase of his capital. The limits of his power are not yet reached, and he would be a bold man who would say when they must be reached, and where their limits lie. Looked at economically, there is always available to him only so much superficies and so much fruitful soil as he has the means and the knowledge to utilise. The development of agricultural skill and technique generally, the employment of manures, growth of population, emigration, scientific discovery, the spread of commerce, the perfecting of the means of transport, increase of wealth in capital and labour—all these have gradually increased landed property to an enormous extent. To the hunter belongs only the surface of the ground : to the peasant who forces his plough down into it belongs also its interior, and the deeper the plough goes, so much more of the land comes into the service of man. In our own time, indeed, the amount of land in far-away countries which is at the disposal of European consumption, has increased in a degree that is alarming to European agriculturists. If we look back on the past, we might almost believe that it has been quite the same with land as with capital ;—that at first the provision of it was very scanty, and that later it has gone on richly and steadily increasing. Certainly the error which this opinion betrays would be no greater than that betrayed by the commonly held opinion that land is quite incapable of being increased. In any case, there can be no doubt of one thing. It is *conceivable* that a time may arrive when all land available for economic purposes has been taken up, and that, notwithstanding, at some later period, so much new land, economically speaking, may come into the world's possession, that a much greater population may be maintained upon it, without even touching the limits of subsistence. And has this conceivable case never been an actual fact? Have we not accounts, handed down to us from primeval times, of over-population and emigration caused by urgent want? Has not the spectre of hunger haunted every land and every people on the face of the earth, and is it not the case that only the most highly cultured of nations, at the height of their development, have been able to escape from its terror?

Still, however that may be,—even supposing it has never actually happened that the limits of cultivation have been reached,—a theory which cannot bring the case of a " universal " land rent under a law remains an inadequate theory. If we have no law for the assumed case that all lands and powers of land bear rent, we have no law for the undeniable fact that all economically employed labour and capital yield a return ; we can say absolutely nothing more than that the better qualities of goods have *more* imputed to them by the amount of their surplus return. We are incapable of learning what shares are to be imputed to the common qualities, which constitute the majority of production goods. The law of a universal land rent, and the universal law of imputation, are identical, and a theory which has no formula for the former confesses its utter inability to solve the problem of the valuation of production goods generally.[1]

---

[1] A further fundamental defect in Ricardo's theory may be pointed out ;— that he has omitted to notice the reaction of land rent upon the return to capital and labour. Rent is certainly dependent upon the current valuations of cost, but, on the other hand, the valuations of ·cost are dependent upon rent, if not in the same degree. The return reckoned to capital and labour is essentially influenced by the amount of capital and labour which is required for working the land, and by the returns which they yield in so doing.

Finally, Ricardo might also be accused of having overlooked the universal importance of the differential valuation (compare Book III. chap. xiii.). Even purely differential valuations may be met with elsewhere than in the case of land, as we saw by the examples just given of wood in a primeval forest and of the herds of cattle in South America. But of course it is in the case of land that we oftenest find the relation which leads to a net differential valuation of the preferable qualities : viz. quantitative superfluity as a whole beside quantitative limitation as regards the best and better qualities. Compare with this Menger, p. 143.

# PART III

## THE NATURAL RETURN TO CAPITAL

### CHAPTER XVII

#### THE PRODUCTIVITY OF CAPITAL

LAND being permanent and indestructible, it is not a matter of surprise that it should continue yielding, year after year, that return which it yields in one year. And if we designate a continually-recurring return as " rent," the rent of land requires no special explanation. It is much the same with the fact that human labour is source of a permanent return. In the case of a healthy person, labour power is renewed constantly after pauses for rest and refreshment.

On the other hand, it is a matter for wonder to find that the perishable powers of the soil, and all the movable means of production, raw materials, auxiliary materials, implements, tools, machinery, buildings, and other productive apparatus and plant, which are consumed, quickly or slowly, in the service of production, are sources of permanent returns,—returns which are constantly renewed, although the first factors of their production may have been long before used up. This brings us face to face with one of the most important and difficult problems of economic theory; with the question, namely, how we are to explain the fact that capital yields a net return.[1]

[1] In what follows I understand by the term capital the perishable or (with the extended meaning explained in the text) the movable means of production. This conception is adapted to the conditions of a communistic state, in which the national income is obtained solely through production. To take note of those

All capital yields, proximately and directly, only a gross return; that is to say, a return purchased by a diminution of the parent capital.   The condition under which this gross return may be the source of a net return is very easily formulated.   In the gross return must be found newly produced all the consumed capital, and beyond this there must be a certain surplus.   This surplus will be net return;—a return which may, permanently and without diminution of the parent capital, be obtained and consumed.

If now we ask whether this condition is actually fulfilled, we find, in the first place, that the nature of capital does per-

forms of capital which serve in the formation of income outside of production, seemed to me out of place, these being too closely connected with the specific conditions of the existing economic order of things.   For the same reason I also refrain from taking into consideration those constituent parts of an undertaker's capital which do not belong to the technical means of production.   I have, however, appended, in Book IV. chap. viii., a discussion of the interest on consumption loans and house rent, and, at the end of Book V. chap. xi., I have looked at the interest which comes from the undertaker's wage fund.

To avoid misunderstanding, I wish once more to emphasise the fact that, among the technical means of production, I do not include the means of subsistence which must be held ready at hand for the labourers.   These are conditions of production, but not its causes.   The cause is here the labourer alone.   And this is no contradiction to our previous statement in Book III. chap. iii.   The things on which the labourer employs his strength, and the things which maintain his strength, stand in totally different relations to the productive return.   The former have a direct influence upon return; the latter influence it only through the medium of the labour power into which they must first transform themselves.   If we wish to make the latter factors of production, it can only be done by regarding the labourer as their first product (compare Book V. chap. vii., on the "costs of production" of labour).   So far as regards his conception of the means of subsistence for labourers I am thoroughly at one with Sax (in particular p. 324), although I explain otherwise the emergence of interest from this part of an undertaker's capital.

Immediately before these pages went to press, Menger's treatise *Zur Theorie des Capitals* appeared in Conrad's *Jahrbücher*.   In this treatise he defends in animated fashion the popular as against the scientific conceptions of capital, and interprets the popular conception as embracing all the parent wealth of an acquisitive economy existing in or calculated in money, without respect to the technical nature of the instruments of acquisition.   As a matter of fact, the circumstance that acquisitive instruments are calculated in money is of decisive importance for their valuation.   To calculate in money means—leaving the form out of consideration—first, to calculate exactly, and second, to calculate with reference to exchange and the unit of all exchange goods which it creates.   We also look at valuation entirely under these two assumptions, although we substitute the internal exchange of goods in a state economy for the exchange of private individuals.   The natural laws we have deduced hold only as regards industries on a large scale and under a highly developed economy.

mit of it.    If capital is, on the one side, perishable, on the
other, it is reproducible.    It serves for production and it is
produced.    Is it, however, produced in sufficient quantity, and
produced from capital itself in sufficient quantity, to fully replace what has been consumed, and leave a surplus beyond ?
Before trying to answer this question I should like to make
one observation of a formal nature.

Capitals which yield gross return may undoubtedly be desig-
nated " productive goods " on this account alone.    They certainly
produce ;  they transform themselves from an unfinished form
of goods to a finished one, or to one that comes nearer a finished
one.    It is, however, preferable to speak of capital as productive
only when it yields a net return.    And in this sense exclusively
we shall understand the " Productivity of capital."

As Böhm-Bawerk has shown, productivity may be either
physical productivity or value productivity.    It is important
that this distinction should be clearly kept before us.    Physical
productivity exists where the *amount* of goods which form the
gross return is greater than the amount of capital goods
destroyed ;  and in the foregoing deduction of the conceptions
of gross and net return we have assumed this physical productivity.    Value productivity exists where the value of the
gross return is greater than the value of the capital consumed.
The task of our theory is, in the last resort, to prove the value
productivity of capital ;  but for this purpose it is necessary
first to prove the fact of physical productivity, as the scaffold-
ing on which the other rests.    The value productivity already
presupposes the determination of the value of capital, but the
value of capital can only be determined when the question of
how to impute the physical return has been answered, because
the value of capital rests on the share of return imputed to it.
Just as the rent must first be ascertained before the value of
any land can be calculated, and just as, generally speaking, the
rules of imputation must be recognised before the value of production goods can be determined, so must also the imputation
of the return to capital first be settled before we can take up
the problem of its value.    In pursuance of our division of the
subject, we have meanwhile only the problem of the physical
productivity of capital to deal with.

There is no doubt that the total return of all three productive factors, land, capital, and labour, taken together, is large enough to replace the capital consumed, and give a net return. This is a notorious economic fact, and as little in need of proof as the fact that there are such things as goods, or such a thing as production. Of course, now and then, a productive undertaking may be unsuccessful, and fail to cover its outlay; indeed many undertakings furnish no usable product whatever. But these are exceptions. The rule is that net returns are obtained,—indeed, net returns of such enormous magnitude, that not only can the millions of human beings be supported, but capital can go on accumulating out of the surpluses.

There remains, therefore, but one thing to ask—whether a share in this undoubted net return can be imputed to the factor capital. But the question can not be put seriously. Why to capital alone should no such share be imputed? Once understood and granted that capital is one of the economic factors of production, to which, with the others, the productive return is ascribed (Book III. chap. iii.), it is also understood and granted that to it belongs by right a share in the net return in which the productive return first embodies itself. Are we to suppose that capital is always in a position to produce only somewhat less than replace itself? This would obviously be an arbitrary supposition. Are we, then, to suppose it capable only of replacing its own loss, however various the success of production may be? This supposition would clearly be no less arbitrary. Whoever denies net return to capital can only do so by denying it any return.

I should fear to repeat myself were I to bring forward any formal proof of the fact that capital does have a share in the productive net return. I shall content myself with mentioning one or two cases which show, in eminently clear fashion, the necessity for attributing net return to it.[1]

---

[1] Among such cases I should include also those where the use of capital increases the previous productiveness of production. Here we see with particular clearness that the additional net return must be credited to the capital. It would, however, be an error to believe that capital can receive a share of net return only when its use has directly increased the previous productiveness of production, or that it would be deprived of this share as soon as the world became accustomed to the increased effects. Experience shows us the productivity of capital even in a stationary economy. On this account all theories are inadequate which derive the productivity of capital solely from its capacity to promote the development of economic life.

Wherever labour is crowded out by capital, as, *e.g.*, where a machine takes over the work hitherto accomplished by human labour—a thing which will happen no less frequently in the communistic state than it does now,—the capital, or machine, must be credited with at least the same return as that formerly imputed to labour. But this was a net return : therefore, the capital or machine must also be credited with a net return. Were the machine capable of reproducing only its own substance as that is worn away in course of use, it would be less effective than human labour, and would not have had power to displace it. But why should a machine such as this be favoured in the imputation more than any other form of capital ? What experience would speak for this ?

In accordance with the universal law of differential imputation, every form of concrete capital of better quality has a higher return imputed to it than the concrete capital of lower quality, and this return is measured by the amount of increase in productive results which the employment of the better qualities brings. And as, when we look at production and its results as a whole, it is only net returns that are taken into consideration, it is thereby proved that, in comparing qualities of capital, the standard of imputation must be taken from the net return.

Whoever employs his capital according to the measure in which he sees it influence the productive net return, employs it well; whoever does otherwise, employs it badly. On this point universal opinion is united now, as it will be in the communistic state. The universal opinion to which we refer is not, however, the untrained judgment of the public in matters of theory, but the ripe expression of experience. [1]

---

[1] The theory of interest, like that of rent, has always been discussed very much by itself; discussed, I mean to say, without any previous examination of the general laws of imputation. The result, however, as regards interest, has been immensely less satisfactory than as regards rent. It is easy to understand that in the case of interest we have to deal with *the* essential point in the problem of imputation, while in the case of rent we have to deal substantially with a detail capable of being conceived by itself,—that, namely, of the differential imputation. Böhm-Bawerk's great work *Geschichte und Kritik der Capitalzinstheorien* (Innsbruck, 1884), translated as *Capital and Interest* (Macmillan), has clearly shown to the scientific world how unsatisfactory all previous attempts at explanation have been.

Ties of family and of friendship bind me too closely to the author to allow of

# CHAPTER XVIII

## THE CALCULATION OF RETURN TO CAPITAL IN PRIMITIVE AND IN DEVELOPED ECONOMIES

THOSE writers who maintain the productivity of capital prefer to take the most primitive economic circumstances in order to make their meaning clear. Thünen, for instance (in his *Isolirter Staat*, 2nd edition, Book II., division I., p. 74) takes his readers to a land in which there is no capital to begin with. In its tropical climate the inhabitants live, in the most literal sense, by the labour of their hands. There a labourer is in a position to produce yearly the total amount required to maintain him for a year—we shall put this down at 100—and, besides that, 10 % more, or 110 units in all. At that he can live and also lay past. And now some man, supporting himself meantime upon his savings from former years, succeeds, after a whole year's labour, in producing a bow, arrows, and a net. He is rewarded for this by being enabled, with the assistance of the new tools, to obtain henceforward a yearly return of 150 units, by means of which he finds time to repair the damage suffered by his little capital through wear and tear, and to maintain it always in the same condition. The total increase to his income per year amounts to 40 units, and this increase is a permanent one in spite of the perishable nature of the capital, because not only is the capital perishable, but it can also be, and is continually being, reproduced. To

any praise of his work from my lips being counted of value by outsiders. I therefore confine myself to remarking that everything contained in the following pages on the subject of the return to capital and the value of capital, was written under the influence of his penetrating criticism, and that, if there is aught of value to be found in it, it could never have originated without that influence. It is not inconsistent with this that I should, nevertheless, arrive at other conclusions than those towards which Böhm-Bawerk—so far at least as may be recognised from the critical and preparatory work already published—appears to point.

*Note.*—Since writing the above, Böhm-Bawerk has published the second part of his work, *Die Positive Theorie des Capitals* (Innsbruck, 1888), translated by me as *The Positive Theory of Capital* (Macmillan, 1891).—*W. S.*

what factor is this increase to be imputed ?   Obviously to the
capital.   To its credit alone can the increase be attributed.
This will be seen, *e.g.*, in the fact that every other labourer
will be inclined to hire the capital at a price which is based
on the calculation and ascription to it of this surplus result.

Similar statements are given by other writers.   They are,
indeed, well adapted to clear up our ideas concerning the
productivity of capital in its most general outlines, and to
persuade the reader to its acceptance.   On the other hand,
they are misleading almost in every detail as regards our
developed conditions of production, and, in particular, they
give a thoroughly false impression as to the measure of
productivity.

In such primitive conditions as those pictured by Thünen,
where capital emerges for the very first time, the return to
capital is calculated at the entire increase of income, which
labour assisted by capital obtains as against labour unassisted.
In other words, the whole "share dependent upon its co-operation" (see p. 91) is imputed to capital as its "contribution."   And
rightly so.   In these most primitive conditions there is a considerable supply of labour power ; indeed, as compared with the
scant occasions for using it, almost too much ; on the other hand,
capital is scarce and greatly in demand.   Much labour must
be expended without aid from capital, and the comparison
between labour assisted by capital and labour unassisted,
forces itself naturally upon every one.   This is no fact found
out by subtle economic investigation ; it is seen practically in
men having constantly to choose between the two kinds of
labour.

But this is very different from the conditions under which
we now live.   Practically such a choice is never placed before
any one.   It would never occur to any one but a theorising
economist, to measure the value of capital by estimating what
would be the amount of loss if capital should not co-operate
at all in the production,—any more than it would occur to any
one to measure the value of labour by estimating the amount
of loss that would ensue should labour refuse its co-operation.
All labour is judged on the quite intelligible assumption that
it is brought into co-operation with capital ; all capital under
the assumption that it is brought into co-operation with

labour.    Production has become ever so much more complicated, and with it the art of calculating production.    The
simple formulæ of former times are not now adequate, and
examples based on them can only be misleading.

How, then, are capital and labour under present conditions
to be distinguished ?    The answer is not doubtful.    According
to that complicated formula, and according to all those rules
which obtain, as regards the imputation of return in general.

The " contribution " of capital is to-day far from amounting to the whole " share dependent upon its co-operation."
While that share is very much equal to the total return of
production, the " contribution " is merely one single quota
alongside of the quotas of land and labour.

Only in one connection has the illustration of Thünen anything to teach us about the measure of the return to capital.
It proves clearly that, in any case, there is a net return to be
imputed to capital—in so far as it is properly employed ; a
return which can be permanently obtained in spite of the
perishable nature of the various items forming the capital, and
in spite of their continual transformation in consumption and
reproduction.    Capital, rightly employed, does more than
simply renew itself ; it yields beyond this a surplus which
must be imputed to it.    This proposition is proved beyond a
doubt, as regards primitive economic conditions, by Thünen
and others ; and in these primitive conditions the progress of
economy generally is shown through the discovery and development of forms of capital.    But will any one assert that what
was the due of primitive capital is not also the due of the
developed modern capital ?


# CHAPTER XIX

### THE IMPUTATION OF GROSS RETURN AND OF NET RETURN

WE have said that capital, rightly employed, shows itself
productive, inasmuch as it reproduces itself with a surplus.
This proposition, although undoubtedly correct as a conclusion,
requires one essential modification.

Do the arrows, bows, and nets—the capital of Thünen's illustration—really reproduce themselves in the strictest sense of the term ? Certainly not. They produce nothing but fish and the spoils of the chase ; in this they exhaust their direct and proximate activity. They do not in the least degree themselves bring forth new arrows, bows, and nets, nor do they give direct assistance in doing so. The return which, in the first place, falls to be imputed to them is, consequently, a gross return in *foreign* things ; things, that is, from among which they cannot replace themselves ; things with which they may possibly be compared in value but not in quantity, and by means of which a physical net return cannot therefore be represented. But we cannot stop short in our consideration at this point : as a matter of fact the indirect efficiency of capital goes much further. The bows, arrows, and nets once obtained lighten the conditions of their reproduction, if they do not actually co-operate in it. They lighten it by means of the extraordinary increase in the gross return of fish and game, as consequence of which immensely more labour than formerly is free to be employed in the creation of capital. Therefore, in the total result, a net return does come in the end to be imputed to these concrete forms of capital, just as if they did directly reproduce themselves with a surplus.

The same argument holds for capital in the developed economy, only that here the conditions are much more complicated and the process, consequently, more difficult to follow. No capital, even in the most highly developed economy, directly reproduces itself ; each produces first a gross return in foreign things, in which, physically, its productivity cannot be seen. The capital of a baker produces bread, that of a miller, meal, that of a peasant, grain. In order that the baker may replace his capital again, he must turn to the miller, and to all the other persons who can provide him with the necessary materials and apparatus for his production. The gross return of every capital must be exchanged against the gross returns of other capitals,—indeed, against those returns which are attributed to land and labour,—in order that the capital may be replaced, and the net return become physically cognisable. The only imputation that ever takes place directly is an imputation of gross return, but from that follows, as a final consequence, an imputation of net return, however circuitous the route may be,—so long, I mean, as the efficiency of capital is considered undiminished, and so long as it is suitably employed. It is just as though every capital did directly reproduce itself with a surplus.

In most cases the return to all the capital invested in one business or one undertaking is grouped in one estimate. It requires no proof, however, that, from the total return, each separate bit of capital (assuming suitable employment) will have its share. Every bit of capital, rightly employed, produces directly a gross return of goods different from itself, and finally, after the necessary exchange between similar gross returns, reproduces itself and yields a net return. In this sense machines, tools, raw materials, auxiliary materials, in short, all forms of concrete capital, the smallest and the most perishable, even those from which, materially speaking, nothing passes over into the product, replace themselves and yield a surplus. From this point of view every piece of coal which is burned for purposes of production creates, in the last resort, another similar piece of coal, and, beyond that, a perishable net return. And, inasmuch as the replaced portions of capital are employed again and yet again, each piece of capital — the smallest and most perishable — becomes the source of a permanent rent.[1]

---

[1] In the exchanges necessary to procure the goods which are to replace the capital, in lieu of the directly obtained goods which form the gross return, goods are, of course, estimated according to their value. Capital goods, are, therefore, estimated at their capital value. To this extent it appears that the knowledge of the value of capital and of the laws which regulate it, must precede the imputation of net return. Only in such a simple instance as that given by Thünen can an imputation of net return be made without a previous knowledge of the value of capital, and this destroys our proof that the imputation of net return is *fundamentally* independent of the valuation of capital. It is, of course, practically impossible to employ this fundamental principle so soon as production becomes complicated. But whenever production becomes complicated every new calculation must practically be laid on the lines of the old ones ; otherwise no conclusion could be come to. Every new determination of value practically presupposes old ones (compare Book III. chap. v. at end). As little, then, as the conclusion can be drawn from this, that theory requires value in order to explain value, so little can it be concluded that, theoretically, the value of capital conditions the imputation of net return.

# BOOK IV

## THE NATURAL VALUE OF LAND, CAPITAL, AND LABOUR

# CHAPTER I

WE have now to retrace our steps. Having made clear the principles according to which the return, jointly obtained, may be imputed to the separate productive factors, we have now to return to the question as to the value of these factors. The general law we are already acquainted with: the value of the product determines the value of the production good. The point which we must now take up is the application of this proposition to the special circumstances of land, capital, and labour.

In this by far the greatest difficulties meet us in the case of capital. It seems as if our explanation of its value came into direct collision with the facts of experience. Assume that a capital, employed for one year and thereby completely used up, yields, at the end of the year, a return of the value of 105 ; experience tells us that the value of the capital will not be estimated at 105, but at a somewhat less amount according to the current rate of interest. At a 5 % rate, *e.g.*, the capital will be estimated at 100. The remainder of the return will be regarded as net return of interest. How does this go with our explanation ? On what ground is this deduction made ? Ought not rather the full value of the gross return to go into the capital value without any deduction whatever ? But if that were so, how should we explain the contradiction of experience which interest presents ? How is the interest to be explained ? Or does natural valuation exclude interest ? Is it, perhaps, merely a phenomenon of present-day exchange and price, which would not re-emerge in the communistic state ?

One of the most conclusive and brilliant among Böhm-Bawerk's critical examinations is that directed towards the attempts to deduce interest from the productivity of capital. Böhm-Bawerk himself in fact arrives at the conclusion that the attempt is hopeless.  To quote his own words : " It was not simply an unfortunate chance that no one found the Open Sesame which had the power to discover the mysterious origination of interest in the productivity of capital.  It was rather that on the road to the truth a wrong turning had been taken.  From the first it was a hopeless endeavour to explain interest wholly and entirely from a productive power of capital.  It would be different if there were a power that could make value grow directly as wheat grows from the field. But there is no such power.  What the productive power can do is only to create a quantity of products, and perhaps at the same time to create a quantity of value, but never to create *surplus* value.  Interest is a surplus, a remainder left when product of capital is the minuend and value of consumed capital is the subtrahend.  The productive power of capital may find its result in increasing the minuend.  But so far as that goes it cannot increase the minuend without at the same time increasing the subtrahend in the same proportion.  For the productive power is undeniably the ground and measure of the value of the capital in which it resides.  If with a particular form of capital one can produce nothing, that form of capital is worth nothing.  If one can produce little with it, it is worth little ; if one can produce much with it, it is worth much, and so on ;—always increasing in value as the value that can be produced by its help increases, *i.e.* as the value of its product increases.  And so, however great the productive power of capital may be, and however greatly it may increase the minuend, yet so far as it does so, the subtrahend is increased in the same proportion, and there is no remainder, no surplus of value " (*Capital and Interest*, translated by William Smart, page 179).

When we turn to land we find also a striking contrast between the apparent demands of our theory and experience. Land yields returns that stretch away into the farthest future. The value of land, then, should surely be not merely twenty or thirty times the annual rent, as experience tells us it is,

but rather an indefinite and incalculable number of times the
annual rent; perhaps it should be estimated as an infinite
amount (see also on this point *Capital and Interest*, page 67).
But the same line of argument may be applied to capital.
Capital also, when well employed, promises to yield its net
return on into the indefinite future, so perhaps its value also
ought to be estimated as an infinite amount.

It will be seen that the difficulties which meet us are not
trifling.   If, nevertheless, I believe that they can be overcome, it is because I trust to the support given by the results
of our investigation into the imputation of return.   None of
the writers who tried to derive interest from the productivity
of capital had this support, and even in Böhm - Bawerk's
critique it is not foreseen.   Have we not in fact found a
productive power, which, although not capable, as Böhm-
Bawerk claims, of creating " more value," can and does create
what amounts to the same thing, " more return "; in other
words, a surplus ?

We shall begin with the most difficult, the theory of the
value of capital.   After what has been said it is clear that
it cannot be taken up without taking up the theory of
interest.

Almost everything in this book will find its complement
in the discussion upon costs which is to follow.


# CHAPTER II

## THE VALUE OF CAPITAL AND THE INTEREST ON CAPITAL

### I.—DISCOUNTING

CAPITAL receives its value from its fruits.   If, then, we are
calculating the final return of any production, and, for that
purpose, deduct from the value of these fruits the capital consumed, with its value, the result will be zero, inasmuch as,
sooner or later, all capital is consumed in production.   The
deduction made must always amount to the value of the fruits,
— indeed, that value measures the deduction — and consequently the value calculation leaves no net return whatever.

Not only is interest not explained ; it is absolutely excluded. And, if we consider that means of production renew themselves again and again indefinitely, and yield results indefinitely, we come across another contradiction of experience, for experience shows that the value of capital is not infinite but always finite and limited.

These are the problems which lie before us for solution when we now go on to examine the value of capital and the interest on capital.

For their solution we may avail ourselves of the results of our analysis of the physical productivity of capital. All capital transforms itself in the last resort into gross return. In this gross return the capital reproduces itself with a physical surplus, the net return. These two facts, which we have already established, will suffice us to deduce the value-productivity of capital, and to solve all the contradictions with experience.

First : all capital transforms itself in the last resort into gross return ; it follows from this that the value of the capital can never exceed the value of the gross return. The value of capital is thus a limited finite amount, although the working of the ever-renewed production extends away into an illimitable future. The materials and apparatus out of which, and with whose help, bread is produced, cannot possibly be worth more than the bread itself. And those things from which the materials and apparatus themselves are produced, and which, consequently, are the producers of bread one stage removed, have, in the prospective gross return —the perishable bread—a maximum limit of value. So with all capitals, however far their primary products may be removed from direct employment in the satisfaction of want. To put it into figures :—if a capital transforms itself sooner or later into a gross return of the value of 105, its own value cannot be put at anything above 105.

Second : in the gross return capital reproduces itself with a physical surplus, the net return. It follows that the capital value cannot be credited with the whole value of the gross return. In the reproduction capital represents only a portion of its own gross return, and can therefore absorb only a portion of the value of that gross return. If, from the value of 105, 5 are set aside as fruits which may be consumed without preventing the full replacement of the capital, only the remainder of 100 can be reckoned as capital value. The prospect of having this residual value of 100 transformed once more, at the close of the next period of production, into the gross return of 105 — by again employing it productively — cannot make any change on this valuation; since the expected return of 105 is always divided in the same way, assuming the same conditions; viz. 100 goes to capital and 5 to the increment on capital.

Gross return and net return are thus the two given amounts from which capital gets its value. The whole difficulty of the problem lies essentially in the recognition of the fact that those two amounts *are* given. For proof of this we refer to our former disquisition upon imputation in general, and the imputation in the case of capital in particular. If physical productivity of capital involves, as we have maintained, the imputation of gross return and the imputation of net return, we have at once a clear and simple principle for the valuation of capital.

There is in common use a definite name for the method of calculating value required by this principle. To fix the present value of a money claim, carrying no interest, which falls due at a future date, we make use, as every one knows, of the method known as " discounting." That is, we deduct the usual interest from the future sum. Now every capital value, —not alone the value of a sum of money but of every perishable productive instrument—is calculated by discounting;[1] that is to say, from the value of the future expected sum of products into which the capital will be transformed, the corresponding net return is deducted. Only that, practically, in discounting money claims, a fixed rate of interest—*i.e.* a definite relation between capital value and net return—is always assumed, and always emerges, while we are explaining the formation of this relation by first discovering the principle for estimating capital value.

Böhm-Bawerk, arguing against Thünen's explanation of interest—which has much in common with that just given— asks with what right it can be assumed that the value of the

[1] Compare Menger, p. 135.

gross return never raises the value of capital to its level, or, inversely, that capital value never depresses that of the gross return to its level ? If a return of 105 can be obtained with an outlay of 100, will there not be competition in production, or levelling of the valuations, until either the outlay come to be valued at 105 or the return at 100, or both settle at some figure half-way between the two ? Böhm-Bawerk is right in raising the question, seeing that he does not start, as we do, with a physical net return to capital. But assuming this physical net return the question is at once answered and settled. So long as the gross return remains large enough to replace the capital and yield a net return, the value of gross return and the value of capital can never be assimilated : there will always be a difference—viz. the value of the net return. This difference could only disappear with the disappearance of physical productivity. So long as it exists, so long does physical-productivity guarantee value-productivity to capital, and so long does capital also create more in value than itself ; —to apply again the words of Böhm-Bawerk, it creates " more value." And if, in order to calculate the amount of capital consumed, the capital value be deducted from the gross return, it is not the whole amount of gross return that is deducted ; the subtrahend is somewhat less than the minuend, and the required residue of interest must be the result.

If this be so, then, in the communistic state also, capital value must be estimated in such wise that it absorbs only a portion of the gross return to capital ; so long at least as capital retains the same efficiency, as an auxiliary of production, which general experience from time immemorial has shown it to do. And for so long, consequently, must it, even in the communistic state, bear interest. Calculation of the net return to capital, and deduction or discount of the same from the gross return, in order to find the value of capital ;—these are natural economic calculations, indispensable in every economy so long as the fundamental conditions of production known to general experience remain in force.

A capital which, in twelve months from the date of possession, yields the same gross return (say 105) and the same net return (say 5), is valued at the date of possession at the same amount (say 100). It is, nevertheless, not a matter of indifference whether the capital comes into our possession now or only at the end of the twelve months, inasmuch as possession now guarantees a return of interest besides. It would, therefore, be incorrect if we were to take the equivalence of valuation put upon capitals in the present and in the future, and argue from that to the full economic equivalence of the present and the future possession. A present sum is always worth more than the same sum at a future date, or, as we may say, the future sum is always worth less, and that in proportion to the futurity of the time when it will come into our possession. If in the course of a year I can make 105 out of 100, the sum of 100 which I shall obtain only at the end of a year, is, to-day, worth only about 95. To reduce future capital values to present value, they must be discounted, just as the values of future gross returns are.

The reader will remember that, in chapter vi. of Book I., we defended the proposition that present and future wants, coming into competition with each other, are, as a rule, to be regarded as equal ; that is to say, the difference in time does not necessitate any difference in valuation. To this proposition we have now to add a second :—that, within the sphere of production, the difference in time *does* necessitate a difference in valuation of the goods employed in production. The two propositions are in perfect accord, and mutually supplement one another. If wants are continuously to find the same satisfaction, equal amounts of return must continuously be produced. And if equal amounts of return are continuously produced, capital must remain continuously the same in substance. But if capital is actually to remain the same in substance, and so is able to yield continuously the same returns, this must find expression in a valuation which ascribes to capital a higher value, the earlier the point of time it comes into our possession. For the earlier the point of time, the earlier, and consequently the greater, the return that may be expected.

The business man who takes note of his own calculations, who tests his recollections and impressions, and asks himself why he calculates interest, and on what principle he graduates the value of his capital, will arrive substantially at the same conclusions as those to which we have just come. The value of goods is derived from their utility ; the value of capital goods from their useful returns; interest represents a net increment to or fruit of capital:—these are the axioms of practical life so much contradicted, even libelled, by theorists. They are axioms which every layman recognises, in his own way, as the motives by which he believes himself guided in his economic operations. A theory which should succeed in vindicating these axioms of ripened experience, which should give a distinct form to the vague impression, and a good and necessary content to opinions not quite conscious of their own *raison d'être*, could have no better testimony to its correctness.


# CHAPTER III

### THE VALUE OF CAPITAL AND THE INTEREST ON CAPITAL
### (*continued*). II.—THE RATE OF INTEREST

INTEREST is the return to capital when that return, with its value, is considered in relation to capital value. The relation existing between capital value and interest, when considered in the individual case, may be described as the percentage of increment; it becomes the "rate of interest" only when it obtains in a large number of connected cases. The rate of interest is the general percentage of increment to all the capital in the market.

The fact that, in one and the same sphere of production, there emerges a general percentage of increment, or at least a constant tendency toward it, arises from the many-sided connections between various kinds of production. In consequence of the comparatively great freedom of choice in the destination of most capital, land, and labour, it is almost always possible to extend any single production at the cost of some other, or to limit it in favour of some other. Of this possibility people will avail themselves whenever, and according as, any one production shows a particularly favourable or particularly unfavourable percentage of increment. In seeking for the most favourable percentage of increment, and in striving towards the equalising of all differences, a general percentage

of increment will be created, or at all events will be aimed
at, so far as there is competition between the various
productions.

The organisations which at present contribute most to the
equalisation of the interest rate are the money markets, where
the principal amounts of capital in the shape of money are
lent.  In the money markets it is, of course, in the first
instance only interest on loans that is determined, but the state
of the loan market in the last instance affects also the return
to production, inasmuch as it influences the extending of
industries carried on with borrowed capital.  Not only loan
capital, however, but also that capital which is the personal
property of undertakers, moves perpetually in the direction of
the highest percentage of increment.  Under a communistic
regime all capital would belong to the one single undertaker,
the state ; capital would no longer be lent for production ; and
the interest on loans would cease to influence the percentage
of increment in production.  But this would simply leave
capital still more free to shift from one production to another ;
it would no longer be hindered by those barriers which the
circumstances of private ownership at present oppose.

Every one knows that the rate of interest, in spite of the
tendencies to equalise it, is never really the same all over.
This is chiefly caused by the fact that the unity or organisation of production is by no means perfect.  There is no such
thing as a united money market, and much less is there anything like a united way of conducting productive business.
The individualism of the present economic order distributes
production among individual undertakings.  These, of course,
under the influence of competition and the desire for gain, are
built into one coherent structure, which to some extent
realises the economic order that an ideal plan of production
would present.  Yet at how many points do we find great
gaps ; how many dislocations through excessive accumulation
of means of production at the wrong places ; how often things
go too quickly, how often not fast enough !  And mistakes like
these are all the greater the more distant the groups compared
are from one another.  The separate branches of agricultural
production may be, relatively speaking, more in harmony
with each other, than, for example, agriculture as a whole

with manufacture as a whole. The transferences from agriculture to manufacturing, and *vice versâ*, take place too seldom to allow of the proper balance between them being maintained.

This results, as we have said, in differences of percentage of increment among the individual productive groups. It is scarcely necessary to emphasise the fact that every difference in rate of interest, arising from this cause, is a misfortune. Every such difference implies a violation of the very first principle of employing goods; that they shall first be used in the most favourable employments, and that the less favourable shall be allowed only in so far as there is not enough of the more favourable. In one group people are content with a less percentage of increment, while in others they may be obtaining higher percentages. The hurtful consequences of this are by no means confined to the use of capital; they go further, and misdirect the production of capital. Capitals which yield a trifling interest are produced far more largely, and capitals which might yield a high interest, to a much less extent than they ought to be.

On the other hand, uniformity in the percentages of increment, and a uniform rate of interest, are, where they exist, proofs, economically speaking, of a well-balanced distribution and disposal of capital. They are proofs that the economically indicated limits of the employment of capital are everywhere equally respected; that nowhere is there any falling short, and nowhere any overstepping of them. In the principle which demands that the employment of capital shall be guided by the rate of interest, and that all employments which fail to return the customary interest be left alone, we find the marginal law brought into one common expression as regards all the different forms of capital. The net return is a definite quota of the gross return, and where the quota of net return is controlled, the direction of capital generally is controlled.

In the communistic state, when production is directed from one point and to one end, the differences in percentage of increment, so far as these are occasioned by the inorganic nature of our system of production, would disappear. Of course, even there, certain differences would still remain; all

those, namely, which could not be further equalised by transferences from one production to another. In the nature of
things, by reason of the variety in the properties of things, no
production can be increased at the cost of others beyond a
certain point, and, on similar grounds, no production can be
limited in favour of others below a certain point. Agricultural
capital could never be completely transferred to trade, nor
trade capital all transferred to agriculture. But what does
observation here show? It shows that those very differences,
which it seems quite impossible to remove, are always removed,
and that through an instrumentality which is permissible even
where transferences of capital are not permissible; by means,
that is to say, of calculation.

How this happens and what it means, we shall now try to
show.

# CHAPTER IV

THE VALUE OF CAPITAL AND THE INTEREST ON CAPITAL (*continued*). III.—THE LAW OF THE UNIFORM CALCULATION
OF THE INTEREST RATE

A CAPITAL which, in a one year's production period, transforms
itself into a gross return of £105, will be valued at £100 if
the general rate of interest be 5 % : the residue £5 is net
return. If the gross return should rise suddenly and greatly,
say, *e.g.*, to £126,—the general rate of interest remaining
unaltered—it appears at first sight that the rise must affect
the net return, and cause it to be calculated at £26 instead of
at £5 as formerly. But, as a matter of fact, is the return so
calculated? It is in one particular case; that, namely, where
the rise is regarded as a solitary instance. But if it is
regarded as permanent the calculation will be different. The
owner certainly reckons the entire increase of £26 as gain,
but he distributes it by putting £20 to capital and £6 to
net return. From this time onward he will reckon his
capital, and consequently his consumption of capital, at £120,

and his net return at £6 ; so that he does not assume an
increment of 26 %, but only of 5 %, corresponding to the
general rate of interest.[1]

In the same way, should the gross return of a capital sink
permanently, while the rate of interest remains unaltered, a
portion of the loss will be written off the capital value, in
such a manner that the relation between capital value and
net return shall again correspond to the general rate of
interest.

In this way it comes about that, where transferences from
production to production are no longer permissible, the individual percentages of increment on individual capitals are, by
calculation, regulated according to the general rate of interest.

The rate of interest which obtains in the particular productive group, or in the particular market to which the capital
in question belongs, is the rate that decides.

The meaning of this act of calculation is easy to understand.   A capital yielding 26 % interest and one yielding
5 %, are not equivalent to one another, although both may
be expressed in the same figures.   Only equal capitals bearing
equal interest are equivalent.   Capitals, then, can be calculated
off-hand—*i.e.* without consideration to the interest they bear
—only where the rate of interest is the same.   That is the reason
why, when the rate of interest cannot be *made* equal, it is at
least calculated as such, by means of shifting the differences
to the capital value, and giving them expression there.

A 3 % capital and a 6 % capital of £100 are not equivalent to one another ; they are put into terms fit for comparison

---

[1] In the above example I assume (1) circulating capital, and (2) circulating
capital whose value is not depressed to a lower level by cheaper costs of production ;—say, a scarce raw material.   Suppose there is an increased demand
for articles made from amber, while amber cannot be obtained in greater
quantities ; it will rise in value.   Those undertakings which work with amber
certainly obtain thereby a rise in their gross returns ; but there is, on the other
hand, a similar rise in the amount deducted for consumption of capital, and
this must be taken into consideration in their estimate of gain.   In the long run
there remains a higher net return, but it is only relatively to the increased
outlay of capital.

A much more complicated calculation has to be made as regards fixed capital,
as also as regards capital whose value is influenced by the costs of production.
I must leave the reader to think out for himself—in the light of the principles
now to be discussed—the corresponding modifications in the valuation of fixed
capital and in the influence of costs.

by calculating the 3 % capital at 6 %, and so reducing the capital to £50, or by calculating the 6 % capital at 3 % and raising capital value to £200.

As a means of simplifying calculation, it might be exceedingly desirable that the rate of interest should be the same in all markets, and in all productive groups. The rate, however, is not the same, and the fact must be reckoned with. If the rate of interest on bonds amount to 4 % and the bank rate to 3 %, it is a consequence of the fact that the two loan markets are separated from one another, and that demand and supply in the one do not approximate to demand and supply in the other, or, at all events, approximate only in trifling degree. This want of touch, however, which renders impossible the equalisation of rates of interest, also renders it less necessary ; it is only when capital is transferred from one market to the other that the difference in rates of interest has any practical importance for the valuation of capital. It is different where one and the same market is concerned. Here capitals are continually valued against each other, and here, therefore, differences in percentage of increment could not be put up with. They are overcome either by regulation of production, or, where that is not practicable, by calculation. In the communistic state, where all capitals would be under a uniform administration, it would be an obvious expedient of calculation to regulate all individual percentages of increment according to the prevailing rate of interest.

We now proceed to further applications of the fundamental proposition that the rate of interest, when possible, should be uniformly calculated.

## CHAPTER V

THE VALUE OF CAPITAL AND THE INTEREST ON CAPITAL (*continued*). IV.—CHANGE IN THE RATE OF INTEREST

IT has just been shown that, when the value of the service of any individual form of capital—*e.g.* a raw material, or a machine—rises or falls, the fact expresses itself in a corresponding elevation or depreciation in its capital value. The net return imputed is, of course, altered at the same time, but only in so far as will bring it again into that relation with the capital value which corresponds with the ordinary rate of interest.

In order that the *general* percentage of increment—the rate of interest—may fall or rise, there must be changes of an extensive kind in the return to the great mass of capitals—brought about through changes in supply, in demand, in technique, in a word, in any of the factors of imputation. A general rise in the gross return to capital, brought about by a great and universally effective invention, would cause a general rise in the net return to capital, and its relation to capital value,—that is to say, in the rate of interest. The capital value might in this instance remain entirely unaltered. Only those capitals which had no part in the effects of the invention, and were in this respect individually separated from the general mass of capital, must necessarily be affected. Where the amount of their services had remained unaltered in the midst of the general increase, in estimating the value of those capitals a greater discount from that amount would require to be made, corresponding to the increased rate of interest. Suppose the rate of interest to rise suddenly from 3 % to 6 %, the value of all capital whose interest remains unaltered at 3 % must be appraised at a correspondingly lower rate.

We have discussed the effect which the individual factors of imputation produce upon the contributions of capital, in sufficient detail to make the derivation of the rules which govern the change in the rate of interest a matter of no difficulty.

One single remark may be added. It is quite a hackneyed proposition that the increase of capital causes a decline in the rate of interest. This proposition is true only with a certain limitation ; it holds only when, by increase of capital, is understood increase in *amount*, without a simultaneous increase in the variety of the forms of capital. Increased variety in capital is synonymous with an advance in technique ; it is one of those facts of economic history to which special attention must be drawn, when it is desired to show clearly the difference between primitive and developed production. Thus to it is due what we know to be the effect of every technical advance ; namely, a rise in the value of the services of capital, as regards individual businesses, and, when comprehensive enough, a rise in the rate of interest. Not until the qualitative advance has been quantitatively used up, and the stocks of the new varieties of capital been multiplied, without other new varieties coming to the front—that is, not until production expands and fills out the newly-set limits,—can the increase of wealth have power, first, to depress the value of the services of capital individually, and, in the long run,— should its compass be sufficiently extensive,—to cause a fall in the rate of interest.

If we look back over the changes in the rate of interest on production over the whole course of economic history, we shall notice an unceasing upward and downward movement, according as advances in production are made, or as the marginal values of the newly - acquired wealth are again depressed by the increment of capital which follows. But through these unceasing fluctuations run great fundamental tendencies, which are, of course, subject to disturbance from opposing tendencies of the rate of interest on consumption loans. Economic history begins at a period when there is almost no capital,—the zero of property in capital as well as the zero of return from capital. From that time onwards property and return, measured absolutely, go on growing so long as the economic world thrives, and has not yet reached the down grade of the movement of value. And the relation between these two—*i.e.* the rate of interest—rises similarly from the beginning, and only begins to fall when the down grade in the movement of value begins to come in sight.

# CHAPTER VI

## THE VALUE OF CAPITAL AND THE INTEREST ON CAPITAL (*continued*). V.—THE VALUATION OF FIXED CAPITAL

UP to this point we have disregarded the circumstance that many capitals—all those called "fixed capitals"—do not exhaust themselves in yielding one single return, but co-operate in several processes of production, and yield several returns before they are finally used up. We were justified in hitherto neglecting this circumstance, as it is of no importance to the principle of the valuation of capital which we had first to establish. Now, however, that the principle has been established, we must go on to this next question. We shall find that the circumstance alluded to does not essentially alter matters, although it certainly renders them much more complicated.

In the case of fixed capital, instead of one single future return there are several returns, and the present value of these several returns must be determined by discounting. If a machine remains capable of work over ten years, the services of all the ten years which are to be imputed to it must be discounted and added up, at their present value, in order to obtain the capital value of the machine. It need scarcely be said that every later service must be estimated at so much less in present value, as the discount must be relative to the terminal point. Further complications are caused by the fact that repairs, and reconstructions, and extensive replacements, frequently take place in fixed capital during the period in which it is wearing out. The outlay which this occasions must be discounted—taking into account of course the period of time at which this outlay may be anticipated. Still further complications, finally, arise from the uncertainty— which increases as the period of wear and tear lengthens —whether the returns expected will actually be received at all. And this also necessitates peculiar deductions, which will be most simply made where people can insure against the danger.

In the case of such fixed capitals as are consumed exceedingly slowly, and, consequently, yield exceptionally many returns, the process of capitalisation frequently takes the place of discounting. Before speaking of this, however, it will be necessary to touch at least upon another somewhat difficult question.

This is the method of calculating the individual percentages of gross return assignable respectively to interest and to wear and tear. If a machine remains serviceable for five years, and yields every year £1000, this yearly income must be divided out between interest and wear and tear (Amortisation) in accordance with a certain law.   In order to find this law, it is best to represent the individual rates of return as annuities.   The first instalment must yield interest for the first year upon the total capital value, all return beyond that is repayment of capital; the second instalment has to yield interest on the capital value remaining after deduction of this repayment, and the residue, which must now be a larger one, serves toward further repayment; and so on, until finally the entire capital is replaced, and interest obtained upon all the portions of capital according to the period of their employment.   The reason for this kind of calculation lies, in the last resort, in the law of the uniform calculation of the interest rate.[1]

# CHAPTER VII

### THE VALUE OF CAPITAL AND THE INTEREST ON CAPITAL
### (*continued*).   VI.—CAPITALISATION

INTEREST is always an aliquot part of capital value, and capital value is always a multiple of interest.   Where interest is 5 %, for example, the interest is $\frac{1}{20}$ of the capital value, and the capital value is equal to 20 times the interest.   It is this fact which renders it possible to determine the value of capital, not by deducting interest from gross return, but by another method which leads to precisely the same result— namely, by means of a corresponding multiplication of interest,

---

[1] Calculated on the figures given above, and assuming a 5 % rate of interest, the value of the machine, on putting into present value the five expected annual returns of 1000, with interest and compound interest, may be reckoned at 4329·48.   The first return of 1000 pays 216·47, as 5 % interest on the capital, while the residue of 783·53 goes to repayment of capital, thus leaving a remaining capital sum of 3545·95.   From the second return 177·30 falls to interest, and 822·70 to the sinking fund; from the third, in the same manner, to interest 136·16, and, to replacement, 863·84; from the fourth, 92·97 to interest, 907·03 to capital; and, finally, from the fifth, 47·62 to interest, and 952·38 to repayment, whereby the entire capital is replaced.

or, to use the ordinary term, by capitalisation. Whether discounting or capitalisation is preferred will depend upon circumstances. With circulating capital discounting is the usual method, as the gross return in this case forms the nearest and clearest basis. With fixed capital, if the wearing out is comparatively rapid, and the gross returns are few in number, discounting will be the preferable method in this case also; but if a long series of gross returns is to be taken into account, capitalisation will be preferred.

Capitalisation is easiest where the gross return contains no quota for wear and tear, and is therefore entirely net return. This would be the case with a capital which never wore out, which promised rent to all eternity, and a rent, moreover, absolutely secure. To carry through the process of discounting here would be laborious in the highest degree; the rent of each separate year would have to be separately calculated, until that rent was reached whose present value was zero; and not till then could the calculation be finished. How much simpler in such a case to multiply the year's rent in accordance with the rate of interest! The result obtained in this fashion agrees with that given by the former and more laborious method, not merely approximately, but with mathematical exactitude, as any text-book of mathematics will confirm. The mathematical formula for the discounting of an eternal rent is simply the formula of capitalisation.

The calculation is a little more complicated when the gross returns contain quotas for wear and tear, and when repairs and the like must be covered and insurance premiums or premiums against risk retained out of these gross returns. In such cases all necessary deductions must first be made from the gross return before we get the net return which is to be capitalised, and this is very often exceedingly difficult in the individual case. The premiums just mentioned are frequently not deducted, but the amount of risk finds instead its expression simply in the rate of interest. The return, for example, of a business regarded as of doubtful solidity will be capitalised at a higher rate of interest, *i.e.* as a smaller multiple.[1]

---

[1] All the separate principles here deduced for the calculating of capital value and interest are followed in practical life and are practically familiar to us. The

# CHAPTER VIII

### INTEREST ON THE CONSUMPTION LOAN.  HOUSE RENT

THE natural principles hitherto laid down for estimating capital value and interest refer only to production.  It must now be asked whether there is also a natural interest which corresponds to the interest given on a loan for consumption purposes, or interest derived from letting of dwelling-houses and the like.[1]

The motives of a debtor who borrows with the view of spending the loan on himself are different from those of an undertaker who borrows to increase his business capital.  The undertaker hopes to obtain both repayment of capital and interest out of the return on the borrowed sum.  The mere debtor cannot hope for this, but must trust that it will be possible for him to repay his debt of capital and interest out of some other income.  He borrows because he needs goods now, and has not got them, while he expects in the future to have them and not to need them to the same degree—at least he deludes himself with some such hope.  Thus in a certain sense interest on production and interest on consumption have a common source.  Both of them relate to a difference in the valuation of present and of future goods, only that the causes which produce this difference are distinct.  In the case of the

theory of them, too, is often given.  But they are always followed and taught under the assumption that the fact of interest and a fixed rate of interest are given.  Nothing is simpler, under such an assumption, than to capitalise a rent, or to show the method of capitalisation.  But the duty of the theorist is to discover these laws, and, at the same time, to explain why such assumptions may be made.  Whence comes interest ?  whence the rate of interest ?  These are our fundamental questions.  All the single laws which we have laid down are confirmed theoretically only if we have succeeded in explaining also the assumption on which they are based, *i.e.* the existence of interest and the rate of interest.

The analysis of the value of land which follows will once more give the reader occasion to notice how difficult it is with the matter in hand to escape arguing in a circle, and to prevent the entrance of any assumption which is itself in need of explanation.

[1] A further form of interest will be discussed in Book V. chap. ii.

productive outlay of capital it is the productivity of capital which causes the difference between present and future; in the case of the consumption loan, it is accidental and personal circumstances,—accidental accumulation of present wants and expenditure, accidental disturbance of income, and so forth. One who finds himself in a situation of urgent necessity is acting quite rationally when he promises—at some future time when he hopes to be more favourably situated—to pay to the person who assists him by an advance of money out of his present difficulty, not only the amount advanced, but an extra, an interest. A sum of £105 at the end of a year may be worth less to him than £100 is at the present moment; he might even promise £150, £200, or more, and yet not be acting irrationally. But if he is to find a person willing to lend him the money, it is essential that every one should not be in the same circumstances of present need and future affluence as himself. It is essential that there should be people who, at the moment, have means which they can do without. And thus it follows that, in an entirely organic economy, such as would exist in the communistic state, the necessary conditions for consumption interest are wanting, inasmuch as all the citizens together would form only one economic subject, and would participate continually, either in the same condition of want, or in the same improved condition of economic well-being.

The interest obtained from the letting of dwelling-houses, and such like objects of consumption wealth, amounts, on an average, to a sum which allows the owner to enjoy—during the period for which the building lasts—interest upon the capital expended in building, and, besides, to provide what the Germans conveniently call "amortisation" of the same; so that, when the dwelling is worn out, he is in a position to replace it. In short, there is assured him, on the average, a *permanent* net return corresponding in amount to the general rate of interest upon property of this kind. During all the long period of time when contract interest on loans was forbidden by law, and violently combated by all theorists, no one thought of objecting to the interest on consumption-wealth. This was always held equitable; and an owner who made over his property to another in perpetuity was regarded as having a right to claim in return a permanent remuneration. If, however, we look carefully, it will be seen that the theoretical arguments employed against interest on loans apply equally to interest on house property, in so far as it brings in more than enough to repay the costs of building. If money be " unfruitful," so are buildings ; and to this extent it is impossible to see why they should bring to their owners a net income lasting beyond the physical duration of the house. Were the owner to retain the house for his own use he would, by the time it tumbled to ruins, possess nothing more of it than, possibly, the value of the materials ;—is it not rather a hard condition that the person who hires the house must rebuild it for him ?

To justify the usual amount of rent on house property, we must go somewhat further back, viz. to the fact that the objects of use which are let must be produced. But if they are to be produced, there must be the prospect that their value will include the full and permanent maintenance of the undertaker's capital, along with the customary return to capital, whether this value be realised through selling or through letting the property. No houses would be built for letting if the prospects of this kind of undertaking were poorer than those of any other ; the interest of hire or let must, therefore, stand at the usual amount of interest on capital. It is an application of the law of costs (see below, Book V.), according to which the customary interest on capital is reckoned among costs. As in all cases, so in this, does the calculation of costs assure the fullest economic distribution of the employments of goods. The more exactly the net income received from the letting of dwelling-houses corresponds with the rate of interest general over the country, the more exactly will the building of houses, and the satisfaction of the need which this meets, correspond with the general condition of production and of the satisfaction of wants. If people were to be contented, *e.g.*, with an exceptionally low return from houses, it would imply a disproportionately ample satisfaction of the want for dwellings. This would stand out from the general economic plane ; and would necessarily be balanced and compensated by limitations in some other direction.

Even in an entirely organic economy, in which the opposition between owner and tenant was abolished, it would be

as needful as it now is to take care that building of houses
corresponded with the general position of production and of
satisfaction. And to this extent we might draw analogies
between the interest of house rent and a calculation, in terms
of value, of the satisfaction given by houses, which would
result in a control of expenditure quite as complete as that
given by house rent.[1]

## CHAPTER IX

### THE VALUE OF LAND

THE value of land is calculated — according to the same
principles as the value of a permanent rent—by capitalising
the rent of land. This is a proposition which is held nowa-
days as self-evident. It was not always so, however, and,
indeed could not always be so. In order to capitalise, a given
rate of interest is necessary; and that an interest rate may
be given, we need capital. To capitalise rent means to multiply it according to principles which are derived, as the name
itself shows, from the valuation of capital.

Imagine an ideal condition of agriculture where no capital
whatever is employed. The land yields produce of all kinds
and in great quantity. In these circumstances the value of
each product can be estimated exactly; the value of each
harvest can be estimated exactly; rent can be fixed exactly;—
but there is no means by which to determine with certainty
how many rents would be required to give the value of the
land.

---

[1] That is to say :—In the present state the due provision of houses for the
people is guaranteed by the consideration that capitalists, investing their money
in house property, will get the ordinary return of interest on capital generally.
Rent must cover replacement as well as interest. In a communistic state,
where the government provided everything, the building of houses would be
controlled by considerations of wants and satisfactions which placed the demand
for houses very much in the same relative position to other satisfactions as now.
No socialist state, for instance, could provide houses in such quantities that
their value was reduced to the mere expenses of building, without disturbing
the marginal plane, and diminishing the total sum of satisfaction obtainable by
the employment of the national capital.— *W. S.*

Why is there no such means in the case of land as there is in the case of capital ? The answer is simple. Capital reproduces itself in the gross return as a part of that gross return. Thus there is a fixed relation between the two " known" quantities, gross return and net return, and the " unknown" quantity, capital value; and this relation gives the measure for capitalisation. Land has not the same double position as productive factor and as product. It produces without being reproduced ; and thus, to determine the value of land, it becomes necessary to bring to our aid the standard for capitalisation which we find in capital.

From this consideration it follows that, so long as capital was scarce, it was impossible to obtain a fixed valuation of land. Every owner of land might estimate its value differently, inasmuch as he might take, as basis of calculation, either a greater or smaller number of yearly rentals, according to varying external circumstances, and according as his judgment was influenced by recklessness or by forethought. An egoist pure and simple, who calculated only with regard to his own lifetime, and to whom his land was of importance only because it secured him a rent for life, would estimate its value according to the probable duration of his life, and would thereby obtain a kind of fixed valuation; at all events, his land would represent to him a finite sum of value and not an infinite one. But one who thought of his children, and of succeeding generations, and took their interests into consideration in estimating the value of his land, would of necessity regard it as an infinite amount. As inconsiderate egoism may be counted exceptional, the value of land must, as a rule, have been estimated as infinite, or, at all events, as an amount incapable of being measured.

As a matter of fact, this probably was the case with primitive economy. In the beginning, where land had any value at all ascribed to it—as, *e.g.*, the pasture lands of nomadic tribes when there was no superfluous amount of such lands,—the opinion must have arisen that here man had to do with an indispensable condition of existence ; a condition which required to be kept up permanently ; and a condition whose importance could not in any way be compared with that of rapidly changing, coming and going, movable goods. The possession of pasture land was a matter of life and death, and the tribe, recognising that its continued existence depended upon the possession, would risk its uttermost to retain it. Even in present times a similar mode of thought may be met with in distant mountainous regions, where the peasant farms his solitary patch of land. His croft is inalienable from him, and its value indeterminable as against other goods. What should the peasant do if he ceased to be a peasant? No sum of money that a buyer might offer could be any temptation to him, unless just then an occasion presented itself to exchange it for another and better piece of land—an unlikely possibility in the circumstances. The peasant's croft is and remains for him a good by itself, the value of it impossible of expression in goods of any other kind,—in fact, indeterminable.

This conception alters only when capital has become more plentiful, and when the landowner has become more familiar with its use and its value. There are two circumstances which bring this about. The one is that land and capital begin to be exchanged for each other, according to the amount of the rents they yield, and thus people use the value of capital to express the value of land. The other, and more important, is that the land becomes more intensively cultivated, and itself employs much capital. Consequently, in every act of cultivation, the question has to be considered, how land and capital should be employed relatively to each other, so as to give the best returns of rent. The same return in crops may be produced by taking more or less land into cultivation, or by employing more or fewer doses of capital, and agriculturists have to decide on these points. Thus land and capital become commensurable in their products; and, whenever civilisation has got this length, it is impossible longer to avoid valuing land according to the fundamental laws of valuing capital. To do otherwise would be to renounce the only possible measure for calculation and economic decisions. Just as capitals can be rightly compared with each other only when calculated at the same rate of interest, so can land and capital be rightly compared only when the valuation of land assumes the rate of interest on capital.

In the communistic state, it is true, the connection between land and capital, brought about by exchange of the one for the other, disappears, but the connection arising from their common co-operation in production remains. The capitalising of land value, accordingly, would remain as now.

# CHAPTER X

## THE VALUE OF LABOUR

To his master the slave is a capital, and his value, like that of an animal, a machine, or any piece of fixed capital, is determined by summing up and discounting all the services which may be expected from him, or, as we may say, by capitalising his net return.

The capital value of free labour, the value of the free labourer, is no object for valuation, any more than his person is an object of economical disposal, or a " good." On the other hand, the individual acts of labour are always objects of economical disposal, and so objects of value, even in the freest community,—even in a community where the labourer himself governs and makes the laws. No economy could be conducted without men recognising not only which labour, in general, is the best and which the worst, but which, in the circumstances, is the more and which the less important, which must be used sparingly and which may be used with most freedom.

The method by which labour is valued is exceedingly simple. The ordinary principles of imputation decide what share of the return may be ascribed to each individual service, and the value of this share obtains directly as the value of the service which produces it. Thus every kind and quality of labour shows a different result according to the available supply, the demand, the support received from complementary goods, and the technical possibilities. At the top of the tree stand the " monopoly " services, when the general economic conditions of the time aid them with technical support and general demand ; at the bottom stand the over - congested branches of labour, particularly unskilled manual labour. Wherever labour power is available in great quantity it is valued as a " cost-good," and suffers from all the disadvantages of this valuation. The marginal employment is always the decisive one,—that employment of the labour in question which brings the smallest result economically permissible.

The socialists would have us believe that the value of every kind of labour should be estimated simply according to time ; that is to say, the duration of the service should alone decide its value relative to other labour,—which assumes, of course, that slovenly labour is reduced to earnest labour, unskilled to skilled labour. This is the extent to which the quality of the labour would be taken into consideration, but no further. Those differences of quality which reside in the task set before the labourer are left quite out of consideration. Common manual labour, higher artisan labour, superior mental labour, are all to be regarded as equal. Does it require any special proof that this is contrary to the natural laws of valuation, and that no economy could last which treated its division of labour in this way ?

The socialists continually overlook the fact—although, indeed, they only follow in the footsteps of most of the economists—that value, in our present condition of society, has two services to perform. The one is to act as title to personal income. In the great round game of income-winning, every one is to receive in the end as much as the value of his stake amounts to ; and in the game the stakes may be wealth as well as personal labour. The man who has much wealth to stake receives, as a rule, much income, even without personal labour, and the man who has little wealth to stake, as a rule receives little, even with the most strenuous expenditure of labour.

The other service of value,—and one usually quite over-looked,—concerns the economical balancing or weighing of goods against goods, and of employment of goods against employment, without regard to distribution among persons, and simply with a view to reach the greatest possible economic results. To this service of value belong *e.g.* those principles which are absolutely indispensable to any economy ;—that every production should be directed so as to obtain the greatest possible return, that no more be spent upon any product than can be made good by its value, that in consumption the good suited to satisfy urgent wants, and therefore the more valuable, should not be spent on a trifling satisfaction, that, generally speaking, the limits of supply and demand, as given in marginal value, should be observed, and so on.

What would the socialists have ?   They wish a regulated economy, in no way worse, and possibly better regulated than that of to-day ; but with this peculiarity that labour shall be the only source of personal income.   The value of land and capital — or the value of the rents of land and capital—shall no longer be imputed to any individual as his outlay or stake ; shall no longer serve any one individual as a title to personal income.   Is there in this claim—the justice of which we shall not here discuss—any force which can abrogate the economical service of value as well as the personal service ?   Because land and capital are no longer to belong to individuals but to the state, must they therefore be regarded by the state as valueless, and be employed in production without regard to the principles of value ?   Because labour is to be the only basis of personal income—measured possibly by the length of time which each man has worked—is labour alone to be considered in production, and is the only measure of its value to be its duration ?   Because there is to be a new order in the distribution of goods among persons, must there be a complete disorganisation in the whole industrial conduct of goods ?

Of course socialists are very far from desiring such a result.   They wish to have a regulated economy, but they expect at the same time to secure that goods are used and employed according to their usefulness.   Does this mean that the usefulness of goods is really the only thing to be considered—not quantity and its changes, not demand with its rise and fall, not the mutual connection of means of production, with all the vicissitudes of favourable and unfavourable coincidence ?   But if usefulness, supply, demand, complementarity are combined, what is this but to value goods according to the utility imputable to them in the given case, instead of according to their general usefulness—in other words, to estimate them according to their value ?

The natural principles of valuation are indispensable, because they serve indispensable economic purposes.   Consequently where these principles are observed, they serve these purposes, and are, in so far, good. In so far as exchange value corresponds with natural value, it is right that it should regulate the economic conduct and disposal of goods, and that in every department, whether as regards land, capital, or even labour. And although the labourer may suffer severely under this law of value, although society generally may suffer with him, although the recompense of the labourer may require to be adjusted, in his own interest and that of society, by a different law ;—still labour cannot be valued according to any other law where its *employment* is concerned. When it comes to employ labour, the communistic state must retain the same law in force, or its economy will become chaos.

Not only the question of payment, but, beyond that, the question of labour in the future, must be kept distinct from its employment. Wherever common labour power is disproportionally abundant, it can, and must, be employed only in producing returns of very trifling value. None the less will it be regarded as an evil that there should be available labour power of such trifling productive capacity, and all efforts towards increasing the services of labour and thus securing it a higher value, are worthy of praise ; all the more so if the small capacity brings a small payment, and thus results, over wide circles of workers, in insufficient satisfactions of wants and wretched conditions.

## CHAPTER XI

### THE VALUE OF PRODUCTION GOODS, WITH REFERENCE TO THE COMPETITION BETWEEN PRESENT AND FUTURE INTERESTS

To distribute a supply of means of subsistence, or other consumption goods, over a considerable period of time, and to value it with regard to the competition between present and future wants, is, at bottom, a very simple task. One would select the highest satisfactions which can be reached on the whole, and these would form the basis for the valuation of the goods, the marginal satisfaction deciding the value of the

unit.   At what point of time the marginal satisfaction will
occur cannot be stated generally.   It may be at the beginning
that the highest satisfactions are possible, as in the case
of stocks which are large and liable to spoil, and cannot well
be preserved for any length of time.   It may be that the
greatest amount of satisfaction can be attained only at the end
of the period ; as when forethought demands that a certain
restraint be observed at the earlier dates in case of possible
accidents.

Not infrequently this task is complicated by the fact that
there is a question between the productive employment of
goods, and their direct employment in the satisfaction of
wants.   Coal, for instance, exerts its power of heating equally
well in the dwelling and in the factory, and so with many other
material goods which may be employed either for consumption
or as capital.   The same will be observed in the case of land ;
a field may either be employed in producing a return, or
be laid out as a park.   And, finally, it is the same with
labour.   It may either be employed as personal service—
domestic service in a house for instance—or used for productive ends.   As all production provides for consumption
sooner or later, the choice between immediate consumption
and productive employment is always a choice between present
or proximate consumption and future or more distant consumption.   The principle which governs this choice is the
one just given ; that employment which, in a consideration of
the whole ground, is found to be the marginal one, decides
the value.   And here again it is impossible to state generally
at what point of time the marginal employment will occur.
It may occur in the present, the period of immediate consumption ; it may occur in the future, the period of productive
employment.   The marginal value of coal might be decided
equally well, either by its service in heating the dwelling or
by its service in the factory.

This consideration may be carried further within the sphere
of production.   Production may be made to yield its fruits
to consumption sooner or later, according to the manner in
which it is directed.   It is possible either to limit production principally to objects of direct consumption,—by which
means the end that is nearest in point of desire is more

speedily reached,—or to direct it on and on, devoting it to the making of production goods themselves, and to ensuring the conditions of great and lasting " rentability "—by which present enjoyment is postponed for the sake of a greater degree of enjoyment in the future.    Not only does the choice of objects of production come into consideration, but many other circumstances also.    Almost every kind of production—with the exception possibly of those strictly dependent upon seasons of the year—permits of a shorter or longer process; almost every production—with still more trifling exceptions—may be carried out " extensively " or " intensively," with slighter means and more temporary results, or with stronger means and more durable results.    In all such cases it has to be decided whether the present, the nearer enjoyment, or the future, the more distant, be preferable.    And finally there is still another peculiar circumstance, which contributes to the competition between present and future interests.    The accomplishment of almost every undertaking demands personal exertion; it thus demands the overcoming of the resistance offered by the natural desire for rest and comfort.    In this connection also the considerations of present and future welfare come into collision.

The principle which must guide one's choice in this respect is in all cases the same, although the difficulty of applying it increases with the complication of the case.    That scheme for the employment of goods which promises the greatest advantage on the whole, must be the one chosen, and valuation—so far as is practicable, marginal valuation—must be adapted to this scheme.

In general, indeed, labour and capital are more concerned in what has just been said than is land.    The motives which make for labour always, or almost always, encounter in the pleasure of the moment a certain resistance which must be overcome.    And capital, as it must continually be reproduced, continually raises the question whether the means necessary for its re-creation could not be employed elsewhere to more advantage.    In this have originated two celebrated theories, intimately related to one another, although they have emerged separately : the one relating to the value of labour, the other to the value of capital.    The former derives the value of labour from the "sacrifices" of labour; this theory we shall discuss later. The other derives the value of capital, or, rather, interest, from the "sacrifice" which, as it asserts, is made by the capitalist in devoting his capital to production instead of directly consuming it. This is the well-known Abstinence Theory, which regards interest as a wage for the abstinence of the capitalist. A few words upon this theory may not be out of place here. After what has just been said there should be no difficulty in forming an opinion upon it.

It is true that, in all cases of the formation of capital, capital might have had another destination than the one actually chosen,—for production is a very Proteus in its capability of taking various shapes; but it is not true—as will now be generally acknowledged—that every capital permits also of being immediately consumed. Since Lassalle's criticism it is unnecessary to waste another word on this point. But even supposing it were true, supposing that every concrete form of capital might be immediately consumed, the abstinence theory would none the less be false. In no way is it possible that a consumption, from which it is economical to refrain, can serve as a measure of value. What kind of sense would there be in this? Goods are of value to us because of what we can obtain from them, and those destinations of goods which are chosen as the economically permissible ones, furnish the basis of value. The consumable nature of capital goods can influence their value only in so far as capital goods are actually devoted to consumption; if capital be consumed the productive stock will be diminished; if much capital be consumed it will be sensibly diminished, and productive value will rise. But even this effect must not be regarded as a one-sided one. The productive employment of capital and the personal consumption of it mutually determine one another. Moreover they determine one another only in consideration of the amount of value employed at the time. On the other hand, neither of them can be *basis* for the other. The circumstance that capital is consumable can no more give value to a foolish employment of it in production, than the circumstance that capital is capable of productive employment can make it consumable, if it be not so in its own nature. The value of an employment must be founded on itself: productive value can be derived only from production, and consumption value only from consumption. The amounts of value gained in the various employments of capital are, of course, compared with each other, so far as is practicable, in the effort to attain to the greatest possible result on the whole: and, moreover, even where they are not compared, they are still put at an equal value with one another in virtue of the particular form of valuation which the marginal law brings with it. As a matter of fact abstinence from consumption is nothing more than a symptom of productive value,—occasionally of so much productive value that the sacrifice of abstinence is at least counterbalanced.

The abstinence theory in its essence bears a striking resemblance to that theory which derives the value of products from their costs. As we shall see immediately, the law of costs does indeed exist as a very good working law of valuation. But costs do not form the foundation of value; they only equalise it: and, moreover, the circumstance that costs are expended makes us conclude for the existence of value. The cost theory, like the abstinence theory—except that it is confined to a narrower sphere—confuses a law of the more or less of value, or more exactly, a law of the equalisation of values, with the fundamental law of valuation. In the one theory as in the other, a symptom, which allows us to conclude for the existence of value, is taken to be its cause and explanation.

# BOOK V

## THE NATURAL COST VALUE OF PRODUCTS

# CHAPTER I

PRODUCTION goods which are capable of being employed in several ways receive their value, as we are aware, from the value of the least of their products, the production of which is economically permissible; that is, from the marginal product or from their contribution to the marginal product. This value attaches equally to all similar articles or similar items of a productive stock, even to those which are actually employed in more remunerative ways. In a stock of iron each part has an equal value with every similar part in the stock, based on the marginal contribution. It is the same with a stock of coal; the same with any available supply of labour of equal quality; the same with any other production good. Assume that, in a productive stock of the class $a$, the item put to the most insignificant use gives a product of 1, every item in the stock will have the value of 1; every item of the class $b$ has the value of 2, if the marginal productive contribution of the class be 2, and every item of the class $c$ has the value of 3, if the marginal productive contribution amounts to 3.

Now, as a rule (the exceptions will be discussed later on) production goods retain that value which is ascribed to them before the beginning of the production—in anticipation of the best possible result,—after the completion of the process of production; that is to say, they retain it still in the products which they have been transformed into. To take the former figures, the product of the elements $10a + 10b + 10c$, will, as a rule have the value $10 + 20 + 30 = 60$, and the product of the elements $10a + 20b + 10c$, will have the value $10 + 40 + 30 = 80$.

This law may be expressed differently according as we state it from the side of production goods or from that of products.

In the former case it runs thus :—similar production goods maintain, as a rule, in every product, first, a similar value, and second, that value as it attaches to them through their marginal productive contribution. This is the correct formula. As the law of costs is usually understood, however, the second clause would be left out; thus giving a formula for relative values, but not for absolute amounts of value.

In the latter case the law runs thus :—the value of a product is, as a rule, a complex obtained by multiplying the quantity of production goods employed by the value of the productive unit, or—taking into consideration the fact that every product is always produced from several productive factors—it is a sum of such complexes ($10a + 10b + 10c$, or $10a + 20b + 10c$, and so on). From this formula, which indicates the absolute amounts of value, there follows another for the relations of value. It is that the values of products which have one productive factor in common are, to each other, in respect of this common factor, as the quantities of it requisite for their production. This is the correct formula. As usually understood the law runs more briefly thus ;—the values of products are to each other as the costs requisite for their production. This, again, is merely a relative, not an absolute expression. Closer consideration shows that it is not possible to apply this relative formula so long as it stands alone. The amount $10a + 20b + 10c$ is not twice as great as the amount $10a + 10b + 10c$, but twice as great only as regards the factor b; the general relation can only be established when the absolute values of a, b, and c, are known. If $a = 10$, $b = 20$, and $c = 30$, the ratio is as 80 to 60; if $b = 100$, it is as 240 to 140.

In the *Ursprung des Werthes* I called products which have one productive factor in common *Productionsverwandt*, which may be rendered in English as "cognate." They represent, as it were, the descending line of this factor, and stand to one another in collateral relationship. All products made from the same quality of iron are cognate. Many products are cognate to each other in more than one respect, *e.g.* products

of iron in the making of which have been expended similar
kinds of labour or similar fuel.  Understood in this sense, it
is always cognate products to which the law just stated
refers.

This is the well-known law of costs.  The task now lies
before us to explain and prove it.[1]

# CHAPTER II

## THE CONCEPTION OF COSTS

WHATEVER economic production goods a man has within his
disposal, whether lands, capital, or labour power, he counts
part of his wealth—although they do not directly increase his
satisfactions; and he does so with just as much right as he
counts those consumption goods wealth which permit of direct
enjoyment.  The possession of production goods gives the
promise of acquiring consumption goods later.  Production,
therefore, not only creates value, it also destroys value.
Only so long as one is taken by surprise at the emergence

---

[1] I have formulated the law of costs only with relation to the so-called costs of
production.  Besides this we speak sometimes of costs, when we refer to expenses
of purchase.  By this is meant the sums of money a buyer has to expend to
obtain possession of goods.  An exactly analogous law obtains as regards these
costs.  All sums of money of equal amount destined for the purchase of goods
have equal value to the one owner, and all goods purchased for money—under
certain assumptions entirely analogous to those conditions which hold as regards
the law of costs in production—have to the one owner a value in proportion to
their costs of purchase (see Book II. chap. ii.).  The law of costs of production
has, however, a more far-reaching importance than the law of costs of purchase,
inasmuch as it is not, like the latter, limited subjectively, but also holds as
regards objective exchange value.  In consideration of these more far-reaching
effects it is entitled to a special statement.

Sax has stated the conception of costs still more comprehensively (see chap.
56 in his *Grundlegung der Staatswirthschaft*).  Nevertheless, important though
the results thus obtained may be, it appears to me that, for the reason just
stated, it is right to hold by the narrower conception of the costs of production,
as against this wider one.

In connection with the present book, see *Ursprung des Werthes*, pp. 97, 103,
and 146; further, in Böhm-Bawerk's *Werth*, pp. 61 and 534; as also Sax,
p. 327; and, finally, the parts referring to this subject in Jevons and Walras.
Menger does not treat of costs.

of productive value, in that it is unexpected, is it reckoned as pure gain. When the Phœnicians—as the fable goes— accidentally came upon glass among the ashes, only the gain of production would be present to their minds; but whoever, thereafter, began to produce glass, and in doing so was obliged to pay attention to the materials of its production, would learn perforce the destructive part of production. If production, on the one side, brings forth products, it limits, on the other, the producing powers. On this account it is every one's duty to see that his production is always directed towards the greatest possible result, in case he should consume more value than he will eventually gain.

This circumstance receives more distinct form and emphasis in the case of production goods capable of many and various employments. Here care must be taken to choose those employments which will prove the most economically efficient, both as regards kind and amount. Circulating capital or labour power devoted to any one production, is thereby absolutely withdrawn from all others; the same is true of fixed capital, and even of unconsumable land, during the period of the production to which they are devoted. In consideration of this fact the devotion of means of production to individual undertakings must always be well considered. It is necessary, for this end, that the man who resolves on the making of one special product, should form an exact idea of the value of all the other products whose manufacture is thereby rendered impossible. But how can this be done? It is done by taking account of the value of their common economic factors of production. In these factors the value of all "cognate" products, without exception, is incorporated. Productive value, consequently, occupies a position of mediation among the whole circle of cognate products. Whenever the value of any class of products falls or rises, and thereby either the extension or the limitation of other branches of production is demanded,[1] the effect is first communicated to productive value, and is then

[1] If, for instance, the price of cotton thread is reduced, thread manufacturers will not pay the former price for cotton yarns. But if cotton spinners are compelled to quote a lower price to thread manufacturers they cannot ask a higher price from cloth weavers. Thus the weavers get their raw material cheaper because of the fall in the price of the cognate product, thread, and this tends to an extension of the cloth manufacture.—*W. S.*

passed on from productive value.    The products and the value of the products adjust themselves, in each individual case, to the productive value, and the productive value indicates the limit of production common to all.

In this way we reach the point of view from which production goods are conceived of as costs.    The first element in it is that the productive employment figures as outlay, as sacrifice, as loss ; the second is that, in virtue of this, attention is called to the equalisation of several connected productions.    To say that any kind of production involves cost, simply implies that the economic means of production, which could doubtless have been usefully employed in other directions, are either used up in it, or are suspended during it.    Costs are production goods when these are devoted to one individual employment, and, on account of their capacity of being other-wise employed, take the shape of outlay, expenditure.[1]    The measure for estimating costs is always the productive marginal utility, as it is found on consideration of all the employments economically permissible.

Thus only those production goods which we have already (in Book III. chap. xii.) called " cost goods," as opposed to " monopoly goods," can be regarded as costs.    Productive elements which admit of only one kind of employment, do not share the multiplicity of conditions necessary for the emergence of what we recognise as costs.    A mineral spring, which can be used only by drawing off its contents and putting them into bottles, must, obviously, stand in a quite different relation to the value of the product from the unskilled labour which fills the bottles, but is capable of a hundred other uses besides. " Monopoly goods " simply take to themselves the value of the products imputed to them, and do not conduct it back again to these products, as do " cost goods,"—while cost goods are the parent goods of the great productive relationships, within which they act as combining forces and equalisers of value. The more various the employments of any productive element are, and the shorter the processes are,—as this continually

---

[1] This definition requires a slight readjustment only in so far as interest and land rent (see below, Book V. chaps. xi. and xii.) are reckoned among costs. Interest and rent—or the goods which constitute them—are not production goods ; they are simply elements of the production calculus, as production goods are.

necessitates new deliberations as to how the goods are to be employed next—the more does their employment in production obtain the character of a sacrifice whose amount must be well weighed if the proper balance of production is to be maintained. Unskilled labour and the commonest kinds of floating capital, are, consequently, the goods to which the conception of costs most frequently applies.

## CHAPTER III

### FOUNDATION OF THE LAW OF COSTS

THE value of costs determines the value of products in two ways. In general it determines it indirectly, by regulating the supply produced; but, in individual cases, it determines it directly by communicating the amount of its own value without any intermediary.

First: as regards the indirect action of costs. In the value of the costs is expressed the expectation of the greatest possible return from production. In order to fulfil this expectation, the relation between the amounts of all cognate products turned out must be well weighed and proportioned. If too much be produced in any one direction a loss will have to be borne elsewhere, which will be more sensible than the gain resulting from the over-production. If too little be produced in any one direction a similar loss will be felt, which it will be impossible to make good by over-production elsewhere. Whether too much or too little has been produced is seen exactly in the value. If the value of products—as it results from the equation between supply and demand—is less than that of the costs, too much has been produced; the costs which should have brought forth products having higher value have brought forth only goods having less value. Where the value of the product exceeds that of the costs, too little has been produced—with one exception which will be mentioned shortly;—the costs have not been employed entirely in bringing forth products of the highest value—the very anticipation of which gave the costs their value. If products, then, are to be produced neither over nor under cost, they must be produced exactly at cost value, if they are to find the most economically advantageous distribution of production.

If we ask why products thus produced—neither under nor over costs—have value, and why they have definite amounts of value, we shall doubtless find that they have themselves alone to thank for it. They create it out of their utility, taking into consideration the amounts produced. The circumstance that costs of a certain value have been expended in making them, is of no consequence as regards their value. The cost value does not determine the use value ; the use value exists of itself, and sanctions the cost value.

Second : as regards the direct action of costs. Under certain circumstances it is economically permissible to produce things whose use value exceeds their cost value, while they must, none the less, be estimated at their cost value. This direct action is the most striking of the two. Assume that the amount of costs necessary for an article has the value of 6, and that the first article produced has a use value of 10, while the use value of a second article would amount to only 1 (compare Book I. chap. iv. and Book III. chap. viii.) : the production must be confined to one article. How is it to be valued ? This will depend upon circumstances. In a moment of extreme danger a weapon will be estimated according to its use value. But suppose a man to be leisurely preparing and equipping himself for an adventuresome journey, he will not think of valuing the best of weapons more highly than the materials and labour available for the purpose of producing and reproducing them. The loss of the weapon can always be made good—supposing one has the necessary leisure and means for its reproduction—by a sacrifice in costs, the amount of which is certainly less than the importance possessed by the weapon itself in a moment of urgent need. A good having a use value equal to 10, and a cost value equal to 6, must be estimated at 6, so long as its reproduction is possible and the satisfaction of want is not prejudiced by the delay.

The same argument as leads to our valuing at marginal utility any single item of a stock which happens to be actually devoted to satisfying a want of higher grade, leads to our valuing at cost value and no more, a product whose specific use value exceeds its cost value, supposing we have also in our possession the means of producing and reproducing it at the proper moment. For, as, in the one case, the marginal use is really the only use threatened, so, in the other, the cost value is the only value threatened. Here is a new application of the marginal law.

Cases of the kind just described attract particular notice on account of the fact that the influence of costs upon the value of products is independent of amounts produced. If the cost value, in the example just given, rise from 6 to 9, or fall to 2, one product only will be produced, and its value likewise will follow the changes of the cost value, and rise to 9 or fall to 2, without the amounts produced being changed. Ricardo, with the keenness of observation peculiar to him, pointed to the consideration of those instances, in which the value of the product adjusts itself to the cost value without any change of amounts, as a very important one from the point of theory. As a matter of fact it is so, although Ricardo was wrong in the place he gave it. He wished to prove from it that costs are fundamentally an independent source of value, whereas, as a matter of fact, it proves simply that costs may, in certain isolated cases, directly determine the amount of the value of products. It is, however, chiefly decisive in that it gives us an insight into the connections of the process of valuation such as could scarcely be obtained otherwise. It gives us, indeed, the most unequivocal and undeniable application of the marginal law that it is possible to find anywhere.

Moreover, even in this case, the fact that costs have been expended is of no importance as regards the value of products. The decisive circumstance is, that costs could again be expended, and secure a higher utility at a less sacrifice of utility.[1]

---

[1] The foundation of the law of costs given in the text appears to be applicable only to natural value, and not to exchange value or price. But it is also applicable to them. The proximate explanation of the validity of the law of costs, in the case of price, is that producers are not willing to sell under cost, and—where there is free competition—are not able to sell over cost. But why is it that they will not sell in the former case, and why does competition make it impossible to sell in the latter? In the last resort it is because every one applies for himself, as well as he is able, the natural laws of valuation, and those laws bring him to that amount of product, or that valuation of what is produced, from which the law of costs results. Competition—*i.e.* the efforts of others who apply the

# CHAPTER IV

## CONDITIONS UNDER WHICH THE LAW OF COSTS OBTAINS

IT is unnecessary to say that products only come under the law of costs. The products which principally come under this law are those which are produced frequently, regularly, and in large amounts, and, in particular, those in the production of which cost-goods are exclusively employed. Products whose manufacture is strictly and narrowly limited by confessedly monopoly goods do not experience the influence of costs at all. All alterations in costs in such cases go, not to products, but to the monopoly factors of production ; every diminution of costs raises, and every increase lowers, the value of these factors.[1]

Such products too as are to be re-employed in production —*i.e.* all produced concrete forms of capital, or " capital goods," as we may call them for convenience sake—come under the law of costs. Thus the valuation of capital becomes an exceedingly complicated matter. One has always to combine two things ;—the return to the capital and its costs. Both amounts stand in mutual relation, and tend, so far as possible, towards equality. The greater the value of the return, the greater the costs that may be expended in producing it ; and the greater will be the expenditure of costs, so far as is practicable and necessary : the smaller the requisite expenditure of costs, the smaller will finally be the value of the return, whether this result from the fact that production finally is correspondingly extended, or from the fact that the valuation of the utility is directly pressed down to the level of the costs. If a machine

same natural laws—then forces him to give expression, in the price which he asks from the consumers, to the valuation which he has made for himself. The actual position of price depends, therefore, essentially upon the actual position of competition, particularly on how far the efforts of competition are limited by the "hindrances to equalisation." These "hindrances" are peculiarly strong in international trade, in which, accordingly, the law of costs holds only very slightly.

[1] Thus in the cotton thread trade neither changes in wages nor in the price of raw material seem to affect prices ; they only increase or decrease profits.— *W. S.*

does very good work, that is a cause for valuing it highly ; but if it can be cheaply produced, the machine itself, and, finally, its products also, will find a low value.    The costs of producing capital transmit their effects right down to the fruits of the capital, however remote these may be, so long as they fall within the producer's field of vision, and can be taken into consideration in the estimates of value.

Products which come under the law of costs do not, however, come under it in all circumstances.    To do so they must come under consideration *as* products, *i.e.* as dependent upon the elements from which they are formed.    If they are estimated independently, if they are valued in isolation and for themselves, their own utility alone—or their marginal utility— will determine their value, without their *productive* marginal utility being taken into consideration at all.

This is most clearly seen in the case of the immediate determination of value by costs.    Why in this case is the valuation made according to costs ?    Because the products can always be obtained again at the sacrifice of the costs, and, just on that account, only when they can be obtained at this sacrifice.    If the possibility of their reproduction be excluded through any circumstance whatever—say *e.g.* that the import of some article is stopped by a blockade, or that demand has increased so rapidly that production cannot keep pace with it,—the value will be estimated at the full amount of the utility (or marginal utility) which the products are expected to give.    As a rule, there are such abundant supplies of all products—partly in the possession of private householders, partly in the larger stores of producers and merchants —that people are provided against the smaller increases in demand.    Valuation by costs is suspended only in the case of large and permanent disturbance of production.    If reproduction remains possible, although at a higher outlay than before, —not, however, coming up to the height of utility,—the law of costs will still obtain, only that the determining amount of costs will have risen.    If demand decrease, or unforeseen supplies increase the stock, to such an extent that the marginal utility falls below the amount of costs, the law of costs will be suspended until marginal utility shall have so far risen as to render production again practicable.

The same applies where costs do not directly determine value, but determine, in the first instance, only the extent of production. The influence of costs ceases so soon as, and so far as, the possibility of production ceases. Here again may be observed the same influence of accumulated stocks—that, through the medium of them, all smaller disturbances in the provision for want are equalised.[1]

When the disturbances which caused the suspension or limitation of the law of costs are over, it again becomes active. So far as is at all possible, men try to conduct production according to a universal plan which embraces all the productions "cognate" at the time. Isolated production prevents complete utilisation of the means of production ; it limits provisions for human want too greatly at certain points, while going too far in other directions, or, what is still worse, leaving production at certain points entirely alone. On this account there is always a tendency to return to the most comprehensive conditions of production, and thus, so far as is possible, to the valuation according to costs.

If society were ever to arrive, in its economic life, at such perfection and control that no plan of production ever miscarried, that there was no interruption in exchange, that no unforeseen loss of goods happened, that all acquisitions of goods could be anticipated to the fullest extent and in the most exact degree, that, finally, the demands should never vary or, at least, that the variations should always be adequately anticipated:—in such circumstances the law of costs would be the only form in which the general law of value would appear as regards those goods in respect to which it holds. It is not to be expected that any disposition of affairs could bring social economy to such perfection. Even in the most perfect condition of society there will be changes, such as must for the moment limit or extend the sphere over which the law of costs holds sway.

If the socialists expect that, in their future state, valuation

---

[1] Up to a certain point costs do—even in such cases as these—directly determine value. All goods that can be supplemented from stocks in warehouses and the like, which stocks again can be renewed through production, thereby appear to us directly as mere combinations of their productive elements. And to this extent it may be said that, on the whole, the cases where costs directly determine value predominate.

by costs will be all-sufficient, they are in error, unless man is able to exert such mastery over the natural conditions of the life of goods, that no harvest shall ever fail, or, indeed, be over-abundant; and, moreover, unless the national life can be assured of a perfectly peaceful course, such as can be conceived of only when war has ceased, when invention is no more, and when no new need ever emerges.

## CHAPTER V

### THE DETERMINING AMOUNT OF COSTS

THE circumstance, as such, that a good has involved costs, and that it has involved a certain amount of costs, does not deter-mine its value. Not only must the conditions under which the law of costs obtains be fulfilled, but the justifiable amount of costs must be observed.

It is only the "socially necessary" costs, the smallest amount of costs required, that determines value, whether the determination is "indirect" or "direct." In cases of "indirect" determination, cost value requires the sanction of use value. Whatever is expended uselessly receives no value, and what-ever is superfluously expended,—expended in excess of what is necessary to obtain the utility,—receives no value. In cases of "direct" determination of value, the important thing from the first is the outlay requisite for reproduction.

The value of products which are economically produced with the smallest cost, must consequently alter should there be, later on, any change in the determining amount of costs. And, in particular, if the amount of costs should become less, the value of commodities produced at the old dearer rate must fall, from the moment when the new and cheap goods are capable of meeting the demand, or even sooner than this, so far as the old stocks are large and dare not be held back in view of the increasing production.

It may be that all the products in demand cannot be produced at the one cheapest rate of cost. Then, of necessity, the amount of costs must rise. The value of goods produced at different costs is determined throughout by the highest cost necessary ; the portion which has been produced at the greatest expense must be valued correspondingly high, if it is permissible to produce it at all at so great an expense ; and the other portion, which has been produced more cheaply, must be valued equally high, because all products of equal quality must have equal value.

All these propositions are well known both theoretically and practically, so far as regards exchange value. It is of interest for us to know that they also obtain as regards natural value.

# CHAPTER VI

## THE LAW OF COSTS AND THE GENERAL LAW OF VALUE

IF the statement of the law of costs just laid down be correct, there can be no doubt regarding its relation to the general law of value.

Between costs and utility there is no fundamental opposition. Costs are goods valued, in the individual case, according to their general utility. The opposition between costs and utility is only that between the utility of the individual case, and utility on the whole. Whoever thinks of " utility " without thinking of " costs," simply neglects, in the utility of one production, the utility of the others. And whoever produces, in the individual case, at the least cost, produces, on the whole, with the highest utility, inasmuch as he thus saves all the opportunities of utility possible, and consequently in the long run utilises all these opportunities to the utmost extent.

Thus where the law of costs obtains, utility remains the source of value. More than this, marginal utility remains the measure of value. The only thing is that utility and marginal utility are no longer determined in a one-sided way within the limits of each particular group of products, but over the entire field of cognate production. Over this field it is always the common productive marginal utility that decides. The result of the productive combination $10a + 10b + 10c$ possesses the common marginal utility of all productive goods of the class A ten times, and so with the classes B and C. It consequently stands in a definite ratio of value to the product resulting from $10a + 20b + 10c$, and this ratio corresponds to the general law of value, according to which separate parts of a stock are to be valued by multiplying the number of items by the marginal utility.  Even products which, in outward appearance and destination, are entirely different from one another, if traced back to the productive elements of their manufacture come ultimately into the same value relations as do the separate parts of a stock.  A cupboard and a table are in themselves different goods ; reduced to their productive factors they are of the same nature, belong to the same class of supply, and receive a corresponding expression of value.  The law of costs is a peculiar and complicated conception of the general law of value, used in a peculiar and complicated case, viz. where the connection of goods with one and the same stock is not apparent from their outward appearance, but can only be recognised after reduction to the productive elements of their manufacture.

This statement would be imperfect if we did not add that the law of costs as regards products is by far the most usual form assumed by the general law of value.  Products of almost every kind are continually being reproduced, and consequently their value must continually be decided by comparing the amount of the productive supplies with the amount of the productive demand.  The vast majority of changes in value are occasioned by the changes which occur in the coming forward of production goods (or in their production, where they are themselves objects of production), as also by technical changes, or changes in the conditions of production which make the quantity of costs necessary to produce the goods greater or less.  Thus it happens that variations in the value of products are traceable, in the majority of cases, to some cause which is to be found in production goods.  Even in cases where the change of value first arises in the demand and in the products, the effect of this circumstance communicates itself, through the medium of the cost goods, to the cognate products, and causes their value to rise or fall.  A product which is " cognate " with a hundred others, will, in all probability, be affected a hundred times by changes in their supply and demand relations, for once that it is affected by a change in its own relations; and all these influences are communicated to it from outside through the cost value. And thus it is that changes in any single supply and demand must pass without leaving any trace, unless they chance to be exceedingly comprehensive, and are, therefore, capable, as against the supply and demand over the whole circle of cognate production, of disturbing the determining marginal utility.

The phenomena of costs are, therefore, a new proof of how greatly the objective conditions of the existence of goods influence the value of goods. How far the value of goods, in its final form of "cost value," is from being the mirror of that subjective fact from which it is derived—the value of wants! The circumstance that cognate products are produced by different quantities of the same productive elements, brings their subjective valuations into a ratio, the terms of which are derived entirely from the objective conditions of production; while the impulses which call for their emergence, as well as the absolute value amounts of the elements whose multiples enter into the ratio, remain subjective, and thus prove the subjectivity of the source and nature of value.

It was impossible that the influence of costs upon the value of products could escape the observation of economists. None the less has recognition by economic theory of the law of costs remained for long very imperfect. It was conceived of only as a relative law—that the value of products was as the quantity of costs; but as to what was the nature of costs, whence they themselves receive their measure, what absolute amounts might accrue to the value of products,—on these points economists were no more capable of saying anything than they were capable of explaining the numerous contradictions which were inevitable so long as costs were conceived as the final cause of the value of products. Possibly it is the greatest triumph of the theory of marginal utility that it fully explains the obscure conception of costs, with which every other theory had to reckon, and with which no theory could come to any reckoning. The labour theory alone has attempted it, but it has thereby—as we shall go on to show—introduced into theoretic political economy the greatest errors that have ever been perpetrated within its sphere.

# CHAPTER VII

## THE SO-CALLED COSTS OF PRODUCTION OF LABOUR

THROUGH a very strange error in judgment the classical school of political economy has put forward the proposition that the exchange value of human labour also is determined by costs of production.

The costs of production of human labour—if we substitute the prosaic personal meaning of this expression for the impersonal and figurative one—would be the costs of producing the labourer. What a monstrous idea! Can it be that there is a " production " of labourers in the same sense as there is a production of material things? Has such a thing ever been said even in the darkest ages of barbarism? Surely another name at least might have been chosen. But leaving the name, let us get to the substance.

The substance is, that, by the cost of production of labour is meant the necessary cost of maintaining the labourer and his family; the means of subsistence which the labourers themselves regard as the minimum necessary to keep themselves in life, in strength, and in ability to work, to bring children into the world, and to bring them up to labour. And as the price of goods can never stand permanently either above or below the costs of production, so it is asserted that the wages of labour can never stand permanently either above or below the existence-minimum. Of course, this proposition can never be understood to apply to any but the commonest and worst paid form of labour, seeing that the better paid labour *does* raise itself above the lowest wage level that can be considered permissible.

On the one side, so far as regards the impossibility of sinking below the minimum, there *is*, as a fact, a close, indeed a frightful analogy between the law of wage and the law of costs. Where the labourer has no other income to spend than his wage, wages cannot indeed fall permanently below the amount marked by the prices of the necessary means of subsistence. If the means of subsistence are scarce and dear, a higher wage must ultimately be conceded. Misery and death are the imperious forces which bring about this result, inasmuch as they reduce the number of labourers until the reduced supply has raised wage sufficiently to cover the necessaries of life.

But how is it as regards the other side ? Is it true that wages can never rise permanently above the costs of subsistence ? Is there the smallest analogy, or even an apparent analogy, between the pressure exercised by the cognisance of cheaper conditions of production upon the valuation of products, and the pressure which might be exercised upon the valuation of labour by cognisance of cheaper conditions of life ? Economists of the classical school assert that there is, and thereby they bring again into the question motives which have as little in common with the considerations that govern the production of goods, as the law of nature, which says that he who can find no means of sustenance must die, has with the considerations that govern the manufacturer who discontinues a business when it fails to return him its costs. The motive which is called upon to prove that wage cannot maintain itself above the minimum of subsistence is the power of the sexual instinct. If means of subsistence become cheaper and more abundant, there is the more room for increase of population, for marrying, producing children, and supporting them. The supply of labourers can go on increasing, and wages go on diminishing, until the maximum of population possible to maintain, and the existence minimum of wage, are again reached. This result *is* possible. But must it ever happen ? Does it always happen ? What has experience to say ? It speaks plainly enough—so plainly that even those who assert that the law of costs obtains for labour find themselves forced to add to that law certain clauses which amount to nullifying it. Thus a clause is added which says that what determines wage is that amount of subsistence which the labourers themselves regard as the permissible minimum, since experience shows that the minimum wage differs from time to time, from place to place, and from nation to nation. But this clause cancels the law. If the opinion of the labourer is to be decisive, there can be no more talk of a compulsory, objective, fixed standard of wage. In yet another direction experience speaks still more con-

clusively.   We notice everywhere that the wage for different
kinds of labour is of varying amount.   Only some of the
labourers, and that not by any means the majority, are always
held down to the lowest possible wage.   But how could this
be the case if the whole position of labour were entirely
governed by the power of sexual impulse as is asserted?
Would not the supply of labour under such a supposition be
overwhelmingly large,—as a rule, and in the' long run at all
events,—and wages be reduced to the minimum in all branches
of production?   Would not all wages be equally low?   The
fact that higher wages are continuously maintained in the
higher branches of labour, is a clear proof that the height of
wage continues to be determined by considerations which are
too powerful to admit of their favourable results being suspended by the sexual instinct; or—what amounts to the same
thing—that the sexual impulse does not possess that destructive
power which is ascribed to it.   And if it does not possess this
as regards one class of labour, it is impossible to see why it
should be held necessary as regards the other class.

If the law of costs were true as regards wages of labour,
it would also be true as regards the natural value of labour.
The forces which are relied on to prove the law of costs
in regard to labour, would, of necessity—if they do act as is
asserted of them—have an equal effect under any social
organisation.   If the sexual impulse were possessed of such
surpassing strength, it would, even in a communistic state,
increase the number of labourers to the highest point which
could be maintained at the existence minimum; only that
here, where the labouring class would include the whole nation,
the consequences would be so much the more comprehensive
and destructive.   To-day's "iron law of wage" would be
extended in the future to an iron law of universal misery.

Modern economists are almost unanimous in repudiating
the application of the law of costs to labour in its older and
cruder form, but, on the other hand, they concede to the consideration of the costs of maintaining the labourer another
effect.   It is the effort of every class of labourers, they say, to
retain the level of life to which they have once attained, making
their claim of wages in correspondence therewith and striving
to realise their claim, besides regulating their marriages and

the size of their families in conformity. The wage, once become customary, is said to have a tendency to maintain itself as a permanency, and to resist the tendencies which would press it down. This law also, if it were a true law of wage, would have to be recognised as a natural economic law, as it also is founded upon a universal force. Experience, however, does not seem to justify it. Do not wages continually rise and fall ? It is to be feared that the quite intelligible wish of the worker to retain a standard of income once reached has not the efficacy ascribed to it, of resisting the chances of an unfavourable issue to labour. If the return to labour falls, the natural value of labour falls, without being in the least prevented by the previous customary level of comfort, and it is in the highest degree likely that its exchange value will fall along with it. For although these do not by any means invariably coincide,—do we not often see wages falling short of natural value ?—as things are, it may be considered an exceedingly rare occurrence that wages are in excess of natural value. The result which might be expected from the postponing of marriage and production of children would, in any case, come much too late ; it could only be felt after years, in a succeeding generation, when circumstances would probably have been long before completely changed. Of course, the desire to obtain the highest possible income is a motive which cannot be considered as quite insignificant among the many motives determining the return from production. It is as fraught with consequences as are intelligence, skill, favourable natural circumstances. But why should this motive be brought prominently forward only as regards the return to labour ? Is it not equally powerful as regards the products obtained from land and capital ? And why should its influence be limited to the amount of income once obtained ? Does it not go beyond this to the procuring of fresh income ? The truth is that men endeavour to make *all* productive returns as large as ever their personal capacities will allow, and that the returns so obtained determine the value of the productive factors,—of labour, as of all the others. It is impossible to consider it even plausible, that a cause shall be effective as regards labour alone, by which the level of wage once reached obtains a peculiar power to maintain itself permanently unimpaired.

Here too the modern economists, who advance such theories, probably do so merely in order to bring the law of wage into correspondence with the general law of the price of commodities. In one as in the other, they start with the false assumption of a fundamental opposition between costs and utility, and wish to find value between the "upper margin of utility" and the "under margin of costs." But even supposing such an opposition did exist, it would not at all events be in the least applicable to labour. It is not possible to force labour into all the economic categories in which material goods by their nature are placed. A producible article is a good, that is, a useful thing—in two respects; firstly, in virtue of its effects—the effects in which it is " of use "; and, secondly, in virtue of its origin and upkeep, in which respects it is materially a matter of property. Labour can only be regarded as a thing in the former respect: in respect of its useful effects the economic use of labour may and ought to be considered. In the latter respect, labour is an affair of persons, and its origin and upkeep cannot be decided by purely economic considerations. It is overstepping the permissible sphere of economic control when the attempt is made to interfere with the personality of the labourer without regard to other considerations; and economic theory goes beyond its sphere when it claims to explain the facts of personal life exclusively by economic considerations.[1]

---

[1] As labour is not the product of the labourer's means of subsistence, so, conversely, the means of subsistence cannot be regarded as the productive factors of labour. In other words, the labourer's means of subsistence are not capital. If labour be a good of the second rank, producing any kind of good of the first rank— a consumption good—the labourer's fund of subsistence is in no way a good of the third rank, producing the labourer ; it is again merely a good of the first rank, a consumption good for the labourer. This has a result of great importance as regards value. Value is communicated, as we have seen, first from the want for goods of the first rank, and then from these to the goods of second rank, and so on through all the ranks. If means of subsistence were capital, they would receive their value from the value of the service rendered by the labourer. But as they are simply means of subsistence, they receive their value from the wants which they provide for.

# CHAPTER VIII

## THE COST THEORIES

I HAVE hitherto almost entirely refrained from criticising outside theories of value. Up to this point, the subject of costs, none of these contains any foreign element whatever. What renders them inadequate is chiefly their inadequate explanation of the true elements of value. Should I have succeeded—as I scarcely dare hope—in proving beyond dispute the theory to which I have given my adhesion, all other theories in themselves are thereby confuted, inasmuch as it completes what they began. Where they have said only half, the whole has been said; where they have only approximated to truth, the truth itself has been found. But it is otherwise —though of course only in the case of some of them,—with those theories which derive the value of goods from costs. They appeal to a foreign element which does not lie in the path I have chosen to follow, and must therefore be dealt with, as it were, on a bye-path of criticism. At the same time, it must be said that this foreign element contains so much that is plausible, that there would be a presumption against any one who passed it by without remark, and a suspicion that his statement did not embrace the entire truth.

As I said, it is only some of the theories of costs with which we are here concerned.

All such theories have this one point in common, that they place costs and utility in opposition to each other, and explain them as dissimilar principles of value. They differ, however, in their manner of treating the principle of costs. Some limit themselves to collating the individual elements of costs, and showing their influence upon value, without answering, or even bringing up, the essential and fundamental question as to what costs really are, and whence they obtain their influence and economic importance. Criticism of these theories is superfluous. They contain no error to criticise. Their fault lies in their silence; in their stopping short at the very heart of the subject.

The rest of the cost theories must be judged differently. They give to the idea of costs an entirely distinct meaning; a meaning which is certainly—taking it all in all—incorrect; but one which, in view of the largeness of its theoretic intention, may be pardoned, and even regarded with some recognition and respect. This division of the cost theories may be marked by the title of Labour Theories, as the element of labour forms their theoretic starting-point. Ricardo's system indicates the high-water mark of the labour theory; the socialist system is its final consequence. Many writers who reject both of these systems, nevertheless take the fundamental motive of the labour theory into their own systems. In fact, there are very few writers who have kept entirely free from it. The critic has consequently a large task before him. I make no secret of it that to do battle with those views, as developed by economic writers, seems to me a matter of considerably more importance that they arise, in the last instance, from popular opinions widely held. The fundamental idea of the labour theory is foreign to no one; everybody has frequently enough had practical occasion to apply it. But for this, Ricardo's system would never have obtained its great hold, and this circumstance may prepare us to expect in the future ever new formulations of the labour theory, should it not be possible meantime to purify theoretically the popular view, and lead it back from its exaggerations, which are easily traceable to the imperfection of popular reasoning, into its true and incontestable form.[1]

---

[1] In his *Werththeorien und Werthgesetz*, in Conrad's *Jahrbücher* for 1888, W. Scharling, one of the latest writers upon the theory of value, has again traced it to the fundamental motive of the labour theory, although with considerable amplification and modification. He derives value from the difficulty of attainment, or, more exactly, from the amount of effort which he who wishes to acquire an object is spared by attaining his end through exchange. I shall not at this point dwell on Scharling's positive work, but rather refer the reader, in regard to his fundamental *motif*, to the succeeding chapter. Only, in passing, I may note that, among the efforts which are to give the standard to price, Scharling includes that (p. 558) "which it costs (at an auction) to distance other bidders," or what it costs "to overcome an owner's disinclination to part from his goods." Both of these efforts have their origin in nothing else than the payment of that very price whose standard they are supposed to explain. In this sense there might be included among the difficulties of attainment the fact that things must be paid for with money, while people are bound to be economical with money. His

# CHAPTER IX

### THE COST THEORIES (*continued*).   LABOUR AS AN
### ELEMENT IN COST

IT cannot well be questioned that, among the costs of any product, the labour necessary for its making comes first. Every product withdraws the labour-power that is devoted to it from other products to which it might have been devoted.    There would be nothing further to say on the subject, were it not that labour calls for economic deliberation as to its employment on a second ground besides that of its utility.   Labour carried too far becomes a burden, and brings a succession of serious personal evils in its train. Where labour brings pain, strain, or danger, there is good reason to think seriously over these consequences ; and, on their account alone, to regard every act of labour as a sacrifice which should be made only if it is certain to be adequately recompensed by its result.    It is in this sense that it is commonly said that production "*costs*" labour, and it is in this sense that most economists conceive of labour as a cost good.

views on the theory of marginal utility are given, in an illustration cited by Böhm-Bawerk, of a boy to whom "the pleasure of eating an apple is more than seven times but less than eight times that of eating a plum." "Let us suppose" continues Scharling "that the father comes and says to his boy : 'Our neighbour has given you permission to pull as many apples from his garden as you wish' ; the boy will at once alter his opinion as to the relation between apples and plums, although his taste for and his enjoyment in consuming the fruit remains unchanged.   But the effort which the possession of one apple saves him from putting forth, is no longer the same." To my mind this illustration, which Scharling advances in opposition to the theory of marginal utility, is really a proof of that theory.   In what way has the situation changed after the father's speech ?   Clearly that the boy may now have as many apples as he will, while formerly he had only one, *i.e.* the available supply has been increased to superfluity.   And thus the result is attained which the theory of marginal utility demands ; the valuation of the apples is entirely altered.   Scharling's opposition would be justified if it were directed against a theory which made value depend simply upon utility and not on marginal utility.   In our theory, along with utility, all the influences are weighed which determine the degree of utilisation, and of estimation of utility, by the supply ; indeed, even those influences which determine the amount of supply by the conditions of production.

Not the utility but the personal sacrifice of the labourer is to determine the economic valuation of labour, and its influence upon the value of commodities.

To decide how much is right in this conception is one of the most difficult tasks of political economy, and, as the theory has developed, one of the most important. Beginning with the idea that labour is valued according to the personal sacrifice it involves, and going on to the wider idea that labour is the only production good, that all products are directly products of labour, and that all costs are labour costs, the conclusion has been reached that the sacrifice of labour necessary for the production of a good is the exclusive source of its cost value, indeed, of its value pure and simple. From its relation to the labour sacrifice the conception of value receives its content, the amount of value its standard. In Adam Smith we find, as was said in the preface, this " philosophical " conception' of value coming into collision with a second " empirical " conception. Ricardo's system aims at proving that this " philosophical " conception is almost realised in the empirical formation of value. Finally the socialists roundly demand its complete realisation, and condemn the empirical deviations as disturbances. In connection with this conception of value, a second conclusion, which relates to the origin and aim of human economy, is drawn from the same premises. Human economy derives its origin, in the last resort, from the fact that goods must be obtained at the price of the sacrifice of labour, and the aim of all economy is ultimately to make the sacrifice of labour necessary for the production of goods as small as possible. And thus, when we endeavour to examine the position of labour as a cost good, we find ourselves plunged into the quarrel of theory as to the fundamental questions of political economy.

The opponents of the Labour Theory do not in my opinion give it full justice. They try to overturn it completely, whereas it is by no means entirely false. It is conceivable, only it does not fit in with facts ; it is, if the expression may be allowed, philosophically right, but it is not empirically realised.

It is possible to conceive of a condition of economic life under which the single consideration of the sacrifice involved in labour would determine the value, both of labour itself and of all products. The widespread recognition which Ricardo's theory has obtained can only be explained by the fact that it is founded upon a conceivable and attractive fundamental idea. Men learned the meaning of " value " as a whole—not as a philosophical conception, but as applied to the circumstances of everyday life—for the first time, and then overlooked the fact that the " value " of actual life was not completely explained.

I shall endeavour to formulate with all possible distinctness those conditions under which the labour theory would apply. This is the best means of enabling us to recognise how far these fall short of realisation in existing economic circumstances.

Suppose that a community—already abundantly provided with all the material auxiliaries for labour—had at their disposal so great a supply of labour power, and so few wants, that they were able to satisfy completely and without delay any desire that they might happen to feel, simply by putting forth the exertion necessary to produce the means of satisfaction. In this case the means of satisfaction so produced would have no value from the consideration of their utility, because—as assumed—they were to be had immediately at all times and in superfluity. On the other hand, the consideration of the exertion of labour required to produce them must give them value. Every product made and possessed would save an effort ; the effort, namely, involved in its reproduction. And, so far, one would have a lively interest in holding on to any possession once obtained. The amount of this interest would depend upon the exertion saved by the possession. A product with a utility expressed by the intensity of 100, and necessitating labour equal to 10, would have a value of 10, and would have no value at all if its reproduction cost no effort.

The conceptions of value and wealth evolved from the assumed circumstances would, formally considered, be such as should arise if value and wealth were derived from consideration of the utility which the goods assure, while, all the time, materially, they would be completely different. Value would be the importance which goods would then have in virtue of the interest every one would feel in securing exemption from the undesirable pain of labour. Wealth would be equivalent to great possessions of goods securing immunity from the pain of labour. The advantage of wealth would be rest. Poverty would not mean want, but only unrest, pain. By a little increase of exertion any advantage of prior possession could soon be overtaken.

That this is not the poverty which the poor man knows : that this is not wealth as men really estimate it : that this is not the value or the economy of which we have any experience :—requires no proving. If merely by pain men could be rich, the very people who are to-day the poorest would long ere this have become the richest. Nothing in reality is as assumed by the labour theory. Our desires are too great, the material resources at our disposal too limited, our labour power too small. No economical possession can be lost without some enjoyment being lost. The idea of utility cannot possibly be separated from the purposes of economy and the conception of value.

There is only one question that may still be asked. It is whether consideration of the sacrifice of labour does not always enter into the valuation of labour as a cost-good, and thus into the cost value of all products, alongside of and bound up with the consideration of the utility of labour. But neither is this the case. It could not be so. Such a possibility is excluded, not empirically but logically. Productive labour can never have value on account of the utility which is dependent upon its success or non-success, and *also* on account of the personal effort which it involves. In what circumstances does an act of labour have use value ? When, in event of its failure, the utility has to be given up, because the labour cannot be put forth a second time ; or when, in the same case, the repetition of the service demands that another use of the labour be abandoned, and its expected utility with it ; in other words, when there is not sufficient labour available to meet the demand, when labour power is not available in superfluity. And in what circumstances would a service be estimated according to the sacrifice involved ? When, in event of failure, one would not need to give up the utility, because it could always be obtained again at no greater expense than the repeated effort; in other words, when all the available labour power had not a predetermined and distinct destination, but when there was always free labour power available in superfluity. Labour could only be estimated at once by its utility *and* by personal effort, if it were at once capable and incapable of repetition; if there were at once a deficiency and superfluity of labour powers. Where the available labour power is less than the demand, labour value will be estimated exclusively according to utility. Where the available labour power is in excess of the demand, it will be valued exclusively with reference to the labour sacrifice.[1]

Even where labour value is estimated by utility, naturally one does not cease to consider the toils and dangers of labour. And although the consideration of these does not directly enter into the value of labour, it will continue to be a consideration so long as toil is felt to be toil, and danger danger. It may even obtain an indirect influence upon valuation, as it must continue to receive economic consideration in several connections.

These connections may be exactly enumerated.

First, before undertaking any labour a man has to consider whether the utility outweighs the effort. Only those acts of labour whose result outweighs the hardship entailed can be reasonably performed. Herein, moreover, is contained

---

[1] It is not at all impossible that, at one and the same place, there may be a lack of labour in certain departments—*e.g.* skilled labour—while there is superfluity in the available supply in others—*e.g.* common hand labour. In such a case the services of the former are estimated by utility, and the latter by amount of hardship. Under primitive economic conditions the "supply of labour power" is frequently too large; not until there has been a considerable advance in civilisation does it become the rule that labour is insufficient. Further, even the labour power of one and the same individual may be too small as regards certain requirements of labour, and at the same time too great as regards others. It happens almost invariably that labourers whose capacity for performing some particular form of service is not sufficient to meet the economic demand for such services, have always sufficient capacity remaining to meet the trifling necessity for labour in their own private lives. With this is connected the fact that labour power is never entirely worn out; after performing the labour of his particular vocation, man refreshes and restores his energy best by light and distracting employments. Even in a country where the economic demand for labour is entirely insufficient, there are not lacking occasions in which labour may be estimated according to the amount of hardship involved. Every individual is continually finding such occasions; and every one thus learns from his own experience the fundamental *motif* of the labour theory.

the reason why labour, estimated by amount of hardship alone, is less highly valued than when it receives its value from its return. This also gives rise to another important issue. The circumstance that expenditure of labour is felt to be a burden, must somewhat affect the selection of employments to which it is devoted. It may occur, as Sax (see note) has forcibly shown, that a less useful employment of labour is chosen before a more useful one, because the latter requires comparatively a greater amount of exertion.

Second, when labour is once decided on, its performance must always be ordered in such a way that the toil and danger are made as light as possible.

Third, the fact that labour is felt to be a burden has the effect of curtailing somewhat the supply of labour as a whole. If labour were not burdensome and exhausting, more labour would be expended than is. And thus the use value of labour is, as we have already suggested, *indirectly* affected, by being placed at a slightly higher level on account of the diminished supply. Services of equal utility, but of different degrees of hardship, are so regulated in regard to value that the more troublesome labour is more highly appraised. But this result can only ensue when the supply is really diminished. Wherever the fear of toil and danger does not have an actively deterrent effect, or where it is overcome by the presence of other motives to such an extent that the supply remains undiminished, the value of labour does not increase. Experience shows that the most wearisome, wearing, and least healthy of employments are valued least highly, because they are the most easily accessible to the great majority, and are consequently the most amply supplied. In the communistic state it would not, in all probability, be in any wise different. The great majority of the citizens will always be suited for the coarsest kind of work only, and those kinds of work are at once the most burdensome and the simplest. And while the communistic state would be plentifully supplied with this sort of labour, so that it could be employed down to the smallest possible return in utility, the better labour powers, in virtue of their more limited number, would require to be economised and have careful consideration given to their employment, just as happens to-day. Utility and not toil would, in

general, afford the standard for the valuation of personal
services.

But we are not finished with our consideration of the
labour theory. Its greatest errors relate to the valuation
which it gives to capital as an element in cost.[1]


# CHAPTER X

## THE COST THEORIES (*continued*).    CAPITAL AS AN
## ELEMENT IN COST

In any complete estimate of costs there can be no doubt that
the figures representing the necessary consumption of capital
must be added to the costs of labour. Of two products
costing equal amounts of labour, that one must be dearer for
which the greater consumption of capital is required. Thus
it has been calculated ever since capital was possessed by man,
and thus it will continue to be calculated, even in the communistic state. The necessity for it is so obvious that even
the adherents of the labour theory bow before it. Even they
admit that the costs of capital co-operate in determining the
value of products. There is nothing for it but to try and
reconcile their theory with this incontestable fact. To do this
there is only one resource, but one so singular that only a
kind of theoretical infatuation could avail itself of it. If all

---

[1] See *Ursprung des Werthes*, p. 103, and also Böhm-Bawerk's *Werth*, p.
42, and, on the opposite side, Sax, chapter 45. Sax, starting from the correct
proposition that only those goods should be produced whose utility outweighs
the burden of labour they involve, appears to me to go rather far in the conclusions he draws, when he says : "If the *Unlust* connected with the want in
question (*i.e.* the *Unlust* which originates from the want not being satisfied) is
less than that of the burden of labour, then the desire for the good will be
a passive one. The want itself ceases to be felt." Only in so far as the desire
is "active" does the expected product receive a value in thought. That, as I
have said, seems to me to go too far. In considering whether a thing should be
made or not, the value, as derived from the expected utility, will be estimated
undiminished ; and, at the same time, the expected toil will be weighed as a
thing by itself. If I hunger but am too lazy to work, I still continue to feel
the hunger, and thus estimate the value of food according to the measure of
my hunger ; only it may happen that the presentation of this value is not
sufficient to overcome my laziness.

costs go back in the last resort to labour, and if the existence
of capital-costs cannot be denied, capital-costs must ultimately
go back to labour-costs—capital must be labour.

The attempt to reduce capital to labour has been made
in two ways, both of them following out the same fundamental idea. Labour must be shown to be the primary
economic element, and capital represented as a secondary or
derivative form of it. Labour value appears as the primitive
economic value from which capital value is derived.

The first of the two efforts made to prove this proposition
is deduced from the manner in which capital works. The effect of
all capital is either to save labour or to increase the result of
labour. Does not a machine save human labour ? Does it
not bring it to greater productiveness ? As a matter of fact,
there are forms of capital which are able to render services
as human labour renders them, and which can, to that extent,
be substituted for labour. But can this be maintained of all
capital ? What labour power, for example, does a raw
material replace ? And, on the other hand, it may undoubtedly be said of many kinds of labour, with equal
right, that their effects are either to save capital or to
increase capital. Capital frequently supplants labour, but
frequently also labour supplants capital. Where wages are
low every undertaker will save his capital and employ more
labourers.

The second attempt is much more important. It points
to the origin of capital. Here we go back to the first begin-
nings of the acquisition of capital. All capital has, in the
last resort—says this theory—been obtained by labour, and on
this ground all capital ultimately represents labour. In the
most varied forms, and illustrated by a perfect wealth of
examples, this thought finds itself in many writers. It is
found in Adam Smith and Ricardo, and it is triumphantly
adopted by the socialists in order to make good their contention that all costs are labour-costs, and that capital is simply
" materialised labour."

It is not easy to imagine greater contradictions than the
labour theory presents when it takes up this line — more
particularly in the extreme socialistic conception of it. Let
the reader judge ! First, the economic valuation of labour

is explained by the peculiar nature of labour — that its employment necessitates personal sacrifice. Then capital, after being recognised as materialised labour, and so labour that has become impersonal, is subjected to the same valuation ;—a proceeding for which there is no possible justification. First, it is asserted that labour is the only productive power ; that it alone produces, creates goods, creates value ; that capital is merely its dead instrument : and then capital emerges from its shell and becomes labour, which contributes its part in determining the cost value of goods. At first it is asserted that capital and labour stand in the strongest opposition to one another, and then every distinction disappears save the one, that capital, like labour, may indeed give value, but may not, like it, receive value. Materialised labour is labour, but no share in the return shall be imputed to it.

It would not be right to entirely reject a theory on account of its contradictions. There might be a kernel of truth in it, and that kernel might be rejected along with the rest. We shall, therefore, submit the contention we are discussing to a further test, though, truth to tell, it will only be to find that seldom, if ever, has so small a truth been clothed in so much error.

As we have seen, products are valued by their costs only when they can be reproduced for the amount of the same. Capital, as a rule, consists of products, and this proposition applies to capital as to other products. Capital may be valued according to its costs *in so far as it can be reproduced for the amount of the costs.* The costs actually expended since the beginning of history in gradually forming our present capital—and it may be noted in passing that no one knows the amount of these costs, and that there has never been offered a less accurate standard for any measurement whatever —are taken as little into consideration as any costs which, though actually expended, would never again be so expended. If all that was wanted economically to replace the capital consumed was to regain it by labour, then capital might be economically measured by labour alone, and would represent economically nothing but labour. If, for instance, coal consumed could be replaced simply by the labourers bringing new coal to the surface, without any assistance whatever beyond the labour of their hands, the coal would be worth just so much labour as was needed to bring it to the surface. If a machine could be made by labourers, without any other assistance than that afforded by other labourers collecting for them valueless materials, and simply using their bodily strength to shape and combine them, the value of this machine would be measured by the quantity of labour that had been expended upon it. So long, however, as capital is consumed in order to produce capital, the factor of capital cannot be dismissed from among the costs of capital, and, therefore, from the costs of all the products of capital ; and, so long as it is credited with the use value which experience assures us may be received from it, this factor will continue to be counted alongside of labour in the estimates of costs.

The idea that capital represents labour and nothing more, may be held so long as economists draw their examples, as they usually do, from the circumstances of a Crusoe or a savage, where the chief features are the slaying of wild animals, primitive bows and arrows, bark canoes, rude axes, and the like—where capital, so to speak, is always conceived of in a state of nature. In face of the complicated economical phenomena of a wealthy and developed society the idea loses all weight. The labour theory, with its assumptions which take no count of historical development, was well enough in a science belonging to the time when men spoke of Natural Rights and the Philosophy of Nature. At that period of history this theory was worth being taken up by any gifted genius who could make it throw a first ray of light into the dark mass of economic phenomena. Even at a later period it might have tempted some thoughtful mind to give a thorough systematic examination to its illusive ideas. But for men who have gone through the school of the founders of our science, and have had the benefit of all the experience and elaboration of these founders, and of their successors, it is only worthy of a schoolboy to hold for ever by the opinions of the first teachers. A great thought may in the long run turn into a childish error.

To the manufacturer who owns it, as to the labourers whom it aids, and as indeed to every one, a machine is an instrument, capable of certain useful work, whose production necessitates a certain consumption of labour, of other machines, of tools, and so forth. What must people think of a science which casts aside this simple definition, and informs the manufacturer that, in his machine, he possesses merely the " materialised " labour, the " previous " labour, of all those who have ever contributed anything towards the complete machine since the making of the first rough tool onward ? It is an ingenious way of looking at things, no doubt, but one that lends extraordinarily little aid towards advancing the practical purposes of economic life. What buyer has ever paid a price, or seller demanded one, what producer ever expended costs, or what chancellor ever laid a tax upon value, based upon such a consideration as this ? Is it conceivable that any one will ever allow his economic conclusions to be guided by such a consideration ? After all, in economic theory we must make up our minds whether we intend to explain economic life, or to pursue after useless and fanciful ideas.

# CHAPTER XI

## THE COST THEORIES (*continued*). INTEREST AS AN ELEMENT IN COST

IN calculating the cost value of his products every undertaker, in addition to the value of the capital consumed, includes interest upon the whole capital sunk and bound up in the production, even on that which remains unconsumed, for the period during which the capital must remain sunk. It is a matter of familiar observation that the exchange value of products, in so far as it is influenced by costs, expresses also the interest thus calculated. If the production of one article costs merely labour and circulating capital, while that of another requires, in addition to the same expenditure of labour and circulating capital, a large outlay of fixed capital, the second product (neglecting, of course, the quota for amortisation) will be considered the more valuable by the interest on the whole fixed capital. The question now arises whether we have, in this circumstance also, a phenomenon of natural value; whether it is in the interest of society generally, or merely in that of the individual undertaker, that interest should be calculated among costs, and whether this principle would require to be observed in the communistic state also.

There is something that strikes one as peculiar in the idea of including interest among costs. Torrens' objection is well known. Interest, he says, is profit, and must first be earned through production as the surplus of return over costs. Thus it is impossible to reckon it among costs.

From the point of terminology Torrens' objection is certainly justified. If we wish, on the one hand, to fix the net return, we shall not impute interest to costs, but if, on the other hand, we are seeking for the cost value of products, interest must be included. In these two cases the term " costs " is used in an entirely different sense. And this is an error in so far as the double meaning remains unnoticed, and is, in any case, a misfortune, whether noticed or not. It would be better to have a second name for the second use of the term.

When we put the name on one side, and examine the actual matter of Torrens' objection, we come to a different conclusion. Here the objection entirely breaks down. It proves too much. It is not only interest that is derived from the return and its value, but the value of capital itself. Torrens' argument expanded runs thus :—the value of products is first ; interest, capital value, the value of production goods generally, second. Right enough up to this point. We have come to the same conclusion, and argued from it that production goods have, as against products, no independent power to create value. On the other hand, we have acknowledged that they do possess the power to equalise the value of products. In virtue of this power, and of no higher one, do they influence cost value generally, and this power cannot be denied to interest, on account of its origin in the return, so far, that is to say, as the conditions in this case are similar to those which hold as regards the elements of costs hitherto considered.

This, as a matter of fact, is the case. As we know, there is a constant tendency towards a uniform rate of increment for all capital in one and the same market, and, on the whole, the rate is realised.  From this it follows, on the one hand, that nothing can be produced whose use value does not at least yield the universal increment on capital—which is an indirect determination of the value of products by interest, in the way of determining the amounts produced.  And it follows, on the other hand, that every product whose use value, regarded by itself, might yield a somewhat higher increment, can be valued only according to the universal rate of interest, to the extent that it can be reproduced at the price of the same—which is a direct determination of value.  If things may not be produced under the general rate of interest, and if they cannot be valued above the general rate of interest, their final value must, along with the other elements of costs, include the interest according to the amount and duration of the capital employed.

The principle of including interest among costs follows from a plan of production which aims at obtaining the highest rate of increment from every employment of capital. And as it results from this, so again has it a reflex influence in controlling the plan and giving it definite limits.  If interest were not estimated among costs, or were not estimated on the whole amount of capital expended, or for the entire length of time during which the capital remains employed, the distribution of capital goods among the individual branches of production could not be so regulated as to attain the highest possible rate of increment.  It would then be permissible to employ capital where it only covered its consumption, but brought no increment, or where it did not obtain the highest increment, or the increment on the whole amount of capital sunk, or the increment over the whole period of time when it was sunk in the productive process.

Under certain circumstances it is necessary to include even compound interest among costs ; that is to say, when the period of time during which the capital is sunk exceeds the period at the end of which interest would usually be expected. Products are themselves re-employed as interest bearing capital, and it is therefore so far profitable to find productions which have a shorter process.  The products of longer processes of production must receive an equivalent against this advantage of having interest on interest at an earlier date, and they obtain it by a corresponding increase in their use value.  Only in this way is the highest degree of utilisation in production as regards time obtained and regulated.

Connected with this is an exceedingly curious conclusion.

In the cost value of products, undertakers include the interest due to that portion of their money capital which they must hold, for paying the wages of their labourers, until the sale of the products takes place.  In the communistic state this money capital would not be required.  It would, therefore, appear that, in the communistic state, the interest expenditure in production would be correspondingly lower, and that the present manner of doing is so far opposed to the natural laws of valuation.  As a matter of fact this is not the case ; in this point also the interest of the undertaker is identical with that of the community at large, and leads to the economic valuation of goods.  The undertaker, in including the interest on his wage fund, simply estimates and expresses—with reference to human labour—the differences in time of employment.  It is not the same thing to employ ten labourers during one year or to employ one labourer during ten years, any more than it is the same thing to employ a capital of £100 for one year or a capital of £10 for ten years.  In the former case as in the latter, the principles of economic action require that, besides ordinary interest, compound interest also be reckoned to the value of the product, if a proper distribution of production is to be attained.

It needs no explanation that, in virtue of this, production is the more limited the longer the period of the process, for the reason that a corresponding increase in the value of the product is required to make the longer process appear sufficiently profitable.  Productions of very long duration must yield a very rich return if they are to bear the burden of the interest which accumulates up till the time when they yield their first return.

# CHAPTER XII

### THE COST THEORIES (*continued*).   LAND RENT AS AN
### ELEMENT IN COST

LAND—understanding the word in that familiar theoretical sense which refers to the indestructible part of land—suffers no loss of substance in production.   Among the costs of agricultural products, consequently, there is nothing to be calculated for what we may call the "substance-value" of land.   Ricardo goes farther than this, and affirms that the rent of land, like the value of land, cannot enter into costs.   This contention is entirely in harmony with his theory that rent is a net differential rent, only ascribable to the better classes of land employed, while the poorest classes, those which are available in superfluity, yield no rent.   If the classes of land which are last employed are free and bear no rent, the determining costs will, as a matter of fact, be made up without consideration of rent, simply by the sum of costs in capital and labour which are applied to the poorest classes of land.   The rent yielded by the better qualities of land originates, as we know, from the surplus return of products which they assure to equal costs of capital and labour and equal value of products.   Rent is, therefore, derived from the return, without finding expression in the value of the products.

It is otherwise if rent is not merely a differential but a general one.   A general rent must enter into costs just as interest does.   It must be included in the calculation if the determining amount of costs is to be obtained.   Where all qualities of lands and all powers of the land, even those of the lowest class, are required to meet the demand, and all bear rent, the circumstance that classes of land of the poorest quality are devoted to a definite production, and so "tied up" throughout the duration of that production, is not a matter of economic indifference.   For, so long as they remain tied up, their services are withheld from other productions to which they might have been devoted.   In case of failure, their rent, which would otherwise have been obtained, is lost. Their rent consequently belongs to and must be included in the cost of the products.

For Ricardo it is of primary importance to persist in maintaining the foregoing contention, that land rent is always differential. His economic system cannot dispense with the proposition depending upon it, that rent does not enter into the value of products. He imagines it possible to bring the value of products under a general law, and consider them simply as multiples of units of capital and units of labour. The intervention of interest already forms a disturbing element in his law, but he believes himself able to prove that the disturbing element thus introduced is of no great importance. But if, besides, the element of rent plays a part in the value, the whole laborious structure of his theory falls to the ground, and his attempt to derive the value of products from labour, and to unite empirical amounts of value with amounts philosophically demanded, is completely over-turned.

For the theory of value which we represent, on the other hand, it is a matter of entire indifference whether the circumstances are such that rent remains purely differential, and thus does not enter into the value of products, or are such as cause rent to become general, and thus to enter of necessity into the value of products. The one case fits into our system as well as the other.

Further, there are certain exceptions to the proposition that a differential rent cannot enter into the value of products. Alongside of those employments of land which may be regarded as the principal ones, and of those forms of rent which might be called the original ones, there exist others which are secondary and derivative. The principal employment of fertile land is in agriculture, but the building of a factory upon land suitable for cultivation is an example of a secondary employment,—of an employment, to express it otherwise, for which land in general will be less required, and which in itself would never exhaust the available supply of lands, as the agricultural demand might easily do. If a fertile field is employed as site for a factory the agricultural rent which, in other circumstances, might be expected from it, will have to be surrendered. The sacrifice of this rent means an outlay of costs which cannot be neglected in calculating the costs of the factory's products. Whatever the amount of the rent, it must be deducted from the value of the products made on that building ground, and it is not till the remainder covers the costs of capital and labour that the calculation is complete.

The case is similar with the ground-rents of dwelling-houses. Ground-rent in a large town is never a simple differential rent. At the periphery of the town, house-rent finds its measure in agricultural rent, and rises towards the business centre, according to desirability of situation. The more valuable for cultivation the land round about the town is, the dearer will be the houses in that town. To this extent agricultural rent acts as a universal element of costs in the calculation of house-rents. The differential rents received from favoured sites do not make houses dearer, but are rather a result of the high valuation placed upon houses in a favourable situation. And in so far as the need for dwelling-houses and the need for business premises compete with each other, does the one employment of land act upon the other as an element of costs.

In following out this line of thought we see that Ricardo's proposition gradually loses its applicability almost entirely, as the cultivation of land becomes very artificial, and the uses of land multiply. The various employments begin to compete with each other, and one has always to make choice among several; thus the differential rents which are surrendered take effect as costs. Ricardo's proposition that the rent of land does not enter into costs, can be legitimately applied only to land devoted of necessity to one distinct use, such as mines, vineyards, and the like.

## CHAPTER XIII

### THE SERVICE OF INDIVIDUAL ECONOMIC VALUE IN NATIONAL ECONOMY [1]

THE supreme principle of economic action being utility, value presents a means by which to grasp the utility of goods in a simplified and comprehensive manner, and so to control the employment of goods. Thus we have described the service of value in economy generally, in doing which we have assumed that value is estimated according to natural laws, and that we are concerned with the valuation of goods in stocks, or marginal valuation.

The return value of production goods and the cost value of products are likewise phenomena of natural marginal value. They afford us a simplified and widely comprehensive estimate of utility in the most complicated circumstances of production. The most heterogeneous kinds of production goods obtain a common measure of valuation through their common products : their return values are multiples of the value of the common marginal products. The most heterogeneous products receive a common measure of valuation through their common elements of cost ; their cost values are multiples of the value of the common cost goods. Different return values, or different cost values, bear the same relation to one another as amounts of goods which are multiples of the same unit. In this way it becomes possible to estimate these value relations in figures, although the value and the amounts of value have their origin in the incalculable intensities of want.

And yet, it is not this consideration that attracts our attention at this point. Now when we have pursued the main threads of the much-tangled web of productive combinations, first from the return up to the co-operating production goods, and then back again from the cost goods to the products, another consideration forces itself to the front : namely, that in any larger economy whatever, particularly in such a one as has

---

[1] See *Ursprung des Werthes*, p. 165.

the compass of a national economy, and is based upon a complicated system of production, it is quite impossible to dispense with value if we wish to have any clear notion of the utility of goods. A Robinson Crusoe does not require the aid of value; he can arrive at a right decision in every instance by simply testing what manner of treatment is likely to secure him the greatest amount of utility on the whole. In a national economy, on the other hand, with a complicated system of production, it is impossible in any way to make the necessary economic decisions by testing the utility of goods *on the whole.* No one can take in the total result of a community's production at a glance. There are too many goods, and too many possible employments of goods, to permit of making one survey of the whole, and one comparison on the whole. Things must be gone into individually; utility must be divided up, and every good have measured out to it its share in the total result; then only is it possible to recognise individually which are the poorer, which the more profitable, and which the best. But how otherwise is utility to be measured out to individual goods than by applying to them the methods of marginal valuation, the principle of which is, to give them that utility which is dependent on the smallest quantity of goods that is yet practically taken into consideration?

And, further, the economical employments of goods result from the relations of supply and demand. It appears then that it would be impossible to discover these economical employments if the amounts of supply and demand were not known numerically. But who knows the amounts of supply and demand in the widely-extended economy of a nation, or, indeed, in the world economy, the relations of which make themselves felt everywhere? Wholesale merchants of course try to make themselves acquainted with them, and do as a fact succeed in obtaining certain figures representing what comes from production, which are tolerably exact, especially as regards large production. But, on the other hand, it is almost impossible for them to obtain, with any measure of exactitude, the equally important figures of demand. If, in spite of this, it can be maintained that economy on the whole is capable of adjusting itself to the variations in supply and demand, this is due solely to the aid afforded by marginal valuation. Value, as marginal value, gives expression in the marginal calculation to the effect produced by the existing amounts of supply and demand, even if these amounts have not hitherto been measured. No owner can attempt to get rid of a good, no buyer can be eager to get one, without this circumstance having an effect on the market, and influencing the sensitive medium of value. Although no one is able, and even though no one should attempt, to figure out the amounts of supply and demand, value shows, with numerical exactitude and down to the finest gradations that people usually make in practical life, the relation between supply and demand in so far as these tend to make themselves felt in exchange. Value shows the effect of causes which in themselves are hidden. And through the fact that we adapt ourselves to this effect, this value, it finally becomes possible to adapt ourselves to the causes, the amounts of supply and demand, and thus to regulate an economy with due regard to economic laws. If at any given point of time the value of all goods remains as it has hitherto been, we may be pretty sure of acting economically and according to the standard of economical insight already obtained, if we retain the disposition of all goods in production and consumption unaltered. If value has altered at any point, it is an indication that the present disposition of goods must be changed, and changed in direct accordance with the change of value. Where value has risen there must new goods be directed, be it for production or for consumption : where it has fallen these goods must be withdrawn. And this transferring of goods from one point to another must be continued until all values are brought once more into equilibrium, and for every stock of goods the law of equal valuation of all its units is re-established.

A knowledge of the values of goods, such as has existed in every economy up till now, is consequently, in itself, one of the most valuable of possessions. It is almost as valuable as the possession of the goods themselves, inasmuch as it is the key to their use. The sum of thousands of years of experience concerning the sources of supply of goods, and the suitability or otherwise of the conditions of their production, as well as concerning the amount of demand for them, is represented in the figures of value handed down to us. Were a nation to lose all remembrance of these, it would be an enormous economic

misfortune.  An almost incalculable period of time, an almost
incalculable amount of error and loss, would have to be gone
through, before the nation could again obtain mastery over the
relations of goods formerly expressed, with numerical clearness,
for each individual good by means of value.

By the socialist programme it is proposed to manage the
counting of stocks and calculation of demand, in the state of
the future, by means of government statistics.  Could this plan
be sufficiently carried out it would be so far possible to dispense
with marginal value.  On the other hand, it can never be
dispensed with where the finding of an expression for the
utility in the individual good is concerned.  To dispense with
it would be equivalent to giving up the attempt to determine
utility in the individual case, and being content with making a
general determination as to the direction of production and
consumption, leaving out consideration of the quantities which
it is desirable to gain or consume.

Here I leave the sphere of conditions of value in private
economies.  Clearly as I realise the imperfection of what I
have tried to do, I yet trust that the reader will have been
convinced that exchange value, as expressed in price, is not
only governed by price competition, but contains a deeper
economic content; that exchange value, although mixed with
foreign elements, unites in itself all the essential elements of
the natural valuation of goods, the valuation which is indispensable to economic action.  If the prices for all similar
goods in one and the same market are equal in amount, it is
because, in the last resort, the valuations of all similar goods
in one and the same economy are equal.  If the prices for all
goods in one stock are fixed at the marginal point, it is because,
in the last resort, the valuations are so fixed.  In so far as
prices represent natural value, an enormous and arduous
mental labour of calculating the exchange value of things is
saved.  By thousandfold weighing and consideration of the
productive and other economical relations, each individual good
gets measured out to it that amount of the total return
which must be directly imputed to it out of the total amount
of the total production, if the goods are to be profitably dealt
with.  I have chosen the word "Imputation" after much deliberation.  It is not only to production goods that return is

imputed and distributed; all goods get imputed and distributed out to them the utility which they give only when co-operating with one another.    There is no satisfaction that is not prepared for and followed by others; all our satisfactions stand in mutual action and reaction with each other. Every man's means are thus linked together.    Individual economic valuation succeeds, nevertheless, in distributing this whole, and imputing to each separate portion of wealth its share of return, in such a way that, as a rule, every one is well advised who, within the sphere of his own individual economy, takes the amount of value thus ascertained as measure for his economic action.

Where exchange value diverges from natural value, something else must of course obtain, but it is beyond our special task to enter on this consideration.

It still remains to show how far natural laws require that individual economic valuation be complemented by the economical considerations of a community, or, more particularly, of a state.

# BOOK VI

VALUE IN THE ECONOMY OF THE STATE

# CHAPTER I

INTRODUCTION

In the exchange transactions of private economies with one another, objective exchange value acts as the economical measure of goods, while, within individual private economies, this part is taken by subjective value as each individual owner estimates it, whether it be subjective exchange value in connection with objective exchange value, or use value independent of it. All these forms of value, reflecting with more or less truth their common prototype, go back to one original form, viz. that which we have indicated as natural value; natural value being, in the last resort, the resultant of two simple fundamental components, quantity of goods and utility of goods. Even such phenomena as land rent, interest on capital, costs, are natural phenomena of value which could be suppressed only by a force so powerful that it would at the same time injure economic life and action itself.

Besides private economies there exist a great many public economies. The question now is whether, in them also, the value of goods holds the same place, and whether in them it takes on any new and peculiar forms. I shall limit my inquiry to the most important of social economies, that of the state, and deal even with it only in the most general way. The theory of social economies is yet in its infancy, and it would be impossible to discuss value in them at all exhaustively without first having thoroughly gone into a great many other subjects. It, therefore, appears to me best to confine myself to an entirely general and comprehensive statement.

State economy divides itself into two great spheres, the economy of income or finance, and the economy of expenditure or administration. Administration, however, belongs to the economy of the state only in so far as it is determined by economical considerations. This is the case mainly where regard is had to the material interests of the people, that is to say, in the economic administration or the economic superintendence of the state; but there is no single form of national activity but must follow economic principles, if only in the second instance; viz. in regard to the careful and economical employment of its resources.

Up till quite recently economists have not, either in finance or administration, recognised in value that importance which, by analogy, might be suspected from its *rôle* in private economy. With regard, in particular, to finance, theory has managed to do almost entirely without value. The principles of taxation have been and are almost always stated without value being mentioned, or if mentioned it has been, at the most, only cursorily touched upon by way of comparison. Taxation gets its warrant in specific considerations, not in general economic ones. We speak of minimum of subsistence, ability to pay, sacrifice of taxation, progressive taxation and so on, almost entirely as if they were facts and conceptions belonging to a distinct sphere, while neither is the relation of this sphere to the fundamental phenomena of all economy made clear, nor is any attempt made to make it clear.

Adam Smith and his school treat the economic administration of the state also in a similar manner. They explain it simply by the necessities of national life, and value never enters into their consideration. Where they do make mention of it exchange value is always understood,—that being the only value which the school, as a rule, recognises. Any peculiar value pertaining to the economy of a state is never discussed, as in general all economic conceptions are borrowed entirely from the circumstances of private economies, and bear their characteristics. Connected with this—as cause and effect—there is a strong tendency to limit the sphere of state economy, and to extend that of private economy. Every theory formulates its conceptions in conformity with its fundamental tendencies, but it strengthens these fundamental tendencies in turn by the logical weight which the conceptions once constructed exert.   A person who recognises no other value than exchange value will, wherever his common sense says that it is a question of value, generally allow exchange value to decide the matter in its one-sided way, or will, at all events, give to it too great a preponderance.   The way in which Adam Smith rejects protection and argues for free trade may be regarded as typical of the school.   The national income is to be measured by exchange value : but thus measured free trade will undoubtedly give the larger income in the near future : consequently, as it is always the income of the present that forms the capital of the future, free trade assures the greatest amount of well-being for all time to come.

In Germany this one-sidedness of the English school was early recognised.   Many writers, as, for instance, Friedrich List, actively combated it.   List placed his " theory of productive forces " alongside of his " theory of value " : exchange value was to be the determining force in private economic relations, whereas, in the economy of the state, " productive force " was to take its place — an antithesis whose inadequacy is most clearly shown from the consideration that " productive forces " are themselves estimated according to exchange value.   Most writers took a different course.   They tried, gradually, and at first altogether academically, to broaden the private economic views of the English School, in such a way as to make them as far as possible applicable to all economic relations.   As regards value in particular, exchange value was traced back to the general conception of use value, and then conceived of as national or social use value.   Thus little by little the theory altered its formal character.   It undoubtedly became more rounded, more plausible, more adaptable, but at the same time more indefinite and inexact.   Without following accurately the further development of this theory, I may point out its most important fact : that the scientific discussion did finally give up its academic hesitation, and, in spite of the slightness of its theoretic foundation, laid down with success and decision principles for the practical formation of a state economy.   Like the financial system of the European states, their economic politics were gradually reformed by the active assistance of theory, although theory itself had not completely accomplished its task, nor, indeed, was quite aware what that task was. The "theory" was a highly-developed technology, capable of giving right direction, although it did not succeed in finding its justification—and with that, of course, its limitation —in absolutely convincing clearness.

The lately published work of E. Sax (*Grundlegung der Theoretischen Staatswirthschaft*) is the first to complete the transition from technology to the theory of national economy, and has thus at last reached a goal aimed at by the German economists through a long and steady development. In the sphere of administration Sax has succeeded in indicating how public interests may have the widest play, while still maintaining a fixed economic conception which holds fast by the essentially economic. The economic is one and the same in all its forms, everywhere entirely distinct from the non-economic. Very important is the application of Sax's work to the sphere of finance—all the more important that here he had almost no predecessors—and that the idea is thought out into details with great clearness. The whole system of imposts rests on value: this simple proposition makes the science of finance for the first time what it should always have been, a part of political economy. "Imposts of all kinds are examples of collective valuation which find their full explanation in the general nature of the phenomenon of value. The truth which finds expression in this formula is directly decisive for the theory of national economy, as a branch of the total theory of political economy, balancing that of private economy. The simplicity of the solution is a guarantee of its correctness. The apple falls from the tree and the stars describe their courses in obedience to one and the same law, that of gravitation. A Robinson Crusoe and a nation numbering a hundred million souls obey one and the same law in their economical transactions, that of value" (pp. 307-8).

The statement which follows is so general and so condensed that I have had but little chance of going into the rich contents of Sax's book. In the interests of the statement I have, moreover, considered it wiser, even where I disagree with Sax, to refrain from the most part from any attempt to prove my divergences with any great exactitude, as, in this portion of my work, even more than in the former, I have neglected the literary aspect of the subject.  Here, as formerly, my task has been to demonstrate, comprehensively and as a whole, what has hitherto been considered only in isolation, if at all.  It appeared to me foreign to the plan of my work, and likely only to increase the difficulty of the task which chiefly concerned me,—that of affording a survey of the whole subject,—were I to let myself be carried away by criticism and polemic into detail which I should not have gone into for its own sake.

# CHAPTER II

### THE PROVINCE OF A STATE ECONOMY

IT is generally assumed that the object of the individual economy is provision for the wants of the individual—that is to say, those wants which the individual feels as an individual ; and that the economy of a community provides for the common or collective wants—that is, those which are experienced by the individual as member of a community, or, to put it differently, the wants of a community.  The economy of a state therefore provides for the wants of the state, *i.e.* those wants experienced by the citizens of a state in consideration of their civic connection with each other.  This conception, however, scarcely corresponds with the actual division of the economic sphere.  National interests, which are undoubtedly to be reckoned under the head of collective interests, are frequently furthered by personal sacrifice and expenditure.  And more numerous instances may be adduced of the contrary case—that individual interests are fostered by collective efforts.  The desire to possess a means of coming and going to one's business, is undoubtedly personal in the highest degree ; but the highways of traffic have been included among the concerns of the commonwealth almost since the beginning of time.  In the communistic state the care of providing for the entire sum of individual wants, would fall altogether to the economy of the state without these wants having changed their nature in any way.  It must, therefore, be some circumstance which does not touch the nature of the want itself that determines the division of the economic sphere.

A simple consideration enables us to recognise what circumstance this is.

The personal ability of the individual is in many cases sufficient to secure him the realisation of his personal wishes. In particular, the sphere within which the individual is capable of making himself felt with effect, is quite extraordinarily enlarged when men have learnt to make use of the division and co-operation of labour. By means of this they enter into combinations and exchange with one another, and thus increase enormously their power of work, while, at the same time, they calculate and distribute out again to the individual the advantages obtained, and thus remain separate from each other, as individuals with individual rights. There are, however, certain results which demand a more intimate kind of connection,—a condition of real community,—and cannot be obtained without it. The desire to obtain these results, which often amounts to the feeling of a peremptory necessity, leads to the formation of the commonwealth.

There are various reasons which may make the attainment of a certain result dependent upon the formation of collective bodies, and upon the carrying out of collective actions.

In the first place may be mentioned the nature of the action in question. For many kinds of action the individual, as individual, is not qualified ; he feels himself too weak, or, it may be, quite incapable. From the first it has devolved upon the state to represent the common weal, in cases where nothing but the solidarity of many or of all is able to create the force that is lacking to the scattered individuals. Only as a united state can a people hope to ward off its enemies, and to protect its citizens when in foreign countries. Only a union of people can succeed in guarding a country's peace, and preserving order against crime within its borders. From the general feeling of justice are obtained the weight and power necessary for the laying down of laws which will bind every one, and for the appointing of judges and officers who will make every one bow before the one common law. And thus numerous interests, partly collective, partly the most ordinary general interests of the individual, lead to an ever-widening extension of the sphere of the state's activity, wherever the opinion prevails that only the state possesses the power of offering any guarantee of the satisfaction, or the full satisfaction, that is desired.

In the case of such actions as are executed in common, there is an overwhelming tendency to bear the burden in common, and to enjoy the results in common. Even if the power of the state is set in motion for the sake of one solitary citizen, the occasion cannot well be judged merely from the standpoint of the interest of that one citizen. The very fact that the power of the state has been set in motion at all, engages the interest of the public, because this power, once set in motion, cannot be allowed to move in vain. All its future success depends on the recognition of this. For this reason the outcome, for instance, of every single criminal or civil process is full of importance to the whole community. Every such process must be so conducted that respect for the law may be strengthened, not shaken. But generally speaking the occasions on which the machinery of the state appears on the scene are, in their origin, matters of great importance and of great compass—frequently, of the greatest importance and the greatest compass ; they are indeed such matters as only the united strength of the whole people is sufficient for. This circumstance of itself makes it impossible, as a rule, to divide out among the individual citizens the result obtained by the combined effort, or even to charge it to the individual according to its effects ; hence the necessity of making the benefit universally accessible, or ascribing it to the people as a whole without further distinction. It happens comparatively seldom that individuals can be indicated and singled out, whose interests are exceptionally concerned, and for whom the services of the state may be exceptionally interposed and charged.

In the second place, just as the results of a war are not to be bought or sold, and a war cannot therefore be carried on as a private matter,[1] so it happens that, among the undertakings for which the means and powers of the individual citizens suffice, there are very many which must be excluded from the

---

[1] This, however, is not the reason why it is reserved for government to carry on wars ; that reason being simply that no private individual possesses the means necessary for it.

circle of private business because of the impossibility of obtaining any profit out of them. The most various circumstances may have this effect. The streets of a town would be useless for purposes of traffic if they were not free to use without payment; this makes it impossible that any citizen should retain public routes for his own benefit. The same principle holds in all cases where goods whose production costs something must be made over to the public free of charge—"quasi-free goods," as Menger calls them. Many undertakings also, although the public interest demands them at once, give promise of return only in the distant future;—so distant indeed that no private individual could be expected to wait for it: this is the case, *e.g.*, as regards many railways. Very often again it is doubtful whether the return of an undertaking will ever be sufficient to cover the costs, while at the same time the results in case of success are temptingly large; here private enterprise would hesitate, either on account of the great amount of capital necessary or for other incidental reasons. Very often there is a scarcity of capable and energetic private undertakers, simply on account of the defective economical development of the citizens. And there are often cases where the goods concerned are, for the private economy, only in process of becoming — still incomplete, unripe, latent; where the goods must first be got at, or the goods that are to supplement and complement them be discovered, before they become capable of rendering any useful service. How much latent labour power there is which must first become conscious of its own existence and train itself, before it can find a market! What hidden wealth may not slumber in a land favoured by nature but uncultivated, its existence suspected, even known, but out of reach owing to the general backward condition of industry, of wealth, of education, of credit, of law, or of peace! And, although, in such a case, there is as yet no secure foundation for private enterprise, what government would not regard it as a duty itself to come forward and take hold, not only in the way of general administration, but by economic undertakings which train and ripen human faculty though they may give no direct return? Sometimes only the want is there, crying urgently for satisfaction, while those who feel it have no power to pay for its satisfaction; in this case no private undertaker can do anything, and the state must step in to mitigate an evil which might grow to be a great public ill.  Many other similar circumstances might be added, all acting in the same direction; that is to say, excluding private enterprise by reason of their unprofitableness, but demanding the activity of the state on account of the importance of the goods concerned.

In the third place, many undertakings which lie within the power of a citizen, and which also hold forth to him a promise of gain, are reserved to the state, for the simple reason that they would put too much power into the hands of the private undertaker, or assure him too great a gain.  The fear is that the exceptional position they would necessarily give to the person who undertook them might be misused.   The businesses which belong to this class are mostly necessary monopolies,—particularly monopolies of great extent, such as the post and the railway.   We do not expect, in an independent private undertaker, the requisite reliableness, or the will to undertake such huge businesses, or to carry them through as we should like ; or we expect that too high a price would be charged for the service. But in all these points people look for something better from a government.   This does not, however, in the least involve that the form of undertaking for profit be entirely rejected. It may be retained, but, with the endeavour to obtain the highest business return, must be conjoined, in some way or other, the endeavour to serve the interests of the public.   In particular, where any considerable want is concerned while the power to pay is wanting, the service must be undertaken at limited prices, — that is to say, valuation according to exchange value must be replaced by valuation according to natural value.   Thus emerges the " public enterprise."  In the communistic state all production would be the affair of the state, and fall under public enterprise, from a consideration which amounts essentially to this ;—that private production is one-sided, and looks to the interests of the richer classes, while putting in the background the interests of the community in general.   Even the affairs of the private household would be, for the most part, given over to the state.

If we cast a glance over the whole series of duties which constitute the economy of the state, it will easily be seen that, apart from the diversity of originating causes just described, they are also distinguished from each other by their *content*. Certain of them—of which the last-mentioned group is the best instance—are very closely related to private undertakings. Like them they have to do with the direct application of labour to goods ; they have to do with detail and with · individual production ; and they are scattered in countless separate actions and occupations — many of these of a similar nature — over countless separate goods. Here it is considerations more remote and far - reaching that exclude private administration in matters where, otherwise, it might be suitable enough. This can be most clearly realised if we consider the businesses of production and of housekeeping as transferred to a communistic state. These would indeed cease to be matters of private economy in the personal sense, but, essentially or technically, they would remain, if the expression may be employed, " economic in detail."

Quite different is the character of the remaining acts of state economy, which chiefly belong to the first and second groups just described. Their duties do not admit of being discharged by private economies for various reasons, but these reasons all lead, in the last resort, to the same issue ;—that such acts are beyond the calculation of the individual, either because their products cannot be bought and sold, or cannot be bought and sold individually. Their results go without money and without price to the public,—either in whole or in great part,—according to what Sax calls the *Princip des allgemeinen Genussgutes*. They are transactions on a great scale, working with large means, and large returns,—returns which it is often entirely impossible to distribute. They assure the general foundations of personal life and of economic action. Their results must be distributed over all the community and not divided out individually, even supposing it possible to conceive of them as distributed to the individual. Of course they are undertaken on account of the utility they promise ; but it is frequently far from certain—as *e.g.* in the case of war —whether the desired result will ever be attained. And even if it is attained its amount can, for the most part, be only approximately determined, partly on account of the wide range which it covers, partly on account of the large number of persons concerned, partly on account of the impossibility of conceiving the individual's share in it, partly on account of the long process of development, and the long time that must elapse before many of its effects emerge. Very often all that one knows of an action is that it must not be neglected, and that we must summon all our forces to undertake it; while it is almost entirely uncertain how in the end the life of the people may be affected thereby. Often it is other generations that must pass judgment upon it.

In the communistic state also, if all economical matters are to devolve upon the state, decisions will certainly be made from this point of view; the affairs of the household and of ordinary production will be kept separate from those of the general economic and state administration. In the former case goods will be estimated at their natural value as that is now determined in private economy, *i.e.* according to marginal value; in the latter case, this form of valuation will be—as we shall go on to show—to a great extent abandoned. Alongside of it, or in its stead, will be placed another form of valuation, which we may best call "national economic" valuation,—a term which certainly does not express the formulas of communism, but those of existing economical conditions.

# CHAPTER III

## VALUE IN THE NATURAL ECONOMY OF THE STATE

SUPPOSE the utopian state of communism actually realised, there also, as we have just seen, where all economic life has become the concern of the state, must the same distinction as now be made between private economy and state economy,— though possibly under different names. On one side must be grouped by themselves all those businesses of the household and of production which are now left in the hands of private individuals, together with many undertakings which essentially belong to private economy, but are at present, for special reasons, conducted by the state. On the other side and distinct from these, must be placed all matters of the general

administration of the state—or of all that is economic in it—
and of economic politics in general.  Of course, there would
be no lack of transferences to and from each group, and whatever might be the ruling consideration in the one group would
have a place in the other.  This does not, however, in any way
conflict with the statement that the leading principles in each
must be different.

In the former, or private economic group, where goods are
capable of being measured very accurately as to their amount
and utility, the main endeavour must be to obtain from every
practically measurable portion of goods the greatest amount of
generally recognised utility.  This endeavour must find its expression in an estimate of value which takes its measure, for each
single good, from the margin at which the most perfectly
utilised supply meets the most perfectly sifted demand.  In the
sphere of production such an estimate of value takes, as we are
aware, the form of an estimate of return or of costs.  The value
of stocks of similar goods must be represented as multiples : the
value of production goods combined in the shape of products
as sums of multiples.  The individual amounts must be calculable—in many instances very exactly calculable—against
each other.  An exact economic calculus must be established,
the advantage and disadvantage of every sufficiently familiar
process being put in figures ; and it must be regarded as the
triumph of economic art to exactly ascertain and exactly
realise that plan which the value calculation indicates as the
best.

In the latter, or national economic group, the first principle
must also be to secure the greatest amount of utility, the
highest well-being of the citizens.  But the utility and its
amount will not be so exactly estimated ; will often, indeed,
as we have already proved at length, be very inexactly estimated.  As the means necessary to achieve the ends of the
state are for the most part very extensive, and the more or
less cannot be so exactly determined, the indefiniteness of the
valuation will be increased from the side of the goods also.
The estimate of value will often be very vague, and in many
cases unanimity of opinion regarding it is not to be expected.
More exact estimates will be obtained only as regards such
goods as are also employed in private economy, by transferring

to them the definite estimate obtained by private economy, and also as regards such goods as are obtained through production. But where national economy makes use of specific goods which do not, either by reason of their employment or origin, take to themselves the estimate of private economy;[1] where national economy stands absolutely and entirely by itself, and seeks to guard public interests by specific public methods; there, in place of the quantitative estimate of the value of goods in masses, will emerge the vague and disputable valuation of interests, influenced by inclinations and passions.[2]

The opposition between natural value in national economy and natural value in private economy reduces itself, in effect, to an opposition between vagueness and definiteness, subjective valuation and exact calculation. Even thus the contrast is sufficiently great to obtain clear and peculiar expression in practical politics. Theoretically, of course, there can never be any doubt as to the relation of the two. Just as private economic interests, where they compete with each other, are ranked according to their relative importance, so the interests of private and of national economy are ranked in relation to each other. The more important aim takes precedence of the less important—this forms the theoretic basis on which the estimate of value is built. But how will this rule work in practice when any doubt arises as to the degree of importance? As a matter of fact, the indefinite nature of national economic valuations must in practice frequently give rise to doubts as to the exact relation which the acts of private and of national economy should bear to each other. Very frequently it is the same goods that may be employed by either private or national economy; in the last resort, indeed, there is nothing but one fund out of which to provide for both, and only a few goods are from the first specifically reserved for one or the other sphere. A characteristic and common instance of the competition between the two interests occurs where an undertaking, which is profitable as a private business as shown by its calculable return in direct results, is maintained, from the side of national

---

[1] We may take as illustration the case of a barren island whose occupation is demanded by military or political considerations.

[2] See note at end of chapter.

economy, to have an unfavourable, destructive, or undermining effect; that is to say, as regards results which are more remote and difficult to follow. Alongside of this we have the converse instance, that an undertaking which is unprofitable as a private business, and whose valuable returns do not cover the costs, may, from the point of view of national economy, be regarded as profitable, whether tending to progress or conservative as the case may be. What holds as regards individual undertakings, also obtains as regards whole groups of these,—of the great acts of legislation and administration, of the various branches and spheres of production, of the activity of the producing class of a nation. It might *e.g.* be disputed whether agriculture or the labouring classes ought to have public subsidy—*i.e.* support which might not be justified, from the point of view of private economy, by the value of the land products or the results of labour, but might be justified if one looked at the maintenance of the stability of the national economy and of the life of the people.

In the communistic state, as in the economy of to-day, there will be no lack of occasions which will continually force people to decide anew between considerations of the quantitative and calculable proximate returns—considerations of direct profit,—and of results more remote and less calculable—considerations of general interests. Suppose that the subject were some technical improvement like the establishing of railways, discussions would undoubtedly arise,—as they did at the time when railways were introduced,—as to their utility, feasibility, and consequences. And even after experience has put an end to the general discussion, there will still continue to be a conflict of opinions as to the more exact relation between the calculable results and the incalculable. Or, possibly, there may be a doubt whether the industry of a people should take the direction of trade or of agriculture; whether the power of the labouring classes should be more utilised, or more economised; possibly, also, whether it would be wise to carry on war, whether preparations should be made for it, or whether it might be better to foster the arts of peace, and so forth. And certainly there will always be one party which calculates, and which looks dispassionately to the profitableness or unprofitableness of any scheme, and another, party which looks far ahead and leaves room for imagination and passion. Under different names the economical opposi- tions of interest to-day will recur. The conflict which we may observe now between exchange value and public interests, depends accordingly—apart altogether from the opposition of personal advantage—upon a difference in economic aims which is inevitable, and arises out of natural economic conditions.

If it must be confessed that, in the communistic state, the private economical valuation of goods is not satisfactory because it sometimes neglects necessary deductions, sometimes essential additions, and so comes out too high or too low, we must *a fortiori* say the same of exchange value in the present order of things, where it goes too far in emphasising the characteristics of the private economy. It is the exact calculation and the incalculable but actually observed influ- ences, that, together, make up the full value of goods. The theorist must admit so much, however hard it is for him, when he considers how greatly economic theory loses by it in exact conception of its formulas and precepts. How simple and how easy to apply any advice whenever only calculable quantities are concerned ;—whatever, calculated by exchange value, yields a profit is economically permissible ; everything else is for- bidden ! And how misty and obscure all theoretical solutions become when they put absolute laws aside, and are obliged to appeal to concrete existing circumstances to decide for them ! In the end it is to politics we must leave the task of deciding, as well as of carrying out its decisions in the concrete—re- membering that politics belongs not only to the politician but to political science. However much the pride of theory may suffer in recognising this, it is a fact not to be gainsaid. In order to observe and understand things, they are often thought of as being less complicated than they really are : and this is right enough when nothing further is intended than to simplify the process of thought by beginning at the easiest. But it is not permissible to call a halt at this point, and apply the solution thus found, without more ado, to reality. This is the sort of thing that might be described as " the disease of theory ": to take things first in the way in which they can be most simply grasped, and then to represent the whole world ac- cording to the picture we have just been able to think out for ourselves ; to take what is most easily grasped, or at all events most precisely grasped, for the actual.

Like every exaggeration this also produces its own reaction, viz. the opposition to all theory whatever. The book which my readers now hold in their hands is a proof that I do not share in this opposition. Possibly it may not prove equally clearly that I consider every other direction of investigation, besides the purely theoretical one, necessary and significant in its own place ; but no candid critic will, I hope, find any reason to dispute this.

That the theory, even when it recognises the influences of national economy upon value, in some sort paves the way for politics, is not likely to be denied. The man who has thought out the theory of value to the end, even within the limits just mentioned, will have cause to point with pride to the help which this has afforded him in political science and practical statecraft. It is a matter of the first importance—one without which no decision can be arrived at,—to recognise that there is a sphere within which the estimate of exchange value is applicable, and another in which it is not. Now if we could define these spheres, even in the most general way; if we could keep entirely and clearly separate the laws of the national estimate and the laws of the private estimate of value, so that every one who followed with sufficient earnestness would be convinced that they corresponded to the essential demands of economic action ; if it were possible, besides, to indicate the directions in which the actual course of things diverges from these laws most frequently and with the most serious results :— in that case the foundation for political action would be so plainly laid down, and would compare so well with all the errors and difficulties which beset its path without these principles, that no one would deny that such a theory had justified its existence. To mention only one special case. The representing of goods by weighed and counted sums of barren metal or paper, and the consequent valuation of goods, and of the well-being they secure, by numbers and figures, by items and weights, is in itself a somewhat mysterious matter ; a matter which a man who wishes to obtain a clear view of things might imagine to have an artificial and unhealthy origin ; a matter which does, in fact, lead many an honest and

intelligent thinker to such a conjecture. It is, then, a conclusion well worthy of consideration when a science succeeds
in proving that such a manner of procedure is, at bottom and
in its own place, sound and simple, and that it would be
impossible to obtain a more exact and distinct measure for
the thousandfold variety of economic satisfactions, than that
afforded, under the necessary conditions, by the natural
marginal value of goods.

### NOTE TO PAGE 229.

Even in private economy, all things considered, one has to deal with masses
of goods and with wants of great compass : private undertakings are in fact more
numerous than state undertakings, and form the principal part of the body
economic.   All the same, the extent of the undertaking, in private economy,
has only to a trifling extent that indefiniteness of valuation which it so easily
gives rise to in national economy.   In private economy one has to deal with
more, but smaller objects ; in state economy, with isolated but more wide-reaching
matters.   In the former all quantities finally resolve themselves into divisible
sums ; in the latter, they do not.   This contrast is so important, and recognition
of it affords so deep an insight into the structure of exchange value, that, at the
risk of repeating myself, I shall try once more to give to it as exact expression as
possible.

There are two considerations which must be carefully taken into account if we
would understand the calculus of private economy.

First : all stocks of goods of a similar kind—and, along with these, all goods
which, as products, relate themselves through costs to such stocks—come within
the range of the marginal law, and are measured as divisible sums made up of the
smallest units, each unit estimated at one and the same value.   This makes it
appear as though all wealth were split up into "atoms," but it is so only in
appearance ; as a matter of fact within the sphere of the marginal law every
"atom" in the whole circle of wealth is valued by this method of measurement ;
not only are all the marginal employments put in evidence but, with and through
them, all permissible employments from the highest down to those standing on
the margin,—only that we are saved the trouble of putting into the calculation
any but the marginal uses.   This makes it possible to calculate even the almost
infinite quantities which are destined to meet almost infinitely various wants.
For the purposes of carrying on ordinary private business, for instance, the whole
enormous agricultural wealth of a nation can be quite properly grasped through
the ordinary economic estimate of the same, even although this estimate, which
only takes stocks and marginal employments into consideration, is very far from
giving expression to the whole importance which those satisfactions that are
provided through agriculture have for the life of the nation.   There is, therefore,
nothing more misleading than to introduce a treatise on the price of agricultural
products by a disquisition upon the importance of agriculture in this latter sense.
The "surplus value" left out from the calculation need not be taken into the
calculation ; for one thing, that it is omitted, not only in agricultural taxation,
but everywhere, and, for another thing, that, as regards detail, a quite adequate
balancing of agriculture against trade, industry, and the other branches of
economy, and also of the individual businesses of agriculture against each other,

may be obtained, if only the margin be everywhere observed down to which wants are satisfied,·production extended, and cost goods expended.

If this same agricultural wealth be considered with regard to the purposes of general economic politics, the point of view changes. We are no longer concerned with innumerable individual goods as opposed to each other, but with that which affects them all in common. Thus agriculture, or great parts of it, become a whole ; then is the time to consider the importance of all its services ; and then we have to face an enormous complex of results which must all be estimated in their entire extent.

Second : by private economy the whole productive return—again taking into account the smallest quantities—is distributed among the complementary productive factors without remainder. The sum of all the "productive contributions" is equal in value to the total return, and the productive value is consequently as clearly calculable as the value of the products. On the other hand, in questions of economic politics, if the destinies of large quantities of production goods have to be weighed all at one time, the estimate of the "contribution" does not suffice. It becomes necessary to undertake the exceedingly difficult task of considering how deep the "complementarity" of the productive factors in its ultimate ground may reach, and how far these factors mutually condition one another—in the way of fructifying or serving as foundation—if they are all at once brought together in masses, or severed from each other. Here, again, in the "contribution" of private economy we calculate only the marginal value, whereas, in the total "co-operation" of national economy, we calculate the more far-reaching and less easily calculable importance of the goods.

This must all be understood with the above-mentioned limitation, that we have here indicated only the leading characteristic of the two economic systems, while each system always shows traces of the other, and the transitions from one to the other escape notice.

## CHAPTER IV

### VALUE IN THE PRESENT-DAY ECONOMY OF THE STATE

THE conduct of economic life, as actually carried on, adds another and a stronger contrast to that which naturally exists between private and national valuation.

The state as it actually exists—unlike the communistic state—has not the management of all economic matters, but only of a trifling portion of them. And, again, all economic goods do not belong to the state. Indeed it does not possess even enough for the proper carrying out of its own objects. As a rule it possesses only the buildings and the fixed plant necessary for the exercise of its public functions. Whatever

beyond is required for the current service must, for the most
part, be handed over to it by the citizens in the shape of
annual contributions from their property and income. The
most important of these contributions are raised, as we know,
in the shape of taxation, and to the consideration of this alone
we shall here confine ourselves.

Schäffle (*Steuerpolitik*, p. 17) has already laid down the
principle on which the goods which form the income of the
citizens should be divided out, between taxes on the one hand
for the satisfaction of public interests, and domestic outlay
on the other for the satisfaction of private wants. He calls it
the "principle of proportionate provision for the wants of the
individual and the wants of the government." The income of
the citizens must always be devoted to those employments
which at the time are the most important. There must not
be too rich an endowment of the public housekeeping at the
expense of keeping down the citizen's, nor of the private housekeeping at the cost of deterioration in the public service.

Sax has developed the same idea still further. Goods
obtain their value from the uses to which they are put.
The correct principle for the appropriation of income to the
purposes of the state is therefore simple; it is the universal
principle of economical employment, viz. that goods be employed in accordance with their value. If the state should
claim too much, it diminishes value, by expending goods for
purposes of state economy which would have a higher value if
employed in private economy. If it claims too little, value is
again diminished—as in this case also the entire importance of
the goods is not realised.

This law obtains its full significance in consequence of the
fact that riches are unequally distributed, and that personal
incomes and, moreover, personal wants are of different degrees.
If every one had the same wealth, income, and wants, all the
citizens would have to contribute the same quota of taxes.
But as this is not so, they must contribute unequal quotas and
again it is value which provides the measure. Every individual
economy, in respect of the relation of supply and demand
peculiar to it, has what Sax calls an "individual *Werthstand*."
The same amounts of goods are valued differently, or, what
amounts to the same thing, the same amounts of value are

expressed in different quantities of goods. To understand this expression of Sax, it may be best to recur to a fact which we have already taken as a starting-point in arriving at the law of price. We said that every intending purchaser who goes on the market calculates to himself, or ought to calculate, the money equivalent of the goods he wishes to buy, *i.e.* the sum of money whose value *to him* will equal the value of the goods, so that it is not economically permissible for him to go beyond it. Now a similar money-equivalent must be calculated for the value which the services of the state have to the individual citizen. More than this money equivalent it cannot, economically speaking, be the duty of any citizen to pay in taxation, but, on the other hand, it is the duty of every one to pay taxes up to this amount in order to meet the costs of the public service.

This acknowledged, the next matter is the more exact estimate of the individual equivalents. The circumstances which decide are wealth, income, and want. The greater the wealth and income, the greater will be the subjective equivalent or the taxation; and the greater the degree of want, the smaller will be the subjective equivalent or the taxation. All the same, taxation cannot simply be fixed proportionally to wealth and income : a progressive rate of taxation is justifiable. The man who only earns enough to sustain the physical minimum of existence has nothing left to give up to the state. I cannot go further than this and show the reasons which Sax gives for the claim of exemption of those who are at the minimum of existence, for the progressive rate of taxation, and all the other familiar claims of modern taxation. While it need scarcely be said that, as the science grows, many things will probably be formulated otherwise, still he has reached the essential matter. In all points which have been indicated as important by economic discussion up till the present, and which developed legislation has called into notice, he has discovered the connection between them and general economic facts and principles, and thus given to what has been empirically reached a basis in theory.

Hitherto, as regards the most important points of the theory of taxation, the science of finance has rested its tenets

on an appeal to the claims of justice.  In this almost unanimous
dependence upon outside and non-economic considerations, the
imperfect condition of that science betrays itself even more than
in its lack of agreement over the purely economic part of its
investigation, and so far as this remains it must resign all
claim to be regarded as an essentially economic doctrine.
Thanks to the labours of Sax this is to a great extent altered.
All the principal requirements of the theory of taxation have
obtained an economic foundation in being derived from the
general economic categories—Want, Goods, Economy, Value.
In spite of this, however, I cannot believe—though this brings
me into opposition to Sax—that the economic basis of taxation
has proved so perfect as to be able to dispense altogether with
considerations of justice.  Without attempting any complete
proof of this statement—which could not be done without
the difficult and tedious work of distinguishing between the
economic and the just,—I should like to advance one single
argument which appears to me sufficiently to corroborate its
correctness.

Sax as we have seen requires that every one pay in taxation the full money equivalent in which, according to his own
individual standpoint of value, is expressed the value of the
services of the state to him.  This claim is certainly absolutely
economic, in so far as it prevents the less able being taxed at
their maximum or above it, while it taxes the more able under
their maximum.  The claim is, further, certainly an economic
one, in so much as it excludes the possibility of any one being
taxed above his maximum.  But in so far it is not an absolutely economic claim ; it rests also upon the legal assumption
of private property ; it would be uneconomic if it could be
proved that private property is itself uneconomic.  But how
would it be if this claim were set against one which demanded
that the rich, and possibly the middle classes also, should
be taxed at their maximum, while the poorer and poorest
classes were taxed below it ?  What could be opposed to this
claim ?  Certainly no absolutely economic consideration ; for
the result of this being realised would be, economically considered, a more perfect satisfaction of the people's want.  The
only thing that could be opposed to it would be the consideration that, as a matter of justice, the same formal fundamental

proposition must hold for all,—equal justice for all ; a consideration which might, perhaps, in the last instance, be traced back to an economic basis, but which, in the present state of scientific development, is simply derived from the feeling of justice, and represents a quite distinct phase of that feeling. It may possibly be that, at a later period of time, it will be declared the duty of the rich to free the poorer classes from all public burdens, in order somewhat to mitigate the privations they suffer from the unequal distribution of wealth. Sax himself suggests (page 522) that, when that time comes, there may be an active endeavour, based on altruistic motives, to extend exemption from the "physical" minimum of subsistence to a "culture" minimum. It is possible that this endeavour might be only a symptom of gradual development in the direction of freeing the weakest and weaker classes, entirely or in part, according to the degree of their weakness, from the burden of taxation.[1]

As it is with the ordering of taxation, so is it, in my opinion, with all valuations in private and national economy, in so far as they have to weigh the conflicting interests of many persons. The principle which will reduce to a common measure of advantage the interests of persons who are differently situated in respect of wealth, has, I think I may venture to say without hesitation, not yet been found. So long as it remains undiscovered, it is impossible in such cases to dispense with some reference to that ranking of personal claims with which the feeling of justice is somewhat satisfied. If we give our assent to the principle of taxation demanded by economic theory, it is only because, without having an entirely strict theoretical justification for it, practical considerations which cannot be rejected compel us to approve of private property, and, moreover, of a degree of its utilisation quite definite and in accordance with modern ideas.

---

[1] Sax (page 522) remarks that, in any case, as regards the over-burdening of the rich, the economic margin is already given in their "individual valuation looking to possible taxation." But even granting that this margin is of purely economic origin, there remains, as we have seen, inside of it, sufficient room for the activity of other than purely economic considerations.

## CHAPTER V

### THE FUNDAMENTAL LAW OF COLLECTIVE VALUATION

IF the burden of taxation is distributed among the citizens in the manner just described, a very remarkable contrast emerges between the law which regulates public imposts, and that law of price (under free exchange on a market uncontrolled by the state) which regulates the burden that must be borne by all individuals when they wish to acquire goods produced or offered for sale by private industry. As return for the services of the state, or as contribution towards meeting the costs of these services, each individual gives the maximum which he is able to give, the full equivalent. In free exchange, on the other hand, the (approximate) maximum is paid only by the marginal purchaser ; the other purchasers get off more cheaply, as the one price is established for all, and no one requires to pay more than the equivalent of the marginal purchaser, even although his own valuation may be much higher. The state, accordingly, takes advantage of the purchasing power of every one in a much more thorough way ; and, more especially, the purchasing power of the wealthier citizens. It does not suffer the rich to pay according to the standard of the poor, but insists that every one shall be taxed in accordance with the full measure of his own personal estimate of the value which the services of the state have for him.

Hence is derived a peculiar law of national economic valuation—as of collective valuation generally. In every self-contained economy equal quantities of goods have an equal value ; similar items, or fractions, or units, of a stock have for their owner the same value. This law holds also in all free economies, and for the economic bodies created by it ; similar goods have on the same market the same price, the same exchange value. But it is different in the case of the national economic body, as, generally, in that of every collective economy which binds together several otherwise independent economic subjects to carry out distinct purposes. Here the goods which belong to the individual economic subjects, and from which the taxes are to be drawn, are valued as unequal,—equal taxes have unequal value, the same value is expressed by unequal taxes. The valuation of individual wealth and income on the part of a government agrees exactly with the individual degree of valuation for purposes of taxation; a government estimates the property of each person exactly as he estimates it himself, and in so far the collective economy is not like a self-contained economy. Not until the government comes to the spending of the taxes does it act in accordance with the universal law; not till then do sums, which were valued as unequal so long as the government had to collect them, come to be equal in value.[1]

Not only, then, does the levying of taxes rest on valuation, but in the levying of taxes is directly expressed a distinct valuation; a valuation which—as regards the wants of the public housekeeping—estimates every good at a lower figure in proportion to the number of other goods which are bound up with it in one individual's wealth, or in proportion to the limited character of the private wants to which it is devoted. In other words, the theory of taxation, in its economic foundations, belongs not to the applications of the theory of value, but to the theory of value itself.

The fact that, when levying taxes, a government, in contrast to the general law of ordinary economic life, rates economic property differently according to the individual circumstances of those who are taxed, has, economically speaking, undoubtedly beneficial results. It allows that the public burdens of the poorer classes be put at a lower figure; it allows the ability of the wealthier to bear taxation to be more fully utilised; and it thus places the taxes where they will cause least injury to the satisfaction of private needs. Were the state to act otherwise; were it to impose equal contributions, like

---

[1] A great deal of the history of taxation may be explained by the fact that people only learnt gradually to distinguish between the valuation of goods in national economy and in free economy. In ordinary economic life one feels injured who has to pay a higher price than any one else; and it can be easily understood that, in face of this rooted opinion, it was hard to introduce the principle that every person should pay more taxation for the same state services according as he possessed more goods for the satisfaction of his wants—and that not simply but progressively.

poll taxes, on every citizen ; it would inflict on the poorer classes privations in no way compensated by the extended indulgence in luxury that would now be possible to the richer.

To this extent it might be desirable that the same principle should also apply in free economic life; that there also each should pay according to the amount of his purchasing power. In this way a universal equalisation of satisfaction might be attained ; if every person were obliged to pay a dearer price according as he possessed more means, riches would offer no advantage, poverty no privation; all would have in the long run the same satisfactions. It need scarcely be said that, so long as our economy remains free, this cannot be. For so long as it is so, every one will strive to buy as cheaply as possible, and sellers will meet buyers in the same spirit—inasmuch as they will make the slightest advance in price an occasion to give the preference to the buyer who offers it, and will not in the least insist on adapting the objective amounts of price to the subjective purchasing power of the buyers. And just because this law of the free economy is so closely united with the freedom of that economy, it would be useless to condemn it for the undoubted evil effects which it directly has upon the distribution of the satisfaction of wants. In order to judge adequately, one must in any case take into consideration as well the effects of economic freedom—or, to put it differently, of private economies and private property — on all other economic relations, and particularly as regards the formation of productive returns. It may very well be that private property gives rise to great inequalities in the satisfaction of wants, while it, nevertheless, secures, even to those who receive the smallest share in the general distribution, an enormously increased satisfaction of want on the whole— the reason being the enormous increase in productive return which it allows and brings with it. And here, perhaps, may be found a reason for the remarkable phenomenon that one and the same community should contain at the same time two such diverse organisations as a free economy and a collective economy. In the former of these it diverges from the natural measure of value in that it over-estimates the goods reserved for acquisition by the rich, while, in the latter, it diverges from it in that it puts all goods possessed by the rich at a low figure so far as the public housekeeping is concerned. In the former the community is governed by a law which spares the rich, except where they come into competition with each other; while in the latter it lays down a law for itself which utilises their purchasing power to a quite unlimited extent. In the former it favours the unequal distribution of satisfactions: in the latter, it helps to equalise them. Such deeply-rooted divergences can only be explained by showing that the two organisations serve different purposes,—purposes in which personal freedom demands different scope.

We could not follow out this line of thought without leaving the sphere of the theory of value, and trespassing into the wide sphere of economic justice and economic philosophy. The explanation of the social organisation within which the valuations take place, is a task with which the theory of value, with its limited means, is not capable of dealing. And it is not only the theory of value which is unequal to this task; only a theory of society, which took into consideration other than merely economic facts, could adequately undertake it.

If now, in closing, there is one thing which, more than another, I wish to repeat with special emphasis, it is the intention which has dominated me throughout the whole work, and in every part of it,—the intention to be, in the best sense of the word, empirical. I may perhaps hope that the attainment of this object has not been disturbed by the fiction—undoubtedly unempirical—of a natural value and of the utopian state of communism. So far as I can judge of my own work, I have nowhere pointed to any foreign non-empirical power in the actuality of economic life. The only liberty I have taken has been to leave out of consideration facts of whose activity there could be no doubt:—the actual imperfections of valuation, the individualism of our economy, and, finally, the inequality of wealth. At the same time, however, I have not neglected to indicate, at all events in a general way, the directions in which these circumstances must of necessity cause value, both in the private economy and in the economy of the state, to deviate from the natural standard. I hope that my statement has not by this means become untrue, though I know very well that it must of necessity be imperfect. But what is incompletely stated is certainly not, on that account alone, non-empirical—if it were so, what statement would be empirical, seeing that we are unable ever to do more than investigate mere fragments of the great organic structure of our world ? All judgment as regards any attempt at investigation must depend on whether the fragment, with which the inquiry is concerned, be large enough and solid enough to have a coherence of its own, and to deserve consideration by itself. If the imperfect description of the phenomena of value, which I have attempted to give, is justified in this sense, it is empirical.

The form of the fiction cannot have misled any one. I might, of course, have stated drily that I intended to abstain from the consideration of certain facts. But like one who wishes to look at certain things undisturbed by the impressions of other things, and aids his senses by spreading a veil over the disturbing objects, I thought to aid imagination by making use of the easily comprehended figure of a communistic society, concerned to abolish in actuality all that I wished to disregard in thought. The fiction which I have employed must be regarded in that light alone, and I trust that the veil has been transparent enough to allow the complete body of phenomena to be clearly outlined at every turn under its slight disguise.

THE END